Nonstate Nations in International Politics

edited by
Judy S. Bertelsen

The Praeger Special Studies program—
utilizing the most modern and efficient book
production techniques and a selective
worldwide distribution network—makes
available to the academic, government, and
business communities significant, timely
research in U.S. and international economic, social, and political development.

Nonstate Nations in
International Politics
Comparative System
Analyses

PRAEGER SPECIAL STUDIES IN INTERNATIONAL POLITICS AND GOVERNMENT

Praeger Publishers   New York   Washington   London

Library of Congress Cataloging in Publication Data
Main entry under title:

Nonstate nations in international politics.

    (Praeger special studies in international
politics and government)
    Includes index.
    1. International relations—Research—Addresses,
essays, lectures. 2. Nationalities, Principle of—
Research—Addresses, essays, lectures. 3. Minorities—
Research—Addresses, essays, lectures. I. Bertelsen,
Judy.
JX1291.N58   327   76-36404
ISBN 0-275-56320-0

PRAEGER PUBLISHERS
111 Fourth Avenue, New York, N.Y. 10003, U.S.A.

Published in the United States of America in 1977
by Praeger Publishers, Inc.

This book is offered both as an early step in an inquiry that is intended to continue, and also as the publication of work on which a number of us have been active for several years. Many persons in addition to the authors of these chapters have contributed to our enterprise. A brief review of the history of our endeavor may be of interest to the reader.

At the 1970 International Studies Association (ISA)/West meetings I presented my first formulation of the nonstate nations systems framework, together with a draft of a study of the Palestinian Arabs. (A much revised version of this work has been published in the Sage Professional Papers in International Studies, vol. 4, 1976, Series Number: 02-043.) A roundtable based on that paper led to commitments by other scholars to produce additional studies; a panel of these papers was presented the following year at the ISA meetings in New York. The group then affiliated as an Internet of the Comparative Interdisciplinary Studies Section (ISS) of the ISA. The Internet structure of CISS has been aided by funds supplied by the National Endowment for the Humanities.

From the outset, the social scientists drawn to the nonstate nation project have shared both an interest in theoretical and methodological problems of comparative/interdisciplinary research, and also a strong involvement with the particular peoples and areas under study. We have attempted at this stage to adhere to a common systems framework, but have allowed each author latitude in applying the terms of the framework to his or her case. We have produced cases that vary in time span covered and in level of detail reported. We hope, however, that by permitting this variation we have avoided the pitfalls of too hasty refinement that might lock us into a premature commitment to a formulation inadvertently biased in a particular cultural direction. My commitment, which I believe is shared by others, is to attempt in the future greater precision of operationalization—but in the light of our independent applications of the systems framework.

Many people have contributed their insights in the preparation of other nonstate nation studies and in commentary and criticism; among them are Rona Fields, Joe Fischbach, Kathleen O'Brien Jackson, Kathleen Knight, Boniface I. Obichere, Charles A. Powell, Helen Purkitt, Greg Wynn, William Hazen, and William Vocke. Fred Riggs, primary organizer of CISS and the Internet structure, aided and encouraged the work in many ways.

CONTENTS

CHAPTER

1

AN INTRODUCTION TO THE STUDY OF NONSTATE NATIONS IN INTERNATIONAL POLITICS
Judy S. Bertelsen

Traditionally, international politics has been viewed as the result of relations between and among nation-states; indeed, international relations has often been viewed primarily as relations between and among the big powers. Recently, however, the impact of nonstate groups has become increasingly visible. A large number of national liberation groups have arisen in recent years, challenging the authority of colonial regimes. Further, "national" movements have developed out of groups conventionally viewed as minorities within an established nation-state. Examples of the latter include tribal-based movements such as the Biafran secession attempt, and the movement that led to the creation of Bangladesh. Movements within the United States include Atzlan (the Mexican-American nationalist movement), a number of Indian or native American groups (both tribally specific and tribal coalition groups, such as the American Indian Movement), and Black nationalist movements such as the Nation of Islam and the Nation of New Africa. The Palestinian Arabs as a general group and as specific subgroups have penetrated the international arena and have been seen not simply as "refugees" within the boundaries of established nation-states but as actors, albeit troublesome actors, from the viewpoints of a number of nation-states.

The systems framework and the Palestinian Arab case (see Chapter 2) are based on the author's monograph, The Palestinian Arabs: A Non-State Nation Systems Analysis, Sage Professional Papers in International Studies, vol. 4, Series No. 02-43 (Beverly Hills: Sage Publications, 1976). This work includes a more detailed treatment of the Palestinian Arab nonstate nation before 1948.

1

The traditional focus of international relations has tended to obscure or ignore the role of nonstate actors. Indeed, the emphasis on nation-states has tended to focus on big-power nation-states, with smaller powers viewed as pawns in a big-power game. Recent assertions of Third World and smaller power unity within the United Nations have raised questions about the comprehensiveness of such a focus. The Third World and smaller power coalitions also have lent credence to the claims of certain nonstate groups, such as the Palestinian Arabs.

What has been the impact of nonstate groups on international politics? Perhaps the best perspective for this question is the vantage-point of such groups themselves. While one cannot adopt the perspective of another, a research design that focuses on the goals of nonstate groups rather than on nation-states may help us to understand the objectives and actions of nonstate actors who attempt to operate in the international arena.

THE NONSTATE NATION PROJECT

In order to see the international arena as a nonstate actor sees it, we have agreed, in this book, to attempt to observe from the theoretical perspective of the nonstate nation (NSN). The NSN is defined as any entity that operates in a manner normally associated with a nation-state but is not a generally recognized nation-state. The defining characteristic of the NSN is its assertion or action implying sovereignty, while not being generally recognized as a sovereign entity. Our definition does not suggest that all NSNs desire complete independence and recognition as separate nation-states. Our definition is not based on the goals of the NSN but simply on the fact that the group enters the international system taking actions usually taken only by nation-states.

Furthermore, while the cases reported in this book all have a history of ethnic cohesion, ethnic identity is not a defining characteristic of an NSN. Nonethnic groups (for example, multinational corporations) might fit the definition under certain circumstances. The multinational corporation provides an example that can help to clarify the definition. The mere fact that a multinational corporation has an impact on the international economy does not make it a nonstate nation. In order to fit the definition the multinational corporation must do something usually done only by nation-states (for example, perhaps, participate in international tariff negotiations). If a corporation's international impact derives instead from its large investments, that impact may be strong, but the corporation is not an NSN. Its impact would probably appear in the "environment" or "resource" categories of NSN analyses.

If an NSN does not necessarily seek complete independence, what are some of the reasons it may have for entering the international arena? A group that has been losing battles within the domestic context of its nation-state may seek to widen the scope of the conflict by moving into an arena that offers more allies or different rules of the game—and therefore perhaps better opportunities for success. (For a discussion of this conflict strategy, see Schattschneider 1975, pp. 15-17). American Indian groups, for example, may not seek complete independence as a nation-state, but they may prefer to deal directly with the U.S. government on the basis of international treaties rather than bargain simply as another special interest group within the welter of groups that operate in the U.S. polity. International treaties and appeals to law offer different rules of the game from those in operation at the level of pluralist interest-group competition for a slice of the public pie. It is plausible that NSN reliance upon international treaty rights is at least partially motivated by consideration of the strategic advantage of operating in the global context by appealing to international agreements.

In many cases, NSN grievances include complaints of restrictions on freedom of expression of national identity. The host nation-state in which the group resides may view the NSN (or certain of its practices) as competitive, subversive, or immoral. The Soviet Union, for example, treats the maintenance of ethnic-religious national identities as reactionary and contrary to Soviet Marxism. Many nation-states have discouraged or suppressed the use of traditional languages. These kinds of grievances, if they are the only grievances, may be redressed by some sort of federal solution, giving the NSN community control over the specified jurisdiction within the federal government's authority. An example of such a solution is Israel's granting of authority over marriage rites to a number of specified religious groups. (While this solution may satisfy the needs of the "strong identifiers," it does not, of course, satisfy the needs of atheists and those who wish to marry across religious groups.) Yugoslavia also has struggled with attempts to devise a workable federal arrangement for its ethnic minorities. Despite variation in level of success of specific efforts, the federal model remains as an alternative to either complete assimilation or complete national independence and sovereignty.

Whatever the motives may be for entering the international context, the NSN desires to remain both durable and audible: We assume that the NSN wishes to continue to exist, and we assume that it wishes to be perceived. These two goals in some cases will be in conflict, however. Insofar as an NSN achieves a high degree of audibility, it may (especially if it is seen to threaten the existence of a currently recognized nation-state) lose durability. In such a case, the greater the audibility, the less the likelihood of durability. The NSN may then choose to "go underground" in order to maintain durability. During the period underground, audibility/visibility will be limited, although it may briefly reappear in sudden acts of violence or other publicity-prone activity. Underground activity often will be directed toward spectacular acts that can be conducted by small numbers of highly motivated partisans willing to make great sacrifices (including possible loss of life). This sort of activity, while not leading to a large membership with high audibility, allows a group to maintain both durability and audibility while under siege.

In the chapters that follow, seven nonstate nation systems will be described and analyzed. Each chapter will also attempt to describe the international context from the perspective of a different NSN. In order to produce comparable studies, the authors have agreed to organize their chapters within a common systems framework. The framework analyzes nonstate nation systems in terms of five categories: (1) decision makers, and, for each decision maker, (2) goals, (3) resources—those things which affect outcomes and are controlled by the decision maker, (4) environment—those things which affect outcomes but are not controlled by the decision maker, and (5) components or missions—the projects undertaken by the decision makers to achieve the goals. (This set of categories has been adapted from a formulation of Churchman 1968.)

If the NSN has more than one decision maker, the resulting set of decision-making subsystems is evaluated by two criteria: (1) unity of purpose, as revealed in goals across decision-making subsystems, and (2) compatibility of components across decision-making subsystems.

Quite separate from the efficiency of the NSN (evaluated in terms of the NSN's own goals), the framework assesses the impact of the NSN in the international context. The framework raises the following kinds of questions: Under what circumstances do NSN decision makers adopt strategies that serve to control or lessen violence, or to involve adoption or escalation of violence? Under what circumstances do NSN decision makers adopt strategies that involve the widening of conflict to include additional nation-states? Under what circumstances do NSN decision makers adopt strategies that produce unity among nation-states or widen cleavages among nation-states? Under what circumstances do NSN decision makers adopt strategies that threaten to weaken or undermine the stability of current nation states (by such means as propaganda, internal subversion, terror, military attack, and so on)?

Obviously these questions do not direct the authors to specific kinds of data. The phrase "under what circumstances" can allow for a number of interpretations, even when there is agreement about the occurrence of a particular kind of impact on the international context. The framework was couched in general terms in order to allow application to a range of cases. The assumption in the framework was that, based on previous attempts to develop formal conflict theory, high specificity of terms can be premature and can produce a Procrustean bed rather than a useful framework. The author's goal was to develop a framework that could guide the production of comparative studies, while allowing sufficient flexibility to include material idiosyncratic to each case.

The chapters that follow serve as an initial effort to systematically compare nonstate nations, the strategies they adopt, and the impacts they have upon international politics. The case studies offer the reader a selection from among the wide range of nonstate nations. It is anticipated that the cases reported here will be followed by increasingly specific identification and definition of the key variables and the relationships between them. The statement of the framework in more defined, specific terms will allow the comparative study of a wider range of cases in a more systematic way. The cases that comprise the next seven chapters of this book vary in time span covered and in interpretation and application of the terms of the framework. But they do provide analyses of a range of nonstate nations within a common, general framework. This stage of research seems necessary and appropriate as a starting point in the study of a subject that has been neglected in much of the literature of comparative international politics. Our ultimate aim is a more refined statement that will allow for explicit definition of key elements and their rules of association in a nonstate nation system. However, at this stage we have been concerned to establish the "lay of the land," and to avoid commitment to a specific framework that might prove useful for analysis of one case, but which is less useful for comparison across a wide range of cases.

REFERENCES

Churchman, C. West. 1968. The Systems Approach. New York: Dell.

Schattschneider, E. E. 1975. rev. ed. The Semisovereign People. New York: Dryden.

2

THE PALESTINIAN
ARABS
Judy S. Bertelsen

The Palestinian Arab case in the period from 1948 to 1976 offers an example of a nonstate nation (NSN) that has operated in a context of nation-states whose interpretations of their national interests have been partially in conflict with the promotion of Palestinian Arab goals. These nation-states also have had varying degrees of interest in promoting Palestinian Arab aspirations. The international context of the Palestinian Arabs has been ambivalent and frustrating but not entirely devoid of resources, a condition faced by a number of nonstate nations.

After the establishment of the state of Israel in 1947–48, Palestinian Arabs relied heavily on the support of Arab state leaders. While these leaders undoubtedly had sincere feelings of Arab brotherhood with Palestinians, they also had narrower notions of national interest—interests which made it useful to be able to control as well as to champion the Palestinian Arab cause.

In this chapter we see the development of the Palestinian Arab NSN from domination by Arab states through a period in which Palestinian Arabs developed the means to veto effectively the actions of those states and thus to push them into policies more preferred by the audible Palestinian Arab groups. The Arab-state interest did not disappear, however. Furthermore, questions remain at the conclusion of the case about the ability of the emerging

---

An expanded treatment of the author's Palestinian Arab (NSN) study is available in monograph form.

Palestinian "government" to govern. Indeed, there remains within the Palestinian Arab groups a debate about
the advisability of taking on, at this point, the respon-
sibilities and liabilities of governing. The problem appears not to be whether or not to govern but when to
govern—will the Palestinian Arabs, by taking on that
task of self-government, weaken the attack on Israel?
There appears to be disagreement within the Palestinian
Arab ranks both on this point and on the question of
possible coexistence with Israel.

—Judy S. Bertelsen

THE PALESTINIAN ARAB SYSTEM
PRIOR TO 1948

Palestinian Arabs have lived for centuries in an environment
dominated politically by other national groups. After the defeat of the
Ottoman Turks in World War I, Palestine became a British Mandate
territory rather than part of an Arab kingdom under Hashemite rule.
Hussein, head to the Hashemite dynasty, trusted McMahon correspondence for assurance that, in exchange for his considerable aid to
British World War II aims against the Turks, he and his sons would
be supported as rulers of a large Arab kingdom, including both the
Arabian Peninsula and "Greater Syria." Instead, secret arrangements
with France prompted Britain to attempt to pay off the Hashemites
with selected kingdoms (eventually Transjordan under Abdullah and
Iraq under Feisal), while France obtained Mandate authority over
Syria and Lebanon. Palestine became a British Mandate, with Jewish
rights to a "national homeland" explicitly asserted through the Balfour
Declaration and maintained as part of the Mandate policy.

Palestinian Arabs, throughout the period of the Mandate, objected to the Balfour Declaration and refused to participate in many
aspects of the Mandate government. Palestinian Arab political activity
tended to organize around the leadership of traditionally powerful
families in the region, in particular the Nashashibi and Husseini clans
(the latter not to be confused with the Hashemite clan, whose patriarch,
Hussein, was based in the Hejaz region of the Arabian Peninsula).
The eminence of the two major Palestinian families was underlined
by the fact that Mandate authorities, after engineering the appointment
of Haj Amin al-Husseini as grand mufti of Jerusalem, arranged to
have the Husseini mayor of Jerusalem replaced by Ragheb Bey
Nashashibi.

The Nashashibi family attempted to develop a working relationship with the British authorities in an effort to curb Zionist immigration
and land acquisition. However, the Nashashibi-led National Defense

party apparently lost its political footing when in 1937 it withdrew from an Arab coalition (the Arab High Committee) dominated by militantly anti-Mandate al-Husseini leadership. When the Mandate authorities issued yet another statement in support of partition, the Nashashibis were discredited in Palestinian Arab public opinion. A number of the al-Husseini leaders left Palestine in the wake of British warrants holding some of them responsible for Arab rebellious activity. The grand mufti of Jerusalem, Haj Amin al-Husseini, eventually returned and continued to act as a militant leader and spokesman for Palestinian Arab claims.

The British, unable to find a solution acceptable to both Zionists and Arabs, turned the matter over to the United Nations, which, after investigation and hearings, established partition in 1947. The state of Israel declared its beginning in 1948.

THE PALESTINIAN ARAB SYSTEM
AFTER 1948

The establishment of the State of Israel signaled a radical restructuring of the Palestinian Arab environment. Many Arabs had objected to British Mandate policies that granted Jews and Arabs similar status as ethnic groups within Palestine. After 1948, however, the Jews existed as a recognized nation-state, while the Arabs had become refugees under the governance of Arab states and UN agencies. Palestinian Arabs who had felt cheated by British Mandate recognition of the "equality" of Jewish and Arab claims to Palestine now felt overwhelming despair and betrayal. The environment after 1948 consisted of nation-states that counted Israel among their number. The environment included the United Nations, an organization that had sought both Jewish and Arab input in its deliberations but which now accepted Israel as a member, while Palestinian Arab status remained unclear.

This chapter will sketch in more detail the outlines of the Palestinian Arab system within the international context, following Israel's establishment as a state. The study will focus on four system states corresponding to four time periods: 1948 to the 1956 Suez conflict, 1956 to the 1967 June war, 1967 through October 1973, and October 1973 through November 1975. For each of these periods the primary decision makers for Palestinian Arabs will be identified, along with the environment, resources, goals, and components for each decision maker. The effectiveness of each of the four Palestinian Arab subsystems will be evaluated. Finally, the impact of the Palestinian Arab system on the international arena will be assessed.

PERIOD I: 1948 TO 1956

The period immediately following Israel's establishment as a state saw Palestinian Arab leadership fragmented. The Hashemite and al-Husseini families continued to maneuver for leadership position, each finding reinforcement through particular Arab states. In addition, the Arab states as a group provided opportunities and support for Palestinian Arab claims. Three Palestinian Arab decision makers can be identified: the two families mentioned above and the Arab states.

Decision Maker A: The al-Husseini Family Environment

With the dissolution of the Mandate and the establishment of the state of Israel, the environment now harbored powerful enemies and competitors of the Husseini family, the state of Israel, and the combination of Transjordan with the Palestinian West Bank, an area that included the Nashashibi family.

Goals and Resources

In pursuit of his goal of Palestine Arab leadership, Haj Amin al-Husseini, the mufti of Jerusalem, relied upon two important new resources—Egyptian support and the formal structure of the Arab League—to augment the resources of religious and popular political leadership already established. The league provided formal recognition of Husseini organizational attempts in Gaza. Egypt supported the al-Husseini efforts as a counterweight to Hashemite ambitions for Palestinian leadership emanating from Jordan.

Component

The major component devised by the Husseinis to foster their leadership ambitions was their attempted government-in-exile. A Palestinian Arab government under the leadership of the mufti and his family was established in 1948 by the Arab League Council. This All-Palestine government, headed by Ahmad Hilmi as prime minister, was fostered in Gaza by Egypt and supported eventually by all Arab governments except Jordan.

The government failed to become an effective organization of Palestinians, however. Gaza was administered under Egyptian military rule. The All-Palestine government, together with the mufti and a few surviving members of the Arab Higher Committee, eventually moved to Cairo. Apparently, the All-Palestine government was not maintained, although Hilmi continued to represent Palestinians in the League Council until his death in 1963 (see MacDonald 1965, p. 91; Lenczowski 1962, pp. 642-45; and Peretz 1970, p. 34).

Decision Maker B: The Hashemites

Goal

The Emir Abdullah, Hashemite ruler of Transjordan, continued
to harbor the goal of a greater Syria (to include, roughly, the area
of the Palestine Mandate, Syria, and Lebanon, as well as Jordan)
under his rule. He publicly announced this goal as early as 1941 and
continued to press for a union of Arab states until his assassination
in 1951 (Lenczowski 1962, pp. 639-45).

Resources and Environment

Abdullah's primary resource lay in his position as head of the
nation-state of Jordan. He faced an environment, however, that included an Arab League with an organized and articulate opponent of
Hashemite leadership: Egypt. Egypt was able to coalesce with old
Hashemite rivals such as Saudi leaders, the al-Husseini family, and
the governments of Syria and Lebanon. The old family-based rivalries
played out their conflicts in the Arab League arena. The environment
also included, of course, the new state of Israel and a substantial
Palestinian Arab population in the West Bank area.

Components

Abdullah appears to have employed at least four major components in his attempt to produce Arab unity under Hashemite rule.
First, he attempted to establish himself as head of "Greater Syria,"
an entity that would have included roughly the present states of
Lebanon, Syria, and Jordan. He opposed and thus denied unified Arab
League support to the al-Husseini efforts to organize an All-Palestine
government. He lost his attempt to establish the Arab League as an
amalgamation of all Arab lands into one state (the vision apparently
fostered by the Hashemite patriarch, Hussein) (see Lenczowski 1962,
p. 640).

While unable to produce his dreamed-of Greater Syria, Abdullah
did succeed in a second component: annexation of the West Bank area
of former Palestine. Although condemned by the Arab League for
this action (see Lenczowski 1962, p. 644), Abdullah successfully
mobilized Palestinian Arab support to secure control of the area. In
his annexation strategy he transformed the Palestinian population itself into a resource. He managed to gain the support of sizable segments of influential Palestinians, who produced rather impressive
displays of organized backing. These included both a conference of
5,000 Palestine refugee notables asking for a protectorate under
Abdullah and an Arab Congress in Jericho asking for annexation of

the West Bank (Peretz 1970, pp. 34-35). Abdullah appointed a new mufti to replace Haj Amin al-Husseini, and he co-opted the major opponent of the al-Husseini family in Jerusalem, Regheb Bey Nashashibi, by appointing the former Jerusalem mayor to the position of minister of refugees, deputy governor of Arab Palestine. According to Peretz, "this act not only strengthened Abdullah's hand against the Egyptians and the Mufti, but added legitimacy to his claims as the successor to leadership of the Palestinian Arabs" (1970, p. 35).

His third and fourth components were unsuccessful: He tried to develop resources in support of his Greater Syria plan by appealing directly to Syrians prior to both the 1943 and 1947 elections to unify with Transjordan under Hashemite rule. These attempts failed in every case (Lenczowski 1962, p. 640). He attempted to negotiate a separate nonaggression pact with Israel, but stopped in the face of Arab League opposition (Lenczowski 1962, p. 644).

Decision Maker C: Arab Governments

Arab governments in 1948 focused primarily on what they perceived as their national interest and only secondarily on the realization of Arab unity in support of Palestinian claims. The governments seem to have been committed generally to the idea of "Palestine liberation," as long as that commitment did not jeopardize their perceived national interests.

Environment

Arab states operated in an environment in which Israel was officially recognized as a nation-state on a par with all other states, although not recognized as such by any Arab states. The United Nations, which included Israel as a member, had set up a special agency, the United Nations Relief and Works Agency (UNRWA), to provide relief aid to Palestinian refugees.

Resources

Arab governments suffered under limitations in both economic and military resources during the period. Either emerging or having just emerged from European imperial domination, these countries were struggling with internal development problems, as well as with conflicts between traditional royalty and reformist or revolutionary challengers.

Each Arab government did have access as a nation-state to the international arena, including the United Nations. In addition, as Arab League members, Arab states possessed a potentially unified voice. The traditional rival Palestinian Arab families functioned as further

resources for the Arab nation-states. The family-based groups
served as allies of individual Arab states competing for leadership
of the Arab world.

Components

Arab governments divided their efforts into major directions:
both support of rival Palestinian Arab factions in order to serve
competing national interests and gestures of unity in support of
Palestinian Arabs. We have already noted that, while both Egypt and
Jordan claimed to support the Palestinian Arab cause, each chose
to support a different rival faction and to exploit factional cleavage
in the pursuit of individual national aims. In general, Arab states
used their positions as UN members to speak in favor of Arab rights
to Palestine. In addition, Palestinians were appointed to the UN
delegations of various Arab states.

Arab governments formalized their commitment to the Palestinian Arabs through Arab League policies. The league council
maintained a seat for a Palestinian representative. According to
Robert MacDonald (1965, p. 87):

> Despite its failure to prevent the establishment of Israel,
> the League Council has continued to act as the legal sur-
> rogate for all Palestine Arabs, maintaining a seat on the
> League Council for the Palestine representative, spon-
> soring the "Palestine delegation" to the United Nations,
> and at least nominally supervising the remaining pieces
> of Palestine in the Gaza Strip and the "West Bank" region
> of Jordan.

While the Arab League Council recognized the All-Palestine government, the support apparently was tenuous (MacDonald 1965, p. 91).
It seems that the council was willing to support this group because,
not in spite, of its lack of resources independent of the Arab nation-
states. The All-Palestine government was an ideologically acceptable
Arab showpiece which did not interfere significantly with the independent decision making of individual Arab governments.

Evaluation of Palestinian Arab System, 1948 to 1956

Palestinian Arabs operated under extremely adverse circumstances in the period from 1948 to 1956. Their major decision makers
harbored conflicting goals. The Palestinian Arabs existed as refugees
while their Jewish opponent had gained recognition as a nation-state.

The goals of the three groups claiming decision-making authority
for Palestine Arabs were at best not integrated and at worst

competitive. The Arab states continued to be united in rhetoric supportive of Palestinian Arab claims but disunited with regard to specific
plans of action.

Disunity in the Arab League mirrored disunity among Arab
states. The sharpest conflict appeared between Egyptian and Jordanian
ambitions for leadership in the Arab world. These international
rivalries paralleled and overlapped the relations between two of the
old Arab families: the Hashemite dynasty in Jordan and the al-Husseini
family, supported now by Egypt.

None of the decision makers was able to define goals which could
unite factions, families, and states under a common strategy. While
parties appeared to agree on general principles, they split over family
and nation-state rivalries for control of decision making.

No group or leader succeeded in becoming audible, independent
of the support of a nation-state. There was no effective leadership
of the "refugee"—only of the Palestinian Arab as sponsored by and
dominated by nation-states (Peretz 1970, p. 30). Palestinian Arabs
did engage in sporadic acts of violence within Israel; the extent to
which these acts represented organized political leadership—or, rather,
spontaneous and personally motivated revenge—is difficult to assess.

Palestinian Arabs found themselves in a position vastly inferior
to that of the Israelis in terms of both audibility and apparent durability.
Whereas Arabs and Jews had had similar positions with respect to
the Mandate government, the Israelis after 1948 enjoyed recognition
as a nation-state, as a UN member, while the Arabs suffered a reduction in status. Arabs were now refugees in relation to an opponent
nation-state. Palestinian Arabs did not have the audibility available
to the state of Israel, either in binational dealings (such as diplomatic
exchanges) or in the United Nations. Further, the Arab refugee status
did not suggest the durability of statehood, but rather threatened extinction as a group, through resettlement in new lands.

PERIOD II: 1956 TO 1967

The Suez crisis produced Palestinian Arab environmental
changes that marked the beginning of a different system-state. Israel's
military capability had been displayed, together with the potential
threat evident from her temporary occupation of the Negev and the
Suez Canal region. The United Nations Emergency Force (UNEF) had
been accepted by Egypt and installed in the Gaza Strip and at Sharm
el Sheikh to aid in maintaining closed borders and in keeping violence
at a minimum.

By 1956 the influence of major Arab Palestinian families appeared
to have been superseded by Arab national influences. Haj Amin el-
Husseini had lost Egyptian support and had moved to Beirut (MacDonald

1965, p. 91). Peretz reports that in many Palestinian homes the picture of Egyptian President Nasser had replaced that of Haj Amin (1970, p. 35). The Hashemites, while continuing to rule Jordan under Abdullah's grandson, King Hussein, appeared to have abandoned their ambitions for expansion into Greater Syria.

Arab government continued to act as major decision makers for Palestinian Arabs. However, the Palestinian Arabs themselves showed evidence of independent leadership: Fatah (the Palestine Movement of National Liberation) surfaced as a visible Palestinian Arab organization.

Decision Maker A: The Arab Governments

Goals

Arab government goals continued to subordinate Palestinian Arab independence or "liberation" to assessments of the national self-interest of the Arab country in question. In the light of Israeli military capability, and in the light of repeated Palestinian raids and reprisals against Israel, the need for control over Palestinian Arab activities became increasingly important. Israeli policy of holding an Arab country responsible for allegedly spontaneous or personally motivated Palestinian Arab border crossings and acts of terror underlined the fact that Arab governments would have to be able to control Palestinian activity if they wished to be able to control their relations with Israel.

In the period following the Suez conflict, Arab governments continued to profess support for Palestinian claims, while increasingly seeking means to control Palestinian activity. The goal of national control seems clearly to have been given precedence over the goal of Palestinian liberation.

Syria did press, from time to time, for more militancy on the part of Egypt or Jordan. However, the motivation apparently derived from inter-Arab governmental rivalry rather than from single-minded commitment to the Palestinians' liberation. Kerr (1971, p. 127) stresses the primacy of Syria's national ambitions when he concludes:

> Despite the Syrians' strident talk of a people's war of liberation, after twenty years of schooling in domestic and inter-Arab factional maneuvering they assuredly had their minds on more practical and immediate matters than the destruction of Israel. . . . When the Syrians provided the Palestinian guerrillas with a base of operations, they knew that Husayn had more to fear from this than Israel—especially when the guerrillas advanced toward Israel by way of Jordanian territory.

Syria apparently was willing to encourage guerrilla actions that suited its national ambitions, although probably not eager to see develop a guerrilla movement capable of independent policy and action.

Environment

As indicated above, the environment included the state of Israel, which had demonstrated its ability to invade and occupy the territory of Arab states.

Resources and Components

The Arab League and the United Nations both offered institutional resources for controlling Palestinian Arab activity. The UNEF provided aid in keeping border crossings and conflicts subdued. The acceptance of the UNEF by Egypt on its soil can be seen as a major component in support of the goal of controlling the Palestinian Arabs and thereby maintaining Egypt's control over its own foreign relations. The UNEF provided a screen, making Palestinian Arab border crossings into Israel more difficult. The danger of Israeli retaliation against Arab governments in response to Palestinian Arab guerrilla activity thus diminished.

The Arab League, while retaining a seat for a Palestinian Arab representative, was clearly dominated by Arab nation-states and run in terms of their national interests. The Arab League thus provided extensive resources for Arab governments. In addition, the Palestinian Arab groups such as the mufti's Arab Higher Committee and the guerrilla organizations functioned as resources used by Arab governments.

Establishment of the Palestine Liberation Organization (PLO) in 1964 produced a "Palestine entity" claiming to represent Palestinian interests, but controlled and contained within the bounds of the security interests of Arab nation-states. From this perspective, the PLO can be seen as a component of Arab state policy. The PLO simultaneously provided both an institution for Palestinian representation and for defusing explosive Palestinian issues. An example appears in reference to the 1964 PLO congress:

One potentially explosive issue, the question of constituting a Palestinian armed force, was resolved in favor of training refugees by the new Joint Arab Command and a plan to establish the "Palestine" units within existing national armies, two devices calculated to keep the Palestinians out of trouble. In the final analysis, moreover, the resolutions of the congress required ratification by

the Arab League Council, thus keeping the activities of
the new organization within an established institutional
framework (MacDonald 1965, p. 93).

The PLO thus served both to develop a "Palestinian" military force
and to assure that the force would not conduct actions independent of
the Arab governments. Peretz has characterized the PLO as designed
by Egypt's Nasser and Jordan's Hussein "to counteract the militantly
precarious policies being pursued by the Syrian Ba'thist leaders, and
carried out in the field by Fatah" (1970, pp. 36-37). (The Syrians, as
suggested earlier, used the Fatah organizations to provoke Israeli
reprisals against Jordan.)

Shukairy, a man generally reputed at the time to be ineffectual,
became both the PLO leader and the official Palestinian representative
to the Arab League Council. He clarified that the PLO did not wish to
challenge Jordan's claim to the West Bank, declaring the PLO's goal
to be the liberation of Israeli-held Palestine. While Egypt continued
to support and aid the PLO, Jordan's King Hussein became disen-
chanted and eventually hostile as Shukairy began organizing Palestinian
military groups in Jordan. Hussein eventually went so far as to invite
his former enemy, the mufti, to return for a visit. Hussein also established political ties with other members of the Arab Higher Committee (Peretz 1970, p. 40).

Decision Maker B: The Palestine Liberation Organization

Although we have characterized the PLO (and its Palestine
Liberation Army, PLA) as a component of Arab state policy, the PLO
began to develop its own resources, thus assuming the role of decision maker.

Resources

The United Nations Relief and Works Agency (UNRWA) indirectly
became a resource for the PLO's Palestine Liberation Army in Gaza.
Because the governing authorities in Gaza refused to report conscrip-
tions of Palestinians into the PLA, the families of those persons were
able to continue to draw UNRWA rations (Buehrig 1971, pp. 96-97).
By indirectly subsidizing the PLA that had originally been established
under Arab state domination, the UNRWA provided a resource to the
PLA, enabling it to develop a bit more independence from Egyptian
governmental control. In addition the educational programs of UNRWA
apparently were used to foster anti-Israeli and pro-Palestinian Arab
attitudes (Buehrig 1971, pp. 155-56).

In addition, the Arab states and the Arab League provided resources: Despite the tendency of Arab states to subordinate Palestinian

Arab interests to pressing nation-state concerns, the stated commitments could be used to pressure for further behavioral commitments.

Decision Maker C: Fatah

Fatah apparently began in 1956 in Gaza as a secret organization
(Nakhleh 1971, p. 192). Unlike the PLO, Fatah was not "sponsored"
by the Arab governments.

Goals

Fatah appears to have been dedicated single-mindedly to the
goal of "liberating" the Palestinian homeland (the entire Palestine
Mandate territory, including the territory of the state of Israel) by
armed struggle. The "Fatah Doctrine" rejected and played down
ideological controversy and the splits that followed therefrom:

> The bloody battle with Zionist occupation is one of sur-
> vival and not over a social ideology, it is a struggle of
> life and death, of being or not being. In such a struggle
> ideological differences ought to disappear and the people
> ought to join together in a broad revolutionary front to
> dismantle the political, social and economic structure of
> the oppressor state, and uproot Zionism from our noble
> soil (translated in Appendix III of Sharabi 1970, p. 49).

Resources

While accurate estimates are difficult, Fatah apparently had
enough resources of people, weapons, and commitment to produce
noticeable commando activity. Fatah received contributions from
private citizens, as well as some encouragement from Syria. Peretz
claims that a "truly popular Palestine Arab consciousness" had developed in the period 1948 through 1967 (1970, p. 41). Fatah appears
to have attempted to turn the environmental element of Israeli military might into a kind of resource by provoking Israeli attacks on
neighboring Arab states.

Environment

Fatah's environment was bleak. According to Nakhleh,

> from 1958 to 1966 Fatah worked against almost insur-
> mountable odds: popular cynicism; inter-Arab govern-
> mental conflict; limited resources; a defeatist apathy
> on the part of the Palestinians, and a concerted campaign

of innuendo and criticism in the Arab press to discredit
Fatah as a group of foreign-supported adventurers (1971,
p. 192).

Of course, the environment did contain Israel and her army, which
Fatah attempted to manipulate.

Component

Apparently the major mission of Fatah was the conduct of military missions to provoke Israeli attack and thus keep the Palestinian
issues alive. Aware of the Arab governments' reluctance to pursue
energetically the Palestinian Arab cause, and cynical about the function of the PLO under the Arab League, Fatah conducted military
operations designed to evoke Israeli response and thus keep the Palestinian cause audible. Fatah is said to have provoked a raid on Samu
(in Jordan) in 1966 and on Syria in 1967 (Kerr 1971, p. 134).

Evaluation of the Palestinian Arab System, 1956 to 1967

While the Arab governments continued to function as a decision
maker for Palestinian Arabs in the years following the Suez conflict,
a new decision maker independent of the Arab governments appeared
in Fatah, the Palestine Movement of National Liberation. While both
decision makers claimed to support Palestinian Arab claims, they
differed in the priority given to Arab-government and Palestinian-
Arab issues. Bluntly put, the fact that these two decision makers
arranged their values in exactly opposite order left them diametrically
opposed.
Given the Arab governments' program to co-opt and control
Palestinian resistance first by the All-Palestine government and later
by the PLO, Fatah faced an acute audibility problem. The strategy of
Fatah commando activities used to provoke Israeli raids made the
existence of Palestinian grievances audible to Arab nations: The
Israeli response could not be ignored, as had the claims of poor and
landless refugees.

PERIOD III: 1967 TO 1973

In the period after the 1967 war, a strong and victorious Israel
dominated the Palestinian environment, occupying the West Bank, the
Golan Heights, and Sinai-Suez. Discredited as potential defenders of
Arab Palestinian interests, the governments of Syria, Jordan, and
Egypt found themselves facing the very simple and basic goal of
Israeli withdrawal from their territory.

While Arab governments continued to act as decision makers for Palestinian Arabs, Palestinian groups not officially sponsored by Arab governments had increased in size and proliferated in number. These groups, representing a wide range of Palestinian opinion, combined into larger umbrella groups in an attempt to coordinate strategy.

Decision Maker A: Palestinian Arab Resistance Organizations

Environment

The Palestinian resistance organizations faced an environment in which Israel occupied parts of the territory of three Arab states. Egypt and Jordan had lost control of large land areas of significant economic importance. Syria had lost a relatively small piece of land—one which was not central to the Syrian economy but which was, after all, sovereign territory of Syria. The environment of course included other Arab countries with commitments to the Palestinians.

The failure of Arab government armies in 1967 coupled with effective resistance by Palestinian Arab forces at the battle of Karameh in 1968 sparked growth of the Palestinian Arab resistance movement as well as proliferation of groups. We shall discuss the two generally recognized to be the most important: Fatah-PLO and the Popular Front for the Liberation of Palestine (PFLP).*

Decision Maker A-1: Fatah-PLO

Although the PLO had originated as a Palestine entity under the tutelage of Egypt and Jordan and as a counter to the rather feisty policies

---

*The Black September Group, a splinter from Fatah, appears to have adopted tactics similar to those of the PFLP. Black September has claimed responsibility for the killing of Jordan's premier, the assassination attempt against the Jordanian ambassador to London, three hijack attempts against planes of Jordan's airline, an explosion in a German plant manufacturing parts for the Israeli air force, and the hijacking of a Belgian plane to Lod airport in Israel (Eric Pace, New York Times, September 8, 1972, p. 12). More recently, the attack on Israeli Olympic athletes has been linked to Black September. The group is thought to have operated in secret coordination with Fatah. As is often the case with alleged clandestine activity, proof is difficult to find. For the moment we must hold final judgment in reserve and simply note Black September's existence and activity.

of Fatah and Syria, the June 1967 war left Shukairy discredited and the guerrillas with new stature. As a result the PLO conducted what amounted to a merger with certain of the commando groups. Half the PLO's National Council seats were given in May 1968 to guerrilla groups (38 to Fatah, 10 to PFLP, and 2 to others). PFLP, which we shall discuss below, did not fully cooperate, however. In February 1969 the PLO's National Council named Fatah leader Yasir Arafat as chairman of the PLO Executive Committee (Kerr 1971, pp. 135-37).

Goals

The goals of PLO-Fatah were essentially the goals established for Fatah: the destruction of Zionism and "liberation" of the Palestinian Arab homeland. With the merger of PLO and Fatah the former PLO assurances of Jordanian West Bank control became less certain. While Fatah did not challenge Arab monarchies, it did seek "liberation" of Palestinian land—and the West Bank obviously had been part of Palestine.

Resources

By February 1969, Arafat, as head of the PLO and Fatah, was leading the combined forces and resources of the PLO, the Palestine Liberation Army (PLA), and its guerrilla forces known as the Popular Liberation Forces. These groups possessed an estimated fighting force (at July 1970) of 10,000 troops and financial backing, including subsidies through the Arab League. Fatah itself was said to possess 15,000 troops. Both PLO and Fatah obtained arms from a variety of sources, including China, and monetary aid from private Palestinian sources channelled through Arab governments (Christian Science Monitor, cited in Peretz 1970, pp. 56-57). UNRWA provided indirect resources, as indicated earlier.

Components

The missions or components of Fatah-PLO under the leadership of Yasir Arafat divided into two classes: operations and coordination. By March 1968, Fatah had begun to conduct a "new strategy of limited large-scale confrontation with Israeli forces" with such features as the battle at Karameh, in addition to guerrilla actions (Nakhleh 1971, p. 193).

When Arafat assumed leadership of the PLO in April 1969 he developed plans to unite the plethora of Palestinian groups into a coordinated whole. By April most major groups except the PFLP (although including three splinters from the PFLP) had combined in the Palestine Armed Struggle Command (PASC), headed by Arafat.

By 1970 a new group, known as the United Command for the Liberation of Palestine was formed, which included the PFLP. A Central Committee headed by Arafat united ten major organizations and established guerrilla jurisdictions within Jordan. Furthermore, a Palestine National Council of Palestinian Arab group representatives was established, taking on the character of a government-in-exile (Peretz 1970, pp. 50-51).

Decision Maker A-2: The Popular Front for the Liberation of Palestine

The PFLP, headed by George Habash, came into being after the June 1967 war. Unlike Fatah-PLO and Arafat, the PFLP did not aim for broad-based unity. PFLP missions were operations aimed against not only Israel, but also the "imperialist" and "Zionist" system that supported her. The enemy consisted of any person or state that cooperated with Israel, as well as any Arab state beholden and/or dependent upon such a collaborator. The enemy thus became Saudi Arabia, Kuwait, Lebanon, and Jordan, as well as the United States and European allies of Israel.

Resources

PFLP monetary resources stemmed from Iraq and private donations. In addition PFLP received arms from East Europe and Iraq. Syria, a major "revolutionary" Arab country, did not tend to support PFLP, as some of its leaders had had connections with old enemies of the Syrian regime (Kerr 1971, p. 134).

The PFLP (as well as other clandestine terrorist groups such as Black September) can be seen as manipulating Israeli military might, transforming it from simply an environmental constraint into a partial resource. The Israeli reprisals provoked by the guerrilla actions served to maintain and renew public Arab militancy and undercut potential developing moves toward accommodation.

Components

One mission or component used first by the PFLP involved the attack of airlines (including hijacking and sabotage of airplanes) doing business with Israel. The hijackings served both to punish Western collaborators and to embarrass Lebanon, Jordan, and Egypt, as the planes hijacked in September 1970 landed in Lebanon, Egypt, and Jordan and were destroyed in Jordan and Egypt. These incidents demonstrated the hijackers' contempt and the inability of the governments to control commando actions within their borders. (These events precipitated the Jordanian attack on Palestinians reported earlier.) The attack at Lod Airport by Japanese guerrillas upheld the "punish all collaborators" mission, in that all nationalities present in the Israeli airport were attacked indiscriminately.

As of July 1970 the PFLP claimed an estimated fighting strength of 4,000 (Christian Science Monitor, cited in Peretz 1970, pp. 56-57). The PFLP, with its Marxist revolutionary ideology, sought allies among revolutionary groups outside the Arab world. While the extent of these contacts is difficult to estimate, some evidence has surfaced through such incidents as the attack on passengers at Lod airport by Japanese guerrillas and the PFLP confirmation of support for that action.

Decision Maker B: The Arab Governments

Goals

Once again, assessments of national interest produced division and disunity among Arab governments with respect to the Palestinian Arabs. As had been the case prior to the June war of 1967, Syria continued to present herself as more militantly concerned with the Palestinian Arabs' liberation than were either Egypt or Jordan. The latter two, having lost control of extensive and valuable land areas (the Sinai-Suez and West Bank areas, respectively), declared their willingness to abide by UN Security Council Resolution 242, which provided both for Israeli withdrawal from occupied territory and for acknowledgment of the rights of all states in the area, presumably including Israel (Lall 1968, p. 309). By contrast, Syria, who had lost control of a much smaller piece of territory, useful primarily for strategic purposes against Israel (the Golan Heights), did not support the resolution (Kerr 1971, pp. 130-32).

Resources (and Environment Constraints)

Arab countries continued to rely upon their big-power allies for military support and continued to attempt to control and use Palestinian Arab groups for the benefit of their national ambitions. After June 1967 the intensity of these relations increased. Egypt became increasingly dependent on Soviet arms and technicians (the resource beginning to take on the character of an environmental constraint); Syria not only collaborated with existing Palestinian resistance movements but sponsored an additional group: al-Sa'iqa (Thunderbolt) (Kerr 1971, p. 134). Syria's development of its own client guerrilla organization appears to have been a clear attempt to channel and control Palestinians and their supporters into strategies that would support Syrian national interests.

Environment

The growing size and proliferating number of Palestinian Arab groups served as an environmental constraint, insofar as these groups could not be controlled completely by the Arab governments. Kerr emphasizes, for example, that the presence of Palestinans meant that Nasser and Hussein "were not free simply to count the benefits and losses for themselves, in any bargain that might be proposed" (1971, p. 132).

Components

The major components or missions of the Arab states after the June war reflected the inter-Arab rivalries, particularly between militant Syria and the more cautious Egypt and Jordan. While Egypt and Jordan were attempting to devise ways to regain the territories occupied by Israel, Syria not only refused to support the UN Security Council efforts but also engaged in activities which exacerbated the conflict. Although she promoted the new guerrilla group, al-Sa'iqa, she avoided provoking Israeli attacks on herself by encouraging anti-Israeli commando activity through the borders of Jordan and Lebanon. Both Syria and Iraq fostered Palestinian guerrilla action, not simply out of opportunistic inter-Arab competitiveness with Nasser, but to serve ideologically revolutionary purposes as well: in Malcolm Kerr's words, "to force the pace, to keep pressure on him [Nasser] from the left, to undermine his new partnership with Husayn, to dissuade him from abandoning the Palestinian and other revolutionary causes altogether" (1971, p. 138).

After a good deal of difficulty and a good many skirmishes between guerrillas in Jordan and government troops, the Jordanian army in September 1970 launched heavy attacks against centers of Palestinian population. Syria aided the guerrillas, although Iraqi troops in Jordan did not (Kerr 1971, p. 149). Nasser and other Arab leaders negotiated a ceasefire between commando leader Arafat and Hussein, leaving the guerrillas badly hurt but not totally destroyed.

In March 1972 Hussein proposed a federal structure for a Palestinian West Bank and an East Bank under his rule (New York Times, March 17, 1972, p. 13). This proposal offered a compromise of increased self-rule for Palestinians, short of complete divorce from Hussein. The suggestion that a "Palestinian entity" should be established which did not include the territory of Israel could be expected to draw severe opposition from militant Palestinian Arab quarters. The proposal appears to have "died for lack of a second." Indeed, the New York Times reported that Fatah claimed responsibility for an explosion in Jordan which was said to be part of a military response to this proposal (April 2, 1972, p. 10). Nonetheless, Hussein's divorce and remarriage to a Palestinian woman in late 1972 appears to be a further effort to increase his credibility with West Bank Palestinian Arabs.

Decision Maker C: Ali al-Jabari and Other Moderates

Muhammad Ali al-Jabari, the mayor of Hebron, was one of the few Palestinian Arab notables who was mentioned publicly as opposing commando programs. It seems plausible that other such Palestinians existed and might have become audible if appropriate environmental and resource changes had occurred.

Goals and Resources

Peretz has identified al-Jabari as one of a small number of influentials who favored a "Palestinian entity on the West Bank separate from either Israel or Jordan" (1970, p. 53). Apparently such persons were willing to coexist in some way with Israel. At present the publicly known Arab resources available to al-Jabari and others like him seem meager, given the extent of organized Fatah and other commando activity. Kerr (1971, p. 153) has suggested, however, that:

> having lost confidence in the benevolence of Husayn, and
> in the utopianism of the Fidayin, some Palestinians might
> now become more inclined to accept a settlement with
> Israel along the lines that Husayn had sought—provided
> only that they could be rid of Husayn himself.

The proposal by Jordan in spring 1972, that an Arab Kingdom be formed including a Palestinian West Bank and a state of Jordan, offered new opportunities to Palestinians such as al-Jabari.

Environment

The environment for these "moderates" includes Western powers and Arab nation-states who might well hope to develop a West Bank state as a workable permanent solution to the national aspirations of Palestinian Arabs. If consensus could be reached among some Arab states and between the United States and the Soviet Union (and China?), such an arrangement might be investigated and established, assuming that significant cooperation and support could be developed so as to make a protracted guerrilla movement impossible to maintain.

The initial rejection by Israel of Hussein's proposal can be seen as hopeful rather than negative, since any proposal immediately

acceptable to Israel would probably be unable to attract significant
Arab support. Although resources publicly available have not given
details, it seems plausible that the plan may have received private
support from big powers and some Arab states, and that Palestinian
Arab support was being sought. Insofar as popular support could be
developed, cutting into popular support for commandos, Arab states
could afford to acquiesce publicly to a solution other than the destruction of Israel.

Evaluation of the Palestinian Arab System, 1967 to 1973

Palestinian Arabs succeeded in the period since 1956 in becoming
audible both within the Arab world and in the larger international context. By provoking Israeli attacks on Arab countries, the Palestinian
Arab commandos forced Arab states, who might have preferred being
deaf to the claims of "refugees," to deal with Israel as an enemy. The
commandos prevented nation-states from agreeing to dismiss Palestinian Arab claims as simply the domestic problem of the Arab states
in which Palestinians currently live. The "revolutionary" Palestinian
Arab movements further extended Palestinian audibility by invoking
an antiimperialist image (in the tradition of Mao, Fanon, and so on),
thus cutting into U.S. pro-Israel sentiment by appealing to U.S. leftist
youth.

Although commando groups succeeded in provoking Israeli
attacks on Arab nations, the commandos themselves were unable to
achieve complete unity. In particular the PFLP persevered in actions
that provoked severe retaliation by the Jordanian government against
commandos in Jordan. In the effort to become audible, the PFLP provoked an attack which threatened to limit the durability of the Palestinian voice, at least as represented by the commandos.

Perhaps Jordanian attacks on the commandos may have developed
caution, allowing the more "conservative" voices such as those of
al-Jabari and friends to become more audible. It is difficult to estimate the amount of support for persons such as al-Jabari. But
assuming that some sort of U.S.—USSR—China accord could be
achieved, it is possible that a viable West Bank Arab entity might
have been established, based on nationalistic Palestinian commitments,
buttressed by big-power agreements, and maintained by both internal
Palestinian Arab support and Israeli acquiescence. Such a "Palestinian entity" could have succeeded in developing both durability and
audibility for Palestinian Arabs, by moving them from the status of
nonstate nation to that of nation-state.

On the other hand, the continuing incidence of terrorist activities
and the surfacing of apparently new groups such as Black September
suggests that some Palestinian guerrillas were "going underground"

in order to maintain durability and surfacing in brief terrorist out-
bursts in order to maintain audibility. The ability of such groups to
attract monetary and popular support in the Arab world appears to
have been linked inversely to the ability of the "moderates," both
Arab and non-Arab, to define a possible and realistic "Palestinian
entity" which could coexist with Israel. If such an entity could be established, offering an improved way of life to the Palestinian Arabs
and satisfying in some way Palestinian national aspirations, support
for the costly and painful road advocated and currently pursued by
the guerrillas might have diminished. Undoubtedly the leadership of
at least some of the Arab states (notably Jordan and probably Egypt,
as well) would be eager to see such a solution develop. Precisely because of this sentiment for peace, however, many of the guerrillas
remained motivated to step up terrorist activity and provoke Israeli
retaliation, both to remain visible themselves and to undercut any
growth of popular support for appeasement or conciliation with Israel.

PERIOD IV: OCTOBER 1973 TO NOVEMBER 1975

Decision Maker A: The Palestine Liberation Organization

Goals

The PLO sought to represent the diversity of Palestinian views
and to develop international recognition and support. Presumably
because of its desire to appeal to a variety of Arab and Arab-Pales-
tinian opinions as well as non-Arab views, the PLO avoided sharpening
the clarity of its goals. Although rumors were voiced about the willingness of Arafat and the PLO leadership to come to some sort of
accommodation with Israel, the PLO continued to maintain that its
goal was the establishment of a "democratic" state including Jews,
Moslems, and Christians, presumably enjoying boundaries that would
include the territory of the state of Israel. In early 1975 the PLO, in
a summit meeting that addressed objections raised by the PFLP and
other "rejection front" groups, issued a statement opposing any
Palestinian entity "for which the price would be the recognition of the
enemy, the conclusion of peace with him and the renunciation of the
historic rights of our people to return to their homeland and to self-
determination" (Keesing's Contemporary Archives, February 10-16,
1975, p. 26961).
    Although the PLO attempted to represent as wide a range of
Palestinian Arab opinion as possible, the organization leaned in the
direction of supporting the establishment of some sort of Palestinian
entity on at least a portion of the land claimed as Palestine. Fatah,

headed by Arafat, the PDFLP (Popular Democratic Front for the
Liberation of Palestine), headed by Hawatmeh (according to Chaliand,
the only Palestinian group that recognized the national character of
the Israeli Jews), and Sa'iqa, the Syrian-sponsored Palestinian group,
all supported the establishment of some sort of Palestinian Arab
national entity. Whatever its ultimate goal may be, the PLO seems
to have given priority to the objective of setting up a Palestinian
national entity over the objective of destroying the state of Israel.

Resources

In addition to its major resources of Palestinian Arab popular
and organizational support, the PLO benefited from a growing sense
of common interest among Arab states. The oil boycott supplied
valuable pressure upon countries previously hesitant or reluctant to
recognize Palestinian Arab national aspirations.

Furthermore, inter-Arab differences, in particular the Syrian
disapproval of Egyptian-Israeli talks and later interim agreement,
led to increased Syrian interest in ties with the PLO.

The United Nations provided additional resources for recognition
of the national-status aspirations of the Palestinian Arabs. In the fall
of 1975, Yasir Arafat was invited to address the UN General Assembly
and was accorded the symbolic treatment usually reserved for heads
of state. The fall 1975 session produced a resolution equating Zionism
with racism. (This resolution, while a blow to Israel, was seen as a
secondary prize to Palestinian Arabs, offered after rejection earlier
by both the Organization of African Unity and the Conference of Non-
aligned Nations of a move to expel Israel from the UN. Both groups,
however, passed resolutions generally supportive of Palestinian Arab
claims and critical of Israel.) Renewal of the UN Golan observer
mission was obtained only after intricate diplomatic maneuvering,
essentially agreeing that the PLO might take part in the January
Security Council discussions on the Middle East.

Environment

Both the Soviet Union and the United States seemed supportive,
in their own ways, of peace-seeking efforts in the Middle East. Although the Soviet Union reiterated its feeling of the "importance of the
participation at Geneva of a representative of the Palestinian Arab
people," the precise identity of that representative was not clear.
Furthermore, the Soviet Union reiterated both the right of Palestinian
Arabs to their own state and the right of Israel to independent state
existence (Facts on File, May 3, 1975, 295:3, and May 10, 1975,
312:2).

Both the PFLP (and its smaller-group allies) and Jordan remained parts of the PLO environment vying for representation of Palestinian Arabs. The PFLP stood ready to oppose any "moderation" or "accommodation" with Israel; the government of Jordan continued to hope to retain sovereignty over West Bank Palestinians.

Components or Projects: Coordination, National Recognition, and Guerrilla Violence

The PLO strategy involved the complex balancing/juggling of three policy strands, which were not always mutually complementary. Coordination involved not only attempting to hold together a coalition of diverse groups but also attempting to discipline persons, such as the Tunis hijackers, who violated stated PLO principles. Although a penal code was established by the PLO, its enforcement remained unclear.

National recognition was developing from a number of non-Arab quarters. For example, the Soviet Union referred to Palestinian "national rights," as opposed to the more vague "legitimate rights." Japan in March 1974 acknowledged the "legitimate rights" while Italy recognized the "national" rights of the Palestinian people. In January 1975 India became the first non-Arab government to accord full diplomatic recognition to the PLO.

While the PLO denounced and attempted to prevent attacks on "third" parties, it condoned attacks on Israeli targets. Various groups in the PLO, including Fatah, the PDFLP, and the PFLP-General Command, conducted attacks on Israelis during this period.

Decision Maker B: The "Rejection Front" Palestinian Arabs:
Popular Front for the Liberation of Palestine and Others

Goals

As indicated earlier, this group opposed any sort of interim or moderate step that might seem in their view to leave open the possibility of accommodation with Israel. A number of the smaller groups in this coalition were also officially part of the PLO. The PFLP, however, withdrew from the PLO.

Resources

Iraq was the primary source of government support. In general the "rejection front" was isolated from effective leadership of large segments of Palestinian and other Arab opinion, although the group retained a kind of "veto" power. The latter was possible because the

"front" was willing to conduct acts of violence designed to disrupt any
developing agreements not to its liking. In general, however, the
rejection front was isolated from effective positive leadership roles.
Most Arab governments seemed to favor Palestinian participation in
an international settlement, whether at Geneva or at the UN Security
Council.

Components or Projects

The rejection front seems to have attempted to do double duty
by both maintaining representatives within the PLO Executive Committee and by having the most audible member (the PFLP) withdraw
in protest against the PLO's apparent tendency to be soft on moderation.
In addition, the rejection front, if it can be defined to include a number of little known or ambiguously identified groups, continued to
attack third parties, for example, a U.S. colonel in Beirut (who was
kidnapped and later released) and the Egyptian ambassador in Madrid
(also later released), the latter allegedly in reaction to Sadat's policy
of interim agreement with Israel.

Decision Maker C: Jordan

Jordan entered only peripherally here, as it did not claim to
speak for Palestinians in general but only for those Palestinians who
had lived as Palestinian-Jordanian citizens. While Jordan was publicly "persuaded" at the Rabat conference of 1974 to give up claims
to authority over the Palestinians, Jordan's position remains unclear
as long as the fate of the West Bank is unsettled. Syria in 1975 was
courting the favor of both Jordan and the PLO; insofar as the PLO is
not able to control the rejection front, the role of alternative parties
such as Jordan may become more significant. Jordan is a generally
recognized nation-state and as such has prerogatives not currently
available to the PLO. While the PLO seems in the ascendancy in
early 1976, the situation is by no means clear or stable. Jordan may
develop further resources, especially given Israeli fears that a
Palestinian state in the West Bank might be used simply as a base
for attack against Israel unless specific guarantees are accorded. *

_____

* The ability of the PLO coalition and Syria to cooperate appeared to falter badly during 1976 as the Lebanese civil war intensified.
The Syrian-PLO ties that had appeared to be a resource in earlier
times later appeared as an environmental constraint. The Syrians
may possibly harbor a desire to establish a "Greater Syria"—to unite

Evaluation of the Palestinian Arab System, October 1973 through 1975

Although the PLO had become the primary Palestinian Arab voice by the end of 1975, it had not established a state, and it had not established its unique claim to Palestinian sovereignty, in that it was not able completely to control the activities of groups acting in behalf of the Palestinian cause. Furthermore, the question of whether or not the PLO was prepared ultimately to coexist with the state of Israel had not been unambiguously resolved. Certainly the public face of the PLO toward Israel was hostile, although speculation continues that at some unspecified future time the PLO, or at least elements within the PLO, might be willing and able to work out an accommodation with Israel.

IMPACT OF THE PALESTINIAN ARAB SYSTEM ON THE INTERNATIONAL ARENA

Whatever its difficulties and disunities, the Palestinian Arab system has had a noticeable impact on the international arena. Following the guidelines set forth in Chapter 1 for estimating that impact, the following observations can be made:

1. Arab governments have tended to move to control violence, while Palestinian groups have been the major sources of increasing violence. The PLO has condemned the use of violence against third parties, although this condemnation has not persuaded all Palestinian groups. Apparently the Arab governments have attempted to control violence in order to maintain control of their own foreign policies. Each government's purpose, whatever the ideological commitment, has been to assure that armed activity involving that government be controlled by that government.

By contrast, Palestinian groups appear to have escalated the level of violence as an attempt to influence the foreign policies of Arab governments—to force the hand of the governments by creating a situation that makes peace with Israel impossible.

2. The attempts by Palestinian groups to increase violence have been grouped in the periods after 1956. The Suez crisis seems to have been a clear watershed point, marking Palestinian Arab loss of faith in the ability or intentions of the Arab governments. The moves

---

in some fashion with all or parts of Jordan and Lebanon—and possibly eventually with the territory of the state of Israel. If so, the Syrians would serve no ultimate objective by supporting a costly and unpredictable PLO ally beyond the point that that ally were cooperative and controllable.

to escalate violence after the 1956 Suez conflict seem to relect a fear that the "self-interest" of Arab governments might lead to a neglect of Palestinian interests in the effort to avoid costly conflicts with Israel. The moves to escalate violence can be seen as an alternative adopted in the face of failure to achieve sufficient success through international institutions (such as the United Nations and the Arab League) and through reliance upon Arab governments as spokesman for Palestinian Arab interests.

3. Two instances of attempts to widen the conflict to include other nations can be identified. The first consists of the use of the United Nations as an arena for discussion and pursuit of Palestinian Arab goals. This approach apparently has been fostered by the Arab governments and continues to this day. The United Nations provides a platform for verbal support of Palestinian Arab claims—an opportunity for Arab governments to show symbolic and verbal solidarity with Palestinian Arabs.

The second conflict-widening action consists of violent guerrilla moves designed to involve countries outside the Arab world. The PFLP and lately Black September have been most active in perpetrating acts of violence against business enterprises and nationals of countries outside the Arab world who do business with or support Israel. It seems plausible to speculate that the latter attempts are related to the failure of the UN moves to produce advancement toward Palestinian Arab goals. The attacks on targets other than Israel seem designed to prevent nation-states outside the Middle East from dismissing the Palestinian Arabs as a "domestic problem" of Israel and her neighboring Arab states. Further, the moves seem aimed at convincing all countries that the problem cannot be solved by either attacking or ignoring the Palestinian Arab claims.

4. Many parties have operated so as to widen cleavages between and among states. This widening seems to derive from the fact that deep cleavages exist between Arab leaders and that any resolute or decisive action inevitably widens further one or another of them. The attempt to avoid widening cleavages leads to a kind of indecision and double-talk, in order to avoid sharpening issues. On the other hand, some states, notably Syria, seem perfectly willing to widen cleavages in order to isolate, highlight, and embarrass opponent Arab states in their vacillation and vagueness.

5. Only one action has been noted that attempted to produce reconciliation betweeen previously opposed states. Abdullah of Jordan made moves after 1948 to establish a separate peace agreement with Israel. He did not succeed. Rather, it is thought that his assassination was motivated by this peace attempt.

6. Both "radical" guerrilla movements and "radical" Arab states have attempted to undermine and weaken the stability of current

nation-states. One target has been Jordan; another target has been
Lebanon. These moves reflect conflicts within the Arab world: current
ideological conflicts between "revolutionaries" and "traditionalists,"
as well as competition among rival Arab leadership movements and
parties that have roots in the period prior to 1948. Because some of
the movements and parties have become the governments of Arab
states, intra-Arab political rivalries include strategies designed to
unseat these governments.

CONCLUSION

The current Palestinian Arab system erupts into the international
context in three general ways: (1) in the provocation or exacerbation
of conflicts among Arab states, (2) in conflicts between Arab states
and Israel, and (3) in the extension by some Palestinian Arab groups
of their target to include non-Middle East states (or nationals of
same) who do business with Israel. These three points of intrusion
into the international context mark three different modes adopted by
various Palestinian Arab groups to achieve audibility and durability
and thereby prevent the nation-states of the world from denying the
national political significance of the Palestinian Arabs. The most
recently developed third mode (moving against nationals of non-Arab
countries and against Israelis in territories outside the Middle East)
seems clearly designed to guarantee that the Palestinian Arabs can
remain audible even if they are successfully controlled within the
Middle East itself.

While Palestinian Arabs do not constitute a nation-state, they
have attempted to serve notice to their international context that it
may not be able to develop a settlement between Israel and its Arab
border states without regard to stateless Palestinian Arabs. If
agreement seems to be in the offing between Israel and Egypt-Jordan-
Lebanon, the conflict between those states and Syria can be exacerbated. If the United States and the Soviet Union should develop some
sort of big-power settlement to be imposed top-down, China may be
brought in as a major supporter of both the Palestinian Arabs and of
potentially dissident Arab states. Splits in both the big outside powers
and the Arab powers provide opportunities for Palestinian Arabs in
developing resources.

We see from this case study of the Palestinian Arabs both the
kinds of strategies and goals that this nonstate nation chooses to
devise in pursuit of its goals and some of the points at which these
strategies are likely to erupt into the international context. By studying
the behavior of the nonstate nation we can gain a new perspective on
international politics, viewing a small but often crucial actor in the
arena apparently dominated but not always controlled by nation-states.

REFERENCES

Alami, Musa. 1949. "The Lesson of Palestine." The Middle East
    Journal 3: 372-405.
Allen, Richard. 1974. Imperialism and Nationalism in the Fertile
    Crescent. New York: Oxford University Press.
Antonius, George. 1946. The Arab Awakening. New York: Capricorn
    Books.
el-Ayouty, Yassin. 1973. "Egypt and the Palestinians." Current
    History, January, pp. 9-12, 39.
Barbour, Nevill. 1969. Nisi Dominus. Beirut: The Institute for
    Palestine Studies.
Buehrig, Edward H. 1971. The UN and the Palestine Refugees.
    Bloomington: Indiana University Press.
Bullard, Sir Reader, ed. 1958. The Middle East, 3d ed. London:
    Boston: Little, Brown
Chaliand, Gerard. 1972. The Palestinian Resistance. Middlesex,
    England: Penguin Books.
Churchman, C. West. 1968. The Systems Approach. New York:
    Dell.
Documents of the Palestinian Resistance Movement. 1971. New York:
    Pathfinder Press.
Dodd, Peter and Halim Barakat. 1969. River without Bridges.
    Beirut: The Institute for Palestine Studies.
Enloe, Cynthia H. 1973. Ethnic Conflict and Political Development.
    Boston: Little, Brown.
Erskine, Beatrice Strong. 1935. Palestine of the Arabs. London:
    G. G. Harrap.
Everyman's United Nations, 8th ed. 1968. New York: United
    Nations.
Facts on File, January—November, 1975.
Fields, Rona M. 1973. "A Comparative Case Study of the Chicano
    and Irish Republican Non-State Nations." A paper presented
    at the International Studies Association meetings, New York
    City.
Fischbach, Joe. 1973. "Non-State Nation: Guinea-Bissau." unpub-
    lished manuscript, University of Southern California.
Forsythe, David P. 1971. "UNRWA, the Palestine Refugees, and
    World Politics: 1949-1969." International Organization, Winter,
    pp. 25-45.
Furlonge, Sir Geoffrey. 1969. Palestine Is My Country. New York:
    Praeger.
Haim, Sylvia. 1962. Arab Nationalism. Berkeley: University of
    California Press.
Heradstveit, Daniel. 1974. Arab and Israeli Elite Perceptions.
    New York: Humanities Press.

Hudson, Michael. 1972. "Developments and Setbacks in the Palestinian Resistance Movement, 1967-1971." Journal of Palestine Studies 1, no. 3: 64-84.

Ismael, Tareq Y. 1970. Governments and Politics of the Contemporary Middle East. Homewood, Ill.: Dorsey.

Jackson, Katheleen O'Brien. 1973. "The Non-state Nation in Northern Ireland." A paper presented at the International Studies Association meetings, New York City.

Jacoby, F. J., ed. Anglo-Palestine Yearbook, 1947-48. London: Anglo-Palestine Publications.

Journal of Palestine Studies, 1-12 (vol. 1-3). Especially "Documents and Source Materials." 1972-74.

Keesing's Contemporary Archives, February 10-16, 1975.

Kerr, Malcolm H. 1971. The Arab Cold War, 3d ed. London: Oxford University Press.

Khouri, Fred J. 1968. The Arab-Israeli Dilemma. Syracuse, N.Y.: Syracuse University Press.

Klieman, Aaron S. 1970. Foundations of British Policy in the Arab World. Baltimore: Johns Hopkins Press.

Knight, Kathleen. 1973. "Bangladesh: Case-study of a 'Successful' N-S-N?" A paper presented at the International Studies Association meetings, New York City.

Lall, Arthur. 1968. The UN and the Middle East Crisis, 1967. New York: Columbia University Press.

Laqueur, Walter. 1972. The Struggle for the Middle East. Middlesex, England: Penguin Books.

Lenczowski, George. 1968. The Middle East in World Affairs, 3d ed. Ithaca, N.Y.: Cornell University Press.

Love, Kenneth. 1969. Suez: The Twice-Fought War. New York: McGraw-Hill.

MacDonald, Robert W. 1965. The League of Arab States. Princeton, N.J.: Princeton University Press.

The Mandates System. 1945. Geneva: League of Nations, April.

Nachmias, David and Robert Rockaway. 1976. "From a Nonstate Nation to a Nation-State: the Zionist Movement, 1897-1947." See Chapter 3 of this volume.

Nakhleh, Emile A. 1971. "The Anatomy of Violence: Theoretical Reflections on Palestinian Resistance." Middle East Journal 25 (Spring): 180-200.

New York Times, July 1973 to November 1974, especially the reports of Raymond Anderson, David Binder, Ed Cowan, Bernard Gwertzman, Richard Halloran, Paul Hofmann, Henry Kamm, Juan de Onis, Eric Pace, Nan Robertson, Alvin Shuster, Hedrick Smith, Terrence Smith, Henry Tanner, and Kathleen Teltsch.

Obichere, Boniface I. 1973. "Guinea-Bissau: A West African Nonstate Nation." A paper presented at the International Studies
Association meetings, New York City.

Peretz, Don, Evan M. Wilson, and Richard Ward. 1970. A Palestine
Entity? Washington, D.C.: The Middle East Institute.

Powell, Charles A. 1973. "Contemporary Scotland as a Non-state
Nation." A paper presented at the International Studies Association meetings, New York City.

Quandt, William B., Fuad Jabber, and Ann Mosely Lesch. 1973.
The Politics of Palestinian Nationalism. Berkeley: University
of California Press.

Rapoport, Anatol. 1960. Fights, Games, and Debates. Ann Arbor:
University of Michigan Press.

Remington, Robin. "Nation vs. Class: The Ethnic Dimension of
Intra-Communist Crisis." Unpublished synopsis for Col-
loquium on Party and Society in East Europe, Berkeley: Center
for Slavic Studies. See also Chapter 7 in this volume.

Rodinson, Maxime. 1968. Israel and the Arabs. Middlesex, England:
Penguin Books.

Safran, Nadav. 1969. From War to War. New York: Pegasus.

Salim, Qais. 1974. "Resistance and National Self Determination in
Palestine." MEIRUP Reports no. 28. Cambridge, Mass.:
Middle East Research and Information Project, May.

Schattschneider, E. E. 1975. The Semisovereign People. New York:
Dryden, reissued from 1960.

Sharabi, Hisham. 1970. Palestine Guerrillas, Their Credibility and
Effectiveness. Washington, D.C.: Georgetown University.

Shepardson, Mary. 1973. "The Navajos as a Non-state Nation." A
paper presented at the International Studies Association meetings,
New York City. See also Chapter 8 in this volume.

Stephens, Robert. 1973. "The Great Powers and the Middle East."
Journal of Palestine Studies 2, no. 4. (Summer): 3-12.

Walton, Richard E. and Robert B. McKersie. 1965. A Behavioral
Theory of Labor Negotiations. New York: McGraw-Hill.

Wolf, John B. 1973. "Black September: Militant Palestinianism."
Current History, January, pp. 4-8, 37.

3

FROM A NONSTATE NATION
TO A NATION-STATE:
THE ZIONIST MOVEMENT, 1897-1947
David Nachmias
Robert Rockaway

The people of this nonstate nation (NSN) claim a land
base that overlaps the claim of the Palestinian Arabs'
NSN. The Zionist groups seem to have been mobilized
earlier than were the Arabs, largely because moving to
Palestine required mobilization as a precondition. The
Arabs, on the other hand, began with a strategic disadvantage common to many status quo groups: Much of the
population tends to assume that the basic pattern of life
will continue along familiar lines.

The Zionists confronted an international context
that showed support for Zionist aspirations in the early
Mandate period but changed to conflict and ambivalence
in the face of increasingly audible Palestinian Arab nationalism. The Zionist groups, however, had organized
what amounted to a government parallel to the Mandate
government. The Jewish Agency served not only as a
quasi government for Jews but as a participatory segment of the Mandate government. In the context of Arab
boycott against the Mandate authority (because of its
treatment of the Zionists as an equally legitimate group),
the effectiveness of the Jewish Agency in dealing with the
British authorities was enhanced. When Britain turned
the Mandate over to the United Nations, the Zionist movement as an NSN continued to participate in the United Nations despite Zionist objection to aspects of the international organization's handling of the matter. In general
the Zionist movement adopted a pragmatic and united-

36

front stance, showing flexibility in dealing with the international context and in dealing with internal disagree-
ments.

—Judy S. Bertelsen

When Theodor Herzl, the founder of modern political Zionism,
returned to Vienna from the First Zionist Congress in Basel, Switzerland, in 1897, he wrote prophetically in his diary: "Were I to sum
up the Basel Congress in a word—which I shall guard against pro-
nouncing publicly—it would be this: At Basel I founded the Jewish
State. If I said this out loud today, I would be answered by universal
laughter. Perhaps in five years, and certainly in fifty, everyone will
know it."[1] It was exactly 50 years later that the United Nations resolved to create a Jewish state by a partition of Palestine.

States, however, are rarely established by resolutions. The
UN resolution can best be regarded as an international act of recognition that a group of people ceases to be a nonstate nation and becomes a sovereign state entitled to all the rights and obligations of a
member of the family of nations. Acts of international recognition
constitute the ultimate goal of nonstate nations striving to attain nation-state status. Characteristically, such a goal, if attained, involves the interaction of two general sets of factors: those common
to all nonstate nations (lack of resources, indifferent international
system, cleavages over strategies, to mention just a few) and those
distinct to a particular nonstate nation.[2] This chapter will demonstrate how these two sets of factors interacted over a period of 50
years, the end outcome of which was the establishment of the State of
Israel. The analysis centers around three periods: 1897 (the meeting
of the First Zionist Congress) to 1917 (the granting of the Balfour
Declaration); 1918 to 1938 (the period between the two world wars);
and 1939 to 1947 (the UN resolution). Each period can be seen as a
stage in the evolution of the Zionist nonstate nation. Furthermore,
each stage has determined to a large extent the course of succeeding
developments.

PERIOD I: 1897 TO 1917

In 1897 the First Zionist Congress, attended by delegates from
every major Jewish community, met in Basel, Switzerland, and
marked the transformation of Zionism from a formless aspiration
into a political movement with an organization which would foster the
Zionist alternative to the "Jewish problem." Zionism as a practical
alternative to the Jewish problem evolved from two main sources.

One relates to the Jewish religion, culture, and tradition; for at least since the Middle Ages, the idea of a return to Zion was a cardinal principle of the Jewish religion.* Jewish survival was linked to the belief that God had promised to Abraham that the Holy Land would belong to his offspring forever. In their dispersion and oppression, Jews found solace in their faith in the eventual return and the rebuilding of the Sanctuary in Jerusalem. The other source relates to the disenchantment from the persuasion of "enlightenment," in which the salvation of the Jews lay in their gradual assimilation to the society and culture of their native lands. A catalytic event which led to the relinquishment of the "enlightenment" was the Dreyfus Affair in France. The false arrest of Alfred Dreyfus, a Jew, in France, citadel of the Enlightenment, and the anti-Semitic reaction which it provoked, served as evidence to many Jews that even in the West the problem of anti-Semitism had only been submerged, not solved. The Dreyfus event led Theodore Herzl to write a manifesto, Der Judenstaat (1896; The Jew State), in which he rejected immigration to the West and insisted that only political action leading to a sovereign state for the Jews would be the solution to the Jewish problem.[3] As a consequence, Herzl established a representative political body, the World Zionist Organization (WZO), which held its first congress in Basel in 1897.

Decision Makers: WZO and Theodore Herzl

The decision makers during this period were the WZO and Theodor Herzl, who, until his death in 1904, exerted tremendous influence due to his position as founder and president of the WZO and to the respect he commanded in both the Jewish and non-Jewish world.

———————————

*The root of the term "Zionism" is the word "Zion" (Tziyon), which originally was the name of a Jebusite stronghold in the Jerusalem area in the tenth century B.C.E. After the conquest of Jerusalem by David, Zion became a synonym for Jerusalem and was used by the Hebrew prophets when referring to the city as a spiritual symbol. With the destruction of Jerusalem by the Babylonians in 586 B.C.E., the name Zion took on a special significance: It expressed the yearning of the Jewish people for a return to their homeland. The longing for return and a restoration of Zion became a cardinal principle and all pervasive element in Judaism after the fall of the independent Jewish state in 70 C.E. For the Orthodox Jew, the return to Zion was an indissoluble part of his faith. In the late nineteenth century the name "Zion" served as the basis for the terms "Zionism" and

The Zionist movement at this time was divided into two trends:
(1) political Zionism, which held that legal and political guarantees
for the Jewish national home must be obtained before beginning large-
scale practical work in Palestine; and (2) practical Zionism, whose
adherents felt that political guarantees could be obtained only after
the Zionists could show practical accomplishments in the resettling
and rebuilding of Palestine. The second trend, which also emphasized
efforts to improve the political and civil status of Jews in the Diaspora, came to exert the dominant influence in the world Zionist movement in the decade before World War I.[4]

Goals

Delegates to the First Zionist Congress shared a common con-
viction that Jews must have a homeland of their own in which they
would constitute a majority of the population, exercise sovereignty,
and be masters of their own destiny. Despite differences between the
"political" Zionists and the "practical" Zionists as to the best way of
achieving this goal, the delegates drafted the Basel Platform which
included this goal-oriented principle: "The aim of Zionism is to create for the Jewish people a home in Palestine secured by public
law."[5]

Resources

Nonstate nations attempt to create tangible as well as nontangible resources. Tangible resources include membership in the
movement, organized branches, finance and propaganda organs. The
Zionist movement tended to be quite limited in tangible resources
during the period. Nevertheless, several achievements are to be re-
corded. In Table 3.1 the official figures on membership in the World
Zionist Organization are presented. Members were required to pay
membership dues—the "shekel" (equivalent to 50 American cents),
which was, until 1920, the movement's main source of income. In
1897, 117 branches were established by the Zionist movement all
over the world, including Palestine. The branches' main functions
were to further the audibility of the movement, to recruit new members, to raise money from non-Zionist Jews, and to establish access
to the governments of their respective countries. The movement also
published an official newspaper—Die Welt—to publicize its goal.[6]

"Zionist" coined by Nathan Birnbaum to express a political orientation to the land of Israel.

TABLE 3.1

Estimated Membership in the World Zionist
Organization, 1899-1913

Year	Members
1899	114,370
1900	96,434
1901	96,626
1903	232,645
1905	137,071
1907	164,333
1909	182,808
1911	175,894
1913	217,231

Source: Stenographisches Protokoll der Verhandlungen des
Zionisten Congresses, II-XVIII (Vienna: 1898-1933).

In 1899 the Jewish Colonial Trust, the first financial instrument of the World Zionist Organization, was established. The objectives of the trust were to promote Jewish settlement in Palestine,
grant credit to prospective settlers, and acquire from "any state or
other authority any concession, decrease, rights, powers and privileges" deemed likely to advance the Zionist case.[7] In 1902 authorized
capital of the trust were 2 million British pounds, of which only
395,000 pounds were subscribed.[8]

Another institution which provided financial resources for the
acquisition of land in Palestine was the Jewish National Fund established in 1901. The aim of the fund was to institutionalize and centralize the purchase of land. The land to be bought by the fund could
be neither sold nor mortgaged, thus remaining in perpetuity the property of the Jewish people; it was to be leased to Jewish settlers for
49-year periods. By 1914 the fund had bought 102,000 acres in Palestine.[9]

Ironically, the Zionists' primary nontangible resource lay in
the anti-Semitic atmosphere in Europe and especially in Eastern Europe and Russia. Anti-Semitism served to raise and strengthen Jewish consciousness and made the Zionist appeal audible and consum-
able in the various Jewish communities. Zionism was also seen as
a viable solution to the Jewish problem by non-Jews and anti-Semites.

That is, were Jews to have a homeland they might migrate from their native countries and terminate the perceived Jewish threat. Anti-Semitism thus contributed to the transformation of Zionism into a political movement claiming to represent a nonstate nation, and at the same time it served as a major resource of the movement.[10]

Another important resource for the movement, at least in its initial stage, was Theodor Herzl. By direct contact and personal diplomacy he brought to the attention of the rulers and governments of Europe and of the Turkish Sultan the desire of the Jewish people to build a national home in Palestine. One of Herzl's aims—the turning of the Jewish problem into a "world political problem"—had been achieved in part as a direct result of his own efforts.

Environment

The Zionist movement was faced with a largely indifferent international system. The Ottoman Empire administered the Palestinian territory in a colonial fashion and Zionist demands for an open policy of immigration and permits to purchase land and settle it were turned down by the Turks, who feared that massive immigration would be accompanied by a loss of sovereignty over the area.[11] With the exception of Britain, which was at first somewhat sympathetic to the Zionist cause and in 1917 partially committed itself to it by issuing the Balfour Declaration, the big powers made themselves available to prominent Zionist leaders but pursued a policy of indifference and nonintervention on behalf of Zionism. Even Pope Pius X, an influential leader in the Christian community, held a private discussion with Zionist leaders. However, their hope for a public statement of support remained unfulfilled. The pope merely stated "We cannot prevent Jews from going to Jerusalem, but we could never sanction it."[12]

Components

The Zionist leadership appears to have utilized at least four major components in its attempt to secure for the Jewish people a publicly recognized, legally sanctioned home in Palestine.

Component 1: Appeal to Christian Community. There were Gentile plans to resettle the Jews in Palestine long before the Zionist movement began to pursue the idea. Some Christians who were sensitive to the Jewish question appreciated the fact that the immigration of the Jews to Palestine might be a way to avoid admitting them to social and political equality, with all the implications that this might entail.

Others thought that Palestine could offer an alternative for Jewish immigrants and refugees unwanted in Britain and the United States. The religious problem of Jews and their place in the Christian eschatological myth motivated still others to support ideas and programs to restore the Jewish sovereignty in their ancient homeland. The Zionist leadership attempted, and to some extent succeeded, in making itself audible to the Christian public and gradually to obtain support for its cause.[13]

Component 2: Appeal to Big Powers. Whereas the appeal to the Christian community could have generated diffuse support, the Zionist leadership sought also to solidify support by obtaining the consent of the various governments, and especially the big powers, for the fulfillment of the claim of Zionism. The appeal to the big powers was made in terms of prospective payoffs to the governments in question. The Turkish government was offered loans and Jewish skill to help it establish economic independence from European powers and develop its resources in Palestine. Germany's Kaiser Wilhelm II was offered relief from his fear of revolutionary socialism, in which Jews were believed to play a significant role. Should Jews emigrate from Germany to Palestine, revolutionary tensions in Germany would diminish. Russia was also offered an immediate solution to its Jewish problem: Jewish emigration would free Russia of its Jews.[14]

The most intense efforts, however, were directed toward Britain. Nonetheless, until World War I, Britain's foreign policy makers were reluctant to publicly support the Zionist cause because the Turkish government might view such a policy as interference with its sovereignty in the Middle East. Britain's national interests, however, shifted upon Turkey's decision to form an alliance with Germany. Britain's search for allies and its firm determination to engage the United States in the war opened opportunities for the Zionist movement. British decision makers were convinced that the Zionists exerted great influence over Jews in America, and that the latter were capable of influencing American policy makers; a pro-Zionist policy would make U.S. Jews pro-Ally and, in turn, would reinforce pro-British sentiments in the State Department.[15] British decision makers also believed that Jews exerted considerable influence in revolutionary movements in Russia, and that a pro-Zionist policy would make these potential influencers keep Russia on the Allied side after the expected collapse of the Czar.[16] Moreover, a pro-Zionist policy might counteract the natural lack of sympathy that the Jews had for a war in which Czarist Russia was on the Allied side. To these considerations Zionist leaders added another one: If the Ottoman Empire should collapse, a strong Jewish community in Palestine would serve

Britain as a reliable and grateful ally and a suitable buffer territory for the defense of the Suez Canal.[17]

In 1917 Britain issued the Balfour Declaration, which was a political document legitimizing the Zionist claim and which gave a boost to the Zionist movement. The Balfour Declaration reads as follows: "His Majesty's Government view with favour the establishment in Palestine of a national home for the Jewish people, and will use their best endeavours to facilitate the achievement of this object, it being clearly understood that nothing shall be done which may prejudice the civil and religious rights of existing non-Jewish communities in Palestine, or the rights and political status enjoyed by Jews in any other country."[18]

Component 3: Settlement of Palestine. In 1897 Jews comprised about 7 percent of the population in Palestine with an estimated 46,000 persons. By 1917 the Jewish population numbered 58,000, approximately 10 percent of the population.[19] This slight increase was considered as a failure by the "practical" Zionists led by Nahum Sokolow and Chaim Weizmann, who urged immediate colonization of Palestine. In this period the movement's mission of "a programmatic encouragement of the settlement of Palestine with Jewish agricultural workers, laborers, and those pursuing other trades" received less attention in comparison to components 1 and 2. The "political" Zionists, who wanted to defer colonizing work in Palestine until political guarantees of Jewish settlement had been obtained, gained control of the movement and set its priorities until 1911. In this year the "practicals" won control; however, the outbreak of World War I foreclosed immediate settlement plans.

Two major waves of immigrants settled in Palestine in this era and established the foundations of the Jewish community. The first wave lasted from 1882 to 1903 and brought some 25,000 Jews, most of them from Eastern Europe. During the ten years of the second wave (1904-13), about 40,000 new immigrants arrived in Palestine.[20] A significant minority of these immigrants, moved by socialist-Zionist ideology, insisted that a Jewish renaissance in Palestine required more than the physical presence of Jews in the country. It required efforts to persuade Jewish employers to employ Jewish labor, which was considerably more expensive than Arab labor; it demanded that Jews take responsibility of defending their own settlements, rather than hiring Arab watchmen, so that the community became self-reliant; and it could be based only on Hebrew as the language of the Jewish settlers. The two waves of immigrants, and particularly the second, began with the implementation of Zionist goals and ideology in Palestine.

Component 4: Strengthening of Jewish National Consciousness. In Eastern Europe there were two elements to which Zionism could appeal. First, among the Orthodox Jews there was the notion that the Jews, God, and Israel (the land) formed an indissoluble partnership. The return to Zion had become a cardinal principle of their faith from the destruction of the Jewish state by the Romans in 70 C.E. The return to Zion was part and parcel of Orthodox Judaism. Second, the Jews of Eastern Europe and especially Russia were aware of their distinctiveness, their difference, and their separation from other Russians. The discriminatory laws and regulations promulgated under the Czars kept them a people apart, "a nation within a nation." Thus, Jews in Russia were conscious of their peoplehood. They had their own language (Yiddish), customs, laws, culture, and history. All that was missing was a territory of their own.[21]

In the West, on the other hand, Jews saw themselves as nationals of their respective countries, albeit of a different faith. To them Judaism did not signify nationality but merely religion. The rise of anti-Semitism in Germany and France in the 1890s shocked them into the realization that no matter how integrated they were into the life and culture of their native lands there would always be a difference, always the specter of anti-Semitism. The only solution for Jews was to completely assimilate and to give up their own traditions, culture, and heritage. For many Western Jews this was not a solution, but a surrender. They wished to be full citizens without having to give up their traditions and culture.

Zionism provided a solution for all these groups, including those who were not religious but wished to remain "Jewish" in a cultural and national sense. For the religious it promised a return to Zion—to Jerusalem. For the nonreligious it promised sovereignty, a national home, a place where Jewish culture could flourish and where Jews could be a nation like all other nations. Zionism thus offered a measure of hope and security for Jews from different backgrounds and citizenships and an immediate solution to anti-Semitism.

While Herzl was alive the political activity of the Zionist movement was conducted in a centralized, personal way. With his passing much of the movement's activity was initiated by strong local leaders such as Chaim Weizmann. Thus after 1904 the above components were organized and directed by national and local Zionist organizations rather than through the central office of the World Zionist Organization.

Evaluation of Zionist System, 1897 to 1917

This period can be characterized by two main achievements: the transformation of Zionism from a formless aspiration into a structured political movement with a worldwide organization and specialized institutions to carry out its goals; and the legitimization of the movement's cause through a policy commitment of a big power. The Balfour Declaration was evaluated by Zionist leaders as the most significant event after the First Zionist Congress.[22]

The Zionist movement attained the Balfour Declaration in spite of limited resources and an indifferent international system. This success can be assessed with reference to three interrelated factors: (1) unanimity of leadership concerning the goals of the movement; (2) concentration of available resources on the most preferred goal; and (3) exhaustion of opportunities.

The Zionist movement presented a united leadership to the external environment. Cleavages and conflicts did take place, especially over matters of strategy. For example, whereas the "practical" Zionists urged immediate colonization in Palestine, the "political" Zionists sought international recognition and political guarantees prior to colonization. The goal, however, was identical: securing a homeland in Palestine. Thus, conflicts over strategy and power positions in the organization were maintained at a level which projected unity.[23]

Consensus over the chief goal and agreement to accept the majority's strategy enabled the leadership to concentrate efforts and resources on specific missions. By the use of diplomacy, personal contacts, and propaganda the movement made itself audible in the highest governmental echelons of the big powers. Finally, the leadership took advantage of opportunities created by the international system. Turkey's alliance with Germany created an opportunity to persuade British decision makers that it was in Britain's national interest to commit itself to the Zionist cause.

PERIOD II: 1918 TO 1938

By 1918 some progress had been made in the purchase of, and settlement on, the land; the principle of a national home in Palestine had been affirmed; and the World Zionist Organization was officially representing Jewish interests in Palestine. When the Ottoman Empire was dissolved at the end of World War I, Britain was given control of Palestine under a League of Nations Mandate, and the Balfour Declaration immediately assumed a greater significance. By the end of this period the Jewish community in Palestine constituted about 30 percent of the country's population. Quite apart from the growing power of the World Zionist Organization, there was in Palestine a relatively large and self-sustaining community organized enough to crystallize its own demands and to design its own strategies. Toward the end of this period the leadership of the Zionist movement shifted decisively to Palestine, where the claim for an autonomous Jewish commonwealth was deeply entrenched. The Zionist leadership continued to act as the major decision maker. They were aided in their efforts by the Jewish Agency but challenged by the Revisionists who, from 1925, can be regarded as an independent decision maker.

Decision Maker A: Labor Zionists

Goals

The Labor or Socialist Zionists had as their goal the establishment of a socialist Jewish commonwealth in Palestine and the "normalization" of Jewish life. This meant, for them, an emphasis on manual labor and agriculture. The Labor Zionists believed that a normal people was one whose labor force was involved in all the occupations in the country. The Jews could only become a "normal" people if Jewish labor were similarly engaged. Manual labor for the Labor Zionists was therefore an absolute moral value, a remedy to cure the Jewish people of its social and national ills. [24]

Resources

The alliance of most socialist Zionist parties and groups was forged at a conference in Danzig in 1932 by the creation of a world union. By 1935 the Labor Zionists succeeded in gaining control of the Zionist movement, which then had over 1 million members (see Table 3.2).

Their success can be attributed to the following factors: (1) They were in the strongest position in the building-up of Palestine. The Histadrut (General Federation of Jewish Labor), organized in 1920, became not only the largest labor union in the country but also the biggest employer in Palestine. By the late 1930s the Histadrut, and through it the Labor Zionists, literally controlled Jewish Palestine's economy. [25] In addition, collective settlements based on socialist cooperation became a leading force in the agricultural development of Palestine. (2) The Labor Zionists, with their charismatic leadership, presented a united front at the Zionist congresses, while the opposi-

TABLE 3.2

Estimated Membership in the World Zionist
Organization, 1921-37

Year	Members
1921	855,590
1923	957,982
1925	938,157
1927	631,151
1929	604,616
1931	627,237
1933	843,607
1935	1,216,640
1937	1,222,214

Source: Stenographisches Protokoll der Verhandlungen des
Zionisten Congresses, XII-XIX (Vienna: 1916-23); Ha-Kongress Ha-
Zioni, XX (Palestine: 1937).

tion remained divided. (3) The rise of Hitler resulted in a flood of
new immigrants to Palestine. Because of their strong economic position in the country, the Labor Zionists provided jobs for the new-
comers, who in turn strengthened the labor movement. (4) The principles of labor Zionism attracted writers, teachers, professionals,
and other intellectuals, which enhanced the prestige of the movement
outside Palestine.

Environment

The Labor Zionists operated in an environment that included a
sympathetic power—Britain; hostile Arab nations and Arab terrorist
groups; a rival Zionist minority faction—the Revisionists; and a supportive Jewish community in Palestine.

In 1922 the League of Nations formally assigned to Britain the
Mandate for Palestine. Jewish public opinion throughout the world
acclaimed the decision with enthusiasm, and the Zionist leaders re-
laid the emphasis on the need for unified endeavor and practical effort in the upbuilding of the country.

With regard to the Zionist cause, the Mandate's operational
objectives were the following: to promote the establishment of a

Jewish national home; to facilitate immigration, settlement, and economic and social development; and to promote self-government and local autonomy. [26] Zionist leaders and the Jewish Agency accepted these objectives as guidelines and attempted to cooperate with the British in implementing them. Although some achievements are worth noting, especially in the development of the Jewish community, the British administration did not undertake any large-scale developments in order to increase the economic absorptive capacity of the country and to raise the general standard of living among the Arabs. The British administration conceived its role mainly in terms of acting as a judge between the parties for an equal division of limited resources.

In response to Arab demands and sporadic violence, the British gradually abandoned the Mandate's operational objectives, especially with regard to the facilitation of immigration and settlement. To this, the policy of the new Zionist executive, now led by the Labor Zionists, was moderation and maximum cooperation with the British who, it was believed, would eventually follow a pro-Zionist policy.

As the strength of the Jewish community in Palestine grew, so, too, did Arab opposition to further Jewish settlement. The Arab population in Palestine had its own nationalist aspirations, and it saw the developing Jewish community as a threat to its ambitions. Palestinian Arabs were also encouraged by the progress toward independence of the neighboring Arab states.

At the San Remo Conference in 1920, Syrian Arab nationalists came out in unmitigated opposition to the Balfour Declaration and demanded the inclusion of Palestine in a united, independent Syria. A Syrian Congress claiming to represent all Arabs in Syria, Palestine, and Lebanon issued the following statement: "We oppose the pretentions of Zionists to create a Jewish commonwealth in the southern part of Syria, known as Palestine, and oppose Zionist immigration to any part of our country; for we do not acknowledge their title but consider them a grave peril to our people from the national, economical and political points of view."[27]

Arab opposition took its first significant violent expression in Jerusalem in 1920, when thousands of pilgrims rioted in the Jewish section of the city. From then on hostilities gradually escalated. In 1921 the Palestine Arab Executive Committee presented a memorandum to Winston Churchill demanding: (1) repudiation of the Jewish national home policy; (2) creation of a national government in Palestine to be elected by the inhabitants of the country in their prewar proportions; (3) cessation of Jewish immigration; and (4) no distinction between Palestine and other Arab countries. [28] Severe violent dis-

turbances were also initiated by Arabs in 1929, 1936, and 1938, when
the disorders assumed the form of organized guerrilla warfare.

Components

Component 1: Colonization in Palestine. With the arrival of the third
wave of immigrants (1919-23) numbering some 50,000, the Jewish
community in Palestine gained substantial strength by constituting 11
percent of the population. Like their predecessors, the new settlers
emigrated from Russia, with many of them having developed strong
roots in the Zionist movement before their arrival. Together with
the experienced settlers they strengthened and extended the initial
settlements and established community services, schools, and a university (The Hebrew University). The Histadrut, Israel's major labor
union, was founded, and efforts were directed to create institutions
of self-government.

The arrival of the fourth wave of immigrants (1924-31) did much
to strengthen the community's foundations. It was larger than the
earlier waves, numbering some 60,000 and, unlike them, consisted
mainly of middle-class Polish immigrants, who settled in the growing
urban areas. A sharp increase in the pace of colonization occurred
during the fifth wave (1932-39). Although these were years of dis-
tress in Europe, the portals to America remained effectively closed
to Jewish immigrants.[29] As a result, 225,000 new immigrants arrived in Palestine in this period. For the first time there was a large
influx from central Europe, which included many professionals. By
the end of this period the Jewish community constituted about 30 percent of the country's population.[30]

The Jewish Agency, charged by the Mandate with "advising and
cooperating with the Administration of Palestine in such economic,
social and other matters as may affect the establishment of the National Home," had become a quasi-governmental institution, with wide
authority in matters affecting the community, and was regarded by
the settlers as their legitimate representative.[31] Toward the end of
the period severe limitations on immigration and land purchasing were
enacted by the British administration as a result of Britain's policy
changes in the area.

Component 2: The Jewish Agency. One of the main tasks of the Jewish Agency during the period of the British administration of Palestine was to represent the Zionist movement and world Jewry at large
before the Mandatory government, the League of Nations, and the
British government in London. Insofar as the British Mandatory government of Palestine was concerned, the Jewish Agency was not en-

titled to take part in the government of the country but merely to cooperate with the Mandatory authorities in matters affecting the development of the Jewish national home. For the Yishuv (Jewish community in Palestine), however, the Jewish Agency became the dominant
force by virtue of its activities in agriculture and urban settlement,
its specialized institutions, and its considerable economic resources.
It was to the Jewish Agency that the Yishuv looked for political guid-
ance. Its role was summed up by the British Government's Peel
Commission (assigned the task of investigating riots in Palestine) in
1937 as follows: "It may be said that the Jewish Agency has used to
the fullest extent the position conferred on it by the Mandate. In the
course of time it has created a complete administrative apparatus.
This powerful and efficient organization amounts, in fact, to a government existing side by side with the Mandatory government."[32]

Component 3: Deal with Arabs. The Zionist Organization as a whole
followed Weizmann's policy of compromise and shared his hopes of
achieving rapprochement with the Arabs. There was a general and
deep-rooted belief that as economic conditions for the Arab population
improved as a result of the Jewish development, the opposition to
Zionism would vanish. The hope for a political agreement with the
Arabs was expressed in formal resolutions of the Zionist congresses.
There were repeated declarations of a desire for cooperation with the
Arab section of the population in the upbuilding of Palestine as a common country for both peoples. In addition, several attempts were
made to negotiate with Arab leaders; these, however, proved abortive.
For example, in 1922 meetings were held between Emir Abdullah of
Transjordan and Weizmann. Shortly after the meetings Abdullah told
a press conference that "a mutual understanding between the Arabs
and the Jews was possible only if an Arab government were established in Palestine."[33] Weizmann denied Abdullah's version, and the
prospective agreement fell through.

     In this period the Jewish community in Palestine followed two
lines of policy, as formulated by the Jewish Agency and the moderate
but dominant Zionist leaders: self-restraint and self-defense. Self-
defense meant that the Jews would defend themselves and their settlements against Arab violence, using arms when necessary. Self-
restraint implied that they would not allow themselves to be provoked
to counterattacks, and they would not engage in indiscriminate reprisals against Arabs. This principle was maintained firmly and e-
voked the praise of the British administration, which, from 1936 on,
helped in the defense of Jewish villages by arming an increasing number of Jews and enrolling them as supernumerary police.[34]

Component 4: The Hagana. The Hagana ("defense") was the underground Jewish army founded in Palestine in 1920 for the purpose of
protecting Jewish life and property against attacks by Arabs. It functioned as a clandestine organization during the entire period of the
British Mandate and was transformed into the Israel Defense Forces
two weeks after the Proclamation of the State of Israel. At times it
was tolerated and even aided by the Mandatory power. On other occasions it was persecuted and openly attacked by the British authorities in Palestine. The Hagana evolved from semiautonomous units
formed in towns and settlements changing from local defense against
Arab attacks into a centralized military machine operating on a national scale in the service of the Zionist movement. It was eventually
employed as a weapon in the fight against the British mandatory power and finally into a full-fledged army.

As part of the Yishuv, the Hagana reflected the strains and
stresses of its political life and its formation and early development
were accompanied by intra-Zionist debates. At first the force was
under the exclusive control of Ahdut Avoda (United Zionist Labor party). With the establishment of the Histadrut, it came under the control of the latter, although admission was open to all. In 1931 the
non-Histadrut elements seceded from the Hagana and formed a separate force which remained independent until 1937, when, under the
impact of the Arab riots of 1936-39, it merged with the Hagana and
was placed under the control of the Executive of the World Zionist
Organization. [35]

Component 5: Policy toward Britain. Conflicts over the Zionist policy
toward Britain were a major bone of contention in these years. The
general Zionist policy, as expressed by Weizmann, emphasized cooperation and a conciliatory attitude toward the Mandatory power.
Weizmann maintained that the safety of the national home could be
secured only through political guarantees by the big powers and
through establishing friendly relations with the non-Jewish inhabitants
in Palestine on the basis of complete parity. [36]

Due to opposition, Weizmann was replaced as president of the
Zionist Organization by Nahum Sokolow, who served for a period of
four years until Weizmann's reinstatement in 1935. In these four
years no basic modification of the Zionist policy with reference to
collaboration with Britain occurred.

In 1937 the Peel Commission published its recommendations on
Palestine. According to the commission, the crux of the Palestine
problem was in the Mandate itself. "The difficulty has always been,
and, if the Mandate continues, will continue with it, that the existence
of the National Home, whatever its size, bars the way to the attain-

ment by the Arabs of Palestine of the same national status as that attained or soon to be attained, by all other Arabs of Asia."[37] Therefore, the Royal (Peel) Commission recommended the partition of Palestine. According to the plan, Palestine and Transjordan were to be divided into three regions: a Jewish State, an Arab State, and a British enclave. Although committing itself to a solution involving partition, the commission was opposed to an immediate creation of two new independent states. The commission's partition plan revealed a radically new approach to the situation in Palestine. All other attempts to deal with the problem, from the very beginning, had assumed that the obligation to the Arabs and the obligation to the Jews were reconcilable. The essence of the Peel Commission's conclusions was that they were not. The commission's report presented the situation as an "irrepressible conflict" between two communities different in constitution and ideas. [38]

The World Zionist Organization advocated the partition plan as a lesser evil. That is, a small Jewish state would be preferable to a crystallized minority status in a hostile Arab state or federation of states.[39] However, Arab opposition to any partition plan coupled with Britain's growing interest in Palestine as a gateway to the Middle East and as an intercontinental bridge joining Europe, Asia, and Africa, and opposition from smaller factions within the Zionist movement and from non-Zionist Jews, led the British to reject the partition plan in 1938.[40]

Decision Maker B: Revisionist Zionists

Goals

The Revisionists, headed by Vladimir Jabotinsky, contended that Zionism should declare that its ultimate goal was a Jewish state within the boundaries of Palestine, that is, extending over the entire area of the Mandate, including Transjordan. In defining a "Jewish state" two indispensible elements were stressed: a Jewish majority and self-government in internal affairs.[41]

Resources

The followers of Jabotinsky had organized the Union of Zionist Revisionists in 1925, and since then the party had steadily grown in strength. In 1935 the Revisionists held a referendum, with an overwhelming majority favoring secession from the World Zionist Organization. They boycotted the Nineteenth Zionist Congress and estab-

lished the New Zionist Organization. The Revisionists were mainly
drawn from the middle class and were supported by the bourgeoisie
and intellectual stratum of Poland and by younger East European Palestine Jews.[42] In Palestine the Revisionists established their own
labor organization, community centers, youth organization, and
published a daily paper.[43]

Another resource was the "Maximilist Zionists" who demanded
full realization of the Basel Program within the historic boundaries
of Palestine; large-scale and rapid economic development with a view
to increasing the absorptive capacity of Palestine; and aggressive
Zionist leadership. The Maximilists were thus sympathetic to the
Revisionist program.

Environment

The Revisionists operated in an environment that was similar
to that of the Labor Zionists, although, of course, it included the
Labor Zionists. The environment also included Maximilists in the
United States, Germany, Poland, and Palestine.

Components

Component 1: Audibility in British Government. Upon the establishment of the New Zionist Organization, the Revisionists attempted to
make themselves heard and to pave access to central authorities in
Britain. The Revisionists succeeded in bringing their platform before
the various committees set up by the British government to investigate
the violent disturbances in Palestine. Thus, for example, the Shaw
Commission, which was created to inquire into the causes of the 1929
riots, invited Revisionist leaders to present their points of view.
Jabotinsky's view was that Britain should actively promote Jewish
colonization to establish a Jewish majority, and that the party's objective was the creation of a Jewish state in Palestine.[44] In 1936,
when invited to the Royal Commission, headed by Lord Peel, Jabotinsky described British policy in Palestine as planless and accused
the administration of being weak and dilatory in dealing with Arab
violence.[45] The Revisionists did not succeed in opening lines of communication with or in influencing the central authorities in Britain.

Component 2: Aggressive Policy toward Arabs. The Revisionists
claimed there was no contradiction between establishing a Jewish
state in Palestine and ousting the Arabs. They did not believe that
the Zionists could expect to obtain Arab consent until after the Jewish
state was established. Revisionist leaders advocated retaliation in-

stead of strict self-defense in 1936-39 as a more effective way to
stop Arab attacks upon the Jews. Jabotinsky's main thesis was that:

> when we hear the Arab claim confronted with the Jewish
> claim—I fully understand that any minority would prefer
> to be a majority; it is quite understandable that the Arabs
> of Palestine would also prefer Palestine to be the Arab
> State No. 4, No. 5, or No. 6—that I quite understand; but
> when the Arab claim is confronted with our Jewish de-
> mand to be saved, it is like the claims of appetite versus
> the claims of starvation. . . the Arab <u>can</u> realize that
> since there are three or four wholly Arab States, then it
> is a thing of justice which Great Britain is doing if Pal-
> estine is transformed into a Jewish State.[46]

Evaluation of the Zionist Movement, 1918 to 1938

The Peel Commission's plan to redivide Palestine and Transjordan into an Arab state and a Jewish state, although rejected by
the British government, marked a radically different conception of
the Palestinian problem. This conception essentially resulted from
the antagonistic and noncompromising policies pursued by the Arabs
in their dealings with the Zionist movement. The Arab riots were
clear manifestations of mutually conflicting aspirations and incompatible goals between two rival nonstate nations.

In the beginning of the period, Zionist leaders perceived the
situation as a nonzero-sum game in the sense that concessions made
by Arabs would benefit both sides; toward the end of the period, the
notion that partition might be the only feasible solution gained approval and considerable support. Thus, whereas the Twentieth Zionist
Congress rejected the specific partition plan, it also empowered the
Zionist executive to negotiate with Britain for a further exploration
of the precise terms on which a Jewish state would be established.[47]

From the beginning of this period there was bitter controversy
among the British, Jews, and Arabs over the proper interpretation
of the Mandate. The Zionists believed that the ultimate object of the
Mandate was the establishment of a national home for the Jews. The
British reaffirmed the obligation undertaken under the Balfour Declaration and the Mandate for Palestine to facilitate the establishment
of a Jewish national home. Unlike the Zionists, however, the British
also strove to develop self-governing institutions for all the inhabitants in Palestine to encourage local autonomy, and to respond to the
Arab demands. In the latter years of the Mandate, as the incompat-

ibility of these goals became clear, the British treated the Jewish homeland as a secondary objective at best. The Arabs, on the other hand, maintained that the establishment of a Jewish state, or a national home, could not be accomplished without forcibly displacing them. These sharp differences in the interpretation of the Mandate led each of the actors to pursue noncompromising policies.

Conflicts within the World Zionist Organization were more intense now and led to a polarization between the majority who held moderate views and a minority—the Revisionists—who advocated aggressive policies toward the British and the Arabs. The Revisionists seceded from the World Zionist Organization and formed the New Zionist Organization.[48] The Labor Zionists gained control of the WZO and shaped its policies with the coordination and consensus of the remaining factions, including the Jewish community in Palestine.

In Palestine, Jewish governing institutions formed a state within a state, functioning alongside the mandatory regime and with many of the attributes of an autonomous government. They were staffed with Jews and were regarded as the real authority by the Jewish community. The Jewish Agency became the mainspring of Jewish self-government. The foundations for an army were also set during this period. The Hagana, founded originally to supply watchmen for Jewish settlements and to defend the Jewish community against Arab attacks, became, by 1936, a well-trained militia.[49] The Zionist movement, then, did not rely solely on the British to achieve its goal but gradually and consistently furthered its own cause in Palestine by its own means.

By 1938 it became obvious to the three actors—Arabs, Jews, and British—that Arab and Jewish goals in Palestine were irreconcilable and that the efforts of the Mandate to pursue reconcilable policies were destined for failure.

PERIOD III: 1939 TO 1947

The new British policy in Palestine was formulated in a White Paper issued in May 1939. The White Paper stated that the framers of the Mandate did not intend that Palestine should be converted into a Jewish state against the will of the Arab population of the country: "His Majesty's Government now declare unequivocally that is is not part of their policy that Palestine should become a Jewish state."[50] Britain's stated aim was the establishment of an independent Palestinian state in which Arabs and Jews would share governmental authority in such a way that the interests of each would be secured. To

advance this goal Britain decided to drastically limit Jewish immigration only if the Arabs acquiesced.

The second event which determined the course of this period
was the traumatic experience of Hitler's persecution of the Jews,
which renewed the basic Zionist myth of self-emancipation and activism. The Zionist myth-image of sovereignty extended its influence
throughout the Jewish world, while its intensity reached ultimate limits among the Zionists themselves. The Nazi holocaust and the new
British policy had a great integrative effect on the Zionist movement
and on the Jewish community in Palestine: a united and determined
leadership emerged.

Decision Maker A: The Zionist Movement

The White Paper was condemned by the Zionist movement and
the Jewish community in Palestine. In 1939 the Twenty-First Zionist
Congress declared its uncompromising hostility to the policy of the
White Paper and denied its moral and legal validity.[51]

Environment

Two major changes occurred in the movement's environment:
first, Britain withdrew its support from the Zionist cause and hostilities broke out between the Jewish community in Palestine and the
British Administration; second, the United States became a major
actor whose support to the movement was crucial. In addition to these
two major changes, the movement had to operate in a hostile Arab
environment and among nonsympathetic Asian nations.

Goals

The major goals of the movement were formulated in 1942 and
incorporated in the Biltmore Program. The chief goals were mass
Jewish immigration into Palestine to give immediate relief to Jewish
refugees and to lay the foundations for the establishment of a Jewish
majority; the purchase and development of unoccupied and uncultivated
lands; and the establishment of Palestine as a Jewish commonwealth.[52]

Resources

With the destruction of European Jewry, the movement's most
significant resource lay in U.S. Jewry, which supplied solidarity and
financial aid and attempted to influence American decision makers.

A second significant nontangible resource was the solidarity of the
Western Christian community. In Palestine, meanwhile, the Jewish
community continued to grow and to develop self-governing institutions, including an army.

Components

Component 1: Resistance to the White Paper. The Zionist movement
declared that it would not acquiesce in the reduction of its status in
Palestine to that of a minority, nor in the subjugation of the Jewish
national home to Arab rule. The movement and the Jewish community took it upon themselves to support illegal immigration and to absorb in Palestine refugees from Nazi terror. David Ben Gurion, the
leader of the Labor Zionists, urged passive and active resistance to
the implementation of the White Paper policy and argued that "the
Jews should act as though they were the State in Palestine. . . ."[53]
Violent anti-British demonstrations took place throughout Palestine,
resulting in the escalation of the government's struggle against illegal
immigration. In 1944 the National Military Organization renewed its
anti-British activities and attacked a number of police stations and
government installations. The British reacted by arresting and deporting members of the organization. In 1945 the Jewish Agency
charged the British administration in Palestine with introducing a
reign of terror in the country "with a view to intimidating the Jews"
into submitting to the White Paper policy.[54]

Having announced that it was determined to defend the Jewish
community from British harassment, to aid in the entry of Jewish
refugees from Europe, and to deprive the authorities of weapons,
which they charged were to be used illegally against the population of
Palestine, the Hagana openly stated its intention to destroy military
installations, to capture arms, and to assist in the admission of immigrants in every possible way.[55] Accordingly, British posts were
blown up as a reprisal action against the interception of Jewish immigrants.

In 1945 the San Francisco Conference discussed the trusteeship
system, and the Zionist movement submitted the following three-point
program: the constituting of a free and democratic Jewish commonwealth; abolition of restrictions on Jewish immigration; development
of the country and aid in immigration and settlement.[56]

Component 2: Control of Jewish Terrorist Groups. As a principle,
the Zionist authorities objected to terrorism and violence. When
dissident bodies (see Decision Maker C-2, p. 85) initiated terrorism
against the British, they were denounced in the most extreme terms.

The Jewish Agency called upon the community to resist the threats of the Jewish "terrorist bands" and to deprive their members of all assistance. On several occasions the Jewish Agency cooperated with the British administration in rounding up terrorists.[57]

Component 3: Deal with Britain. Relations between Britain and the Zionist movement went from bad to worse. In 1945 the Anglo-American Inquiry Committee reported that "Palestine is an armed camp. We saw signs of this almost as soon as we crossed the frontier, and we became more and more aware of the atmosphere each day. Many buildings have barbed wire and other defenses. . . . It is obvious that very considerable military forces and large numbers of police are kept in Palestine. The police are armed; they are conspicuous everywhere."[58] The continuing stubborn resistance in Palestine, the Anglo-American Inquiry Committee's recommendation to increase legal immigration into Palestine coupled with President Truman's support, together with opposition in the British Parliament and public sector convinced the British government that the Mandate was impossible. In February 1947 Britain referred the Mandate on Palestine back to the United Nations.

Component 4: Appeal to the United States. With the destruction of European Jewry and the growth of U.S. influence in international affairs, U.S. Zionism had become one of the most important factors in the world movement. The events in Europe after the outbreak of the war and U.S. reluctance to admit Jewish refugees as immigrants increased U.S. Jewry's sympathies for Zionism and Palestine. U.S. Jews became overwhelmingly pro-Zionist and sought to exert influence on their government. An indication of their success is seen in a statement published in 1942 calling for the establishment of a Jewish national home, which received the endorsement of 68 U.S. senators and 194 congressmen.[59] The Zionist movement succeeded in creating a climate of opinion favorable to Zionism among legislators, church dignitaries, the press, and the public in general. In 1947 President Truman gave his assent to the partition scheme and to the establishment of an independent Jewish state.

Component 5: Support the UN Partition Proposal. Upon Britain's turning the Mandate back to the United Nations, the General Assembly approved the creation of a committee (UN Special Committee on Palestine, UNSCOP) to investigate the Palestine question and to make suggestions for a settlement. Zionist leaders invited to appear before the committee were united in the opinion that only the partition of Palestine and the establishment of a Jewish state could solve the

Jewish problem and stop the violence in Palestine. The UNSCOP majority came out in favor of partition and the establishment of a Jewish
state and an Arab state.

Component 6: Mobilize Nation-State Support. Upon the publication of
the UNSCOP recommendation for partition, the Zionist movement
directed all its effort and resources to obtain the support of nation-
states in the scheduled vote of the UN General Assembly. Britain,
the Arab countries, and most of the Asian nations were strongly opposed to partition. The U.S. position was unclear, but the State Department was against establishing a Jewish state. The Soviet Union's
aim to diminish Western influence in the Mediterranean was expressed
by unexpected support for a Jewish state. The Zionist leadership concentrated on influencing the uncommitted countries—especially the
United States. The assumption was that an American propartition
stance would secure positive votes by other Western nations. The
Zionist Organization of America, the pro-Zionist public, and sympathetic Christian churchmen were all asked to persuade President
Truman to favor the partition plan. In October 1947 President Truman gave his assent and in November the vote was taken in the General Assembly. The motion in favor of partition was carried by 39
to 13. The British Mandate was due to end on May 14, 1948, with the
State of Israel coming into being at the same time. David Ben Gurion
read out the Declaration of Independence: "By virtue of the natural
and historical right of the Jewish people and of the resolution of the
General Assembly of the United Nations, we hereby proclaim the establishment of the Jewish State in Palestine to be called Israel."[60]

Decision Maker B: New Zionist Organization

The New Zionist Organization (NZO) was the Revisionist Party
which had seceded from the World Zionist Organization in 1935. The
New Zionists represented a small group relative to the Zionists in
the WZO. Nevertheless, they were a strong decision maker forcing
the Zionist leadership to adopt a less conciliatory and more activist
approach toward Britain. When, in 1946, Zionists and non-Zionists
adopted in substance the "independent Jewish state" demand of the
New Zionists, the latter rejoined the WZO.[61]

Environment

The New Zionist Organization was opposed by all the actors in
the environment, including the leadership of the World Zionist Organization and the Jewish Agency.

Goals

The NZO's goals included the following: to reconstitute Palestine, including Transjordan, as a Jewish state; to guarantee the right of any Jew to enter Palestine at any time ("to bar Jewish immigration is a crime, to break the bar a duty"); and to establish a Jewish army.[62]

Resources

The NZO's main nontangible resource lay in the growing disappointment with the British policy, and the restrained reaction of Zionist leaders to Arab violence. At the same time the NZO increased its tangible resources by establishing its own labor union, youth organizations, and community services.[63]

Components

Component 1: Noncooperation with Britain. The 1939 White Paper met with the condemnation of the NZO, which demanded absolutely no cooperation with the British government and advocated civil disobedience in the forms of mass demonstrations and illegal immigration to Palestine.

Component 2: Deal with Arabs. The Jewish independent state was to include Transjordan, and the Jews were to constitute a majority of the population. Arab violence was to be met with counterviolence and retaliation.[64]

Decision Maker C-1: The Irgun (National Military Organization)

The Irgun was founded in 1937 by a group of leaders of the Revisionist Zionists and their autonomous youth movement. The Irgun placed great emphasis on a political and diplomatic offensive in favor of Jewish demands in Palestine. As the British stiffened their policies, the Irgun decided on a new tactic of armed resistance to British policy. From January 1944 the Irgun took the position that Britain violated its trust by adopting the White Paper and had thus forfeited its very right to rule in Palestine. Britain was henceforth to be considered an illegitimate, foreign occupying force.[65]

Environment

The Irgun operated in an environment that included a hostile
British administration, rival Arab terrorist groups, a nonsympathetic
and critical World Zionist Organization, and antagonistic non-Zionist
Jews. Its moral and financial support came from the extremist faction of the New Zionist Organization. Toward the end of the period,
the NZO adjusted ideologically to the Irgun.

Goals

The Irgun's major goal was independence for Palestine as a
Jewish commonwealth comprising its then Jewish population and the
Diaspora Jews who were prevented from living in Palestine because
of the White Paper.[66]

Resources

The Irgun's most significant nontangible resource lay in its
powerful appeal to the Jewish community as a whole. It responded to
the "deep revulsion which predisposed Jews, despairing of help in
their need from the Gentile world, to welcome the emotional release
of risking the all-or-nothing choice in a fight for their own survival."[67]

Components

Component 1: Retaliation against Arabs. The Irgun advocated and engaged in retaliation against Arabs, a tactic which was perceived to
be the only effective way to stop Arab attacks against Jews.[68] The
bombings carried out in Arab areas succeeded, above all, in satisfying the Jewish community's desire for revenge.

Component 2: Fight British Mandate. The Irgun engaged in smuggling
Jewish refugees into Palestine and in sporadic violence against the
British. It also organized mass demonstrations to express the Jewish community's discontent with regard to the policies carried out by
the British administration.

Decision Maker C-2: The Stern Group

The Stern Group—"Fighters for Freedom of Israel"—was a
small, underground, right-wing terrorist group.

Environment

The group operated in a hostile international environment and a strongly antagonistic Jewish environment. The WZO and the NZO disapproved and actively sought to repress the group.[69]

Goals

The major goal was to drive the British out of Palestine. The leadership believed that assassination of high government officials was an indispensible step toward this end.[70]

Resources

The monetary resources of the group stemmed mainly from private donations and acts of robbery.[71] The leadership acquired its military training while serving in the Polish army. The Stern Group sought allies among the extremists in the Irgun, but had little success.

Component: Terrorize British Administration. The enemy, according to the Sternists, was Britain; the aim, therefore, was to sabotage British installations in Palestine and to assassinate high government officials. In 1944 members of the group assassinated Lord Moyne, the British resident minister in the Near East.[72]

Evaluation of the Zionist System, 1939 to 1948

Fifty-one years after the establishment of the World Zionist Organization the State of Israel was proclaimed and the ultimate goal of the Zionist movement was realized. The period 1939–48 was a continuation of the preceding efforts to work out a suitable solution to the Jewish problem. In the first period (1897-1917), anti-Semitism had been a major factor in the establishment of the movement. In the third period, the destruction of the Jewish community in Europe heightened the intense demand to establish a Jewish commonwealth.

In this period the three chief decision makers aimed at common goals: to facilitate mass immigration into Palestine, giving immediate relief to the Jewish refugees; to establish a Jewish majority in Palestine; and to establish eventually a Jewish state. In the beginning of the period, decision makers differed on matters of strategy. While the Zionist Organization and the Jewish Agency advocated moderation, passive resistance, and active diplomacy to gain audibility and durability, the Irgun and the terrorist groups engaged in violent resistance.

As the British policy in Palestine stiffened, so did the attitudes of the Zionist leadership. Toward the end of the period the entire Jewish community engaged in passive and active resistance, and the decision makers collaborated in a united front.

The unity of the leadership, the solidarity of the Jewish community in Palestine, and the support of the Zionist rank and file, especially in the United States, contributed most in persuading the nation-states to approve of the partition of Palestine and the establishment of a Jewish state. The UN resolution legitimized that which had been created by the Zionist movement. David Ben Gurion, Israel's first prime minister, conveyed this idea shortly after Israel was founded:

> Nor did the State suddenly emerge by being proclaimed—
> no, its beginnings were set by three generations of pio-
> neers, from the builders of Petah Tiqvah to the pipelayers
> in the Northern Negev. The proclamation marked but the
> historical climax of their work of creation, to which we
> owe our newfound national dignity, our economy, culture
> and administration. Our resistance to the Arab states,
> likewise, was no magic combustion or conjuring of strength
> out of thin air, nor explosion from an uncanny, invisible
> source. Our youth and our Yishuv were trained for it by
> the acts and education, the organized planning, of the
> Hagana for years past, by the first Jewish watchman and
> the heroes of Tel Hai. Therein lies the secret. [73]

IMPACT ON INTERNATIONAL CONTEXT

The interactions of nonstate nations with their respective environments, with nation-states, and with international organizations bear different degrees of impact on the international system. For example, once a nonstate nation is officially accepted into the family of sovereign nations a precedent is established, and this, in turn, reinforces the claims of other nonstate nations for de facto and eventually de jure recognition. With the establishment of the State of Israel, several significant precedents have been established, the most general of which are discussed in this concluding section.

First, and perhaps most significantly, the Zionist movement has modified the criteria for laying claim to nation-state status. Attributes such as a well-defined territory, control over the territory, and an operating central government have given way to a more socio-cultural characterization. Thus, a common heritage and an aspiration to be regarded as distinct are sufficient for a people to begin to demand the status of a nation-state. Obviously, this heritage/aspiration would not automatically result in the creation of a state. Nevertheless, a sociocultural characterization provides a nontangible resource to a nonstate nation for both strengthening its internal cohesion and making it more audible among potentially supportive audiences.

The prestate Zionist movement attempted, and to a large extent succeeded, to exert a considerable impact on three interrelated parts of the international context: (1) public opinion within nation-states; (2) aspects of the nation-states' foreign policies; and (3) commitments from the League of Nations and later from the United Nations.

We have shown that the Zionist decision makers channeled much of the resources to mobilize Jewish and non-Jewish public opinion in a variety of nation-states. Such diffuse support was presumed to find expression in the foreign policies of the involved nations, but more significantly to facilitate access to major sites of international decision making. Indeed, with no political access nonstate nations cannot advance their cause. A nonstate nation's decision makers must create formal and informal opportunities to be heard and make their plight salient. The mobilization of public opinion was sought by Zionist decision makers in both peaceful and violent manners. With the establishment of the movement and up to the Balfour Declaration all Zionist decision makers made use of peaceful means such as personal connections, fund raising meetings, statements to the mass media, and statements of intent in formal and informal gatherings. The movement's propaganda organs played a significant role in this regard. However, in response to Arab hostilities coupled with Britain's changing policies, the more militant decision makers chose and utilized violence. This violence, in turn, polarized the parties in conflict, but at the same time it widened the scope of conflict to include more audiences, the majority of which took a pro-Zionist stand. The involvement of numerous and diverse publics in the Arab-Zionist conflict has contributed, to a certain extent, to the democratization of foreign policy making: publics in the various democratic nation-states took positions and brought up demands to the legislative and executive branches of their respective governments.

The escalation of the conflict forced nation-states to take clear-cut policy commitments. With the changing international order in the post-World War II era, and the crystallization of rival blocks, nation-states were less reluctant to get involved in the affairs of nonstate nations. For both humanitarian and political reasons, nation-states made themselves more open to the appeals of the Zionist decision makers. With this change of attitudes, Zionist decision makers could advance their cause more effectively. Advocating a partition plan rather than a more inclusive program made the Zionist demands seem less radical and more compromising than those advanced by Arab decision makers. Moreover, the formal commitments made by nation-states served an integrative function within the rival blocs. Thus, a greater measure of cohesion resulted both within the Western bloc and the Arab bloc.

The third major impact of the Zionist movement was on international organizations. Zionist decision makers saw the various international organizations as sites for both publicizing their cause and eliciting commitments. The League of Nations got involved in the Zionist cause in a limited manner by issuing the Mandate. The Mandate, however, served the Zionist decision makers as a stepping stone to demand a greater measure of involvement in governance. Britain was to some extent neutralized by internationalizing the Zionist issue. Despite the apparent Balfour commitment, Britain attempted to extricate itself from the conflict by turning the matter over to the United Nations. Moreover, Zionist decision makers could publicize their cause in a more immediate manner as participants in the UN organization. The United Nations took an active role in international disputes and served as a neutral site for dealing with the Zionist-Arab confrontation. The organization has legitimized the Zionist cause and eventually contributed to the establishment of the State of Israel. Furthermore, Britain's assignment of the Palestine Mandate problem to the United Nations contributed to the development of the international organization as a body to deal with significant international problems.

NOTES

1. Theodor Herzl, The Complete Diaries of Theodor Herzl, ed. Raphael Patai and trans. Harry Zohn, 5 vols. (New York: Thomas Yoseloff, 1960), vol. 2, p. 581.

2. Judy S. Bertelsen, "The Nonstate Nation in International Politics: A Systems Framework," in Nonstate Nations in International Politics, ed. Judy S. Bertelsen (New York: Praeger, 1976).

3. Theodor Herzl, "The Jewish State," in The Zionist Idea, ed. Arthur Hertzberg (New York: Atheneum, 1971), pp. 204-26.

4. Encyclopedia of Zionism and Israel (New York: McGraw-Hill, 1971), p. 1265.

5. Nahum Sokolow, History of Zionism, 1600-1918, 2 vols. (London, 1919), vol. 1, p. 268.

6. Ismar Elbogen, A Century of Jewish Life (Philadelphia: The Jewish Publication Society of America, 1966), p. 282.

7. Encyclopedia of Zionism and Israel, op. cit., p. 620.

8. Ibid.

9. Ibid., pp. 627-28.

10. Walter Laqueur, A History of Zionism (New York: Holt, Rinehart and Winston, 1972), p. 590.

11. Elbogen, op. cit., p. 291.

12. Laqueur, op. cit., p. 130.

13. Ben Halpern, The Idea of the Jewish State, 2d ed. (Cambridge, Mass.: Harvard University Press, 1969), pp. 251-52.

14. Laqueur, op. cit., p. 109; Elbogen, op. cit., pp. 291-92.

15. Halpern, op. cit., pp. 272-75.

16. Leonard Stein, The Balfour Declaration (London: Vallantine-Mitchell, 1961), pp. 341-48.

17. Ibid., pp. 144-45; p. 127; Laqueur, op. cit., p. 183.

18. Esco Foundation for Palestine, Inc., Palestine: A Study of Jewish, Arab and British Politics, 2 vols. (New Haven, Conn.: Yale University Press, 1947), pp. 107-08.

19. Encyclopaedia Judaica (Jerusalem, 1971), vol. 9, pp. 477-78.

20. Leonard Fein, Politics in Israel (Boston: Little, Brown, 1967), pp. 16-18.

21. Elbogen, op. cit., pp. 200-23; Howard M. Sachar, The Course of Modern Jewish History (New York: Delta Books, 1963), pp. 240-69.

22. Laqueur, op. cit., p. 204.

23. Elbogen, op. cit., pp. 300-03.

24. Laqueur, op. cit., pp. 270-337.

25. Sachar, op. cit., p. 382.

26. Esco, 1, op. cit., pp. 234-40.

27. Paul Hanna, British Policy in Palestine (Washington, D.C., 1942), p. 43.

28. Esco, 1, op. cit., p. 264.

29. Saul Friedman, No Haven for the Oppressed (Detroit: Wayne State University Press, 1973), pp. 17-37.

30. Esco, 2, op. cit., pp. 664-84.

31. Encyclopedia of Zionism and Israel, op. cit., pp. 757-60.

32. Ibid., p. 613.

33. Esco, 1, op. cit., p. 571.

34. Yehuda Bauer, From Diplomacy to Resistance: A History of Jewish Palestine, 1939-1945 (New York: Atheneum, 1973), pp. 11-12.

35. Encyclopedia of Zionism and Israel, op. cit., p. 445.

36. For Weizmann's views see Chaim Weizmann, Trial and Error: The Autobiography of Chaim Weizmann (New York: Schocken Books, 1966).

37. Esco, 2, op. cit., p. 837.

38. Christopher Sykes, Crossroads to Israel, 1917-1948 (Bloomington: Indiana University Press, 1973), pp. 167-69.

39. Weizmann, op. cit., p. 387.

40. Sykes, op. cit., p. 195.

41. Esco, 2, op. cit., p. 621; see also Vladimir Jabotinsky, Der Judenstaat (Vienna, 1938).

42. Esco, 2, op. cit., p. 749.

43. Esco, 1, op. cit., pp. 362-63, 404.

44. Joseph Heller, The Zionist Idea (New York: Schocken Books, 1949), p. 149.

45. Esco, 2, op. cit., pp. 802-04.

46. "Evidence Submitted to the Palestine Royal Commission (1937)," in Hertzberg, op. cit., pp. 559-70.

47. Sykes, op. cit., p. 174.

48. Israel Cohen, A Short History of Zionism (London: Frederick Muller, 1951), p. 137.

49. Bauer, op. cit., pp. 11-12.

50. Esco, 2, op. cit., p. 902.

51. Ibid., p. 930.

52. Ibid., pp. 1084-85.

53. Ibid., p. 929.

54. Ibid., p. 1200.

55. Ibid., p. 1202.

56. Ibid., p. 1196.

57. Ibid., pp. 1045-46. In 1944 the Jewish Agency cooperated with the Mandatory police in rounding up and deporting 279 Sternists and Irgun followers (Sykes, op. cit., p. 257); also see Bauer, op. cit., p. 326.

58. Esco, 2, op. cit., p. 1200.

59. Ibid., pp. 1113-14.

60. Cohen, op. cit., p. 224.

61. Halpern, op. cit., p. 39.

62. Esco, 2, op. cit., pp. 1135-36.

63. Esco, 1, op. cit., pp. 362-63; Laqueur, pp. 339-83.

64. Halpern, op. cit., p. 43.

65. Sykes, op. cit., p. 248.

66. Halpern, op. cit., p. 358.

67. Ibid.

68. Laqueur, op. cit., p. 375.

69. Esco, 2, op. cit., pp. 1043-49.

70. Ibid., p. 1043.

71. Bauer, op. cit., p. 311; Laqueur, op. cit., p. 377.

72. Esco, 2, op. cit., pp. 1046–49.

73. David Ben Gurion, The Rebirth and Destiny of Israel (New York: Philosophical Library, 1954), pp. 223–24.

4

THE KURDISH
NONSTATE NATION
Charles Benjamin

Like the two preceding nonstate nations (NSNs), the Kurds
were encouraged in their nationalist aspirations by the
settlements at the end of World War I and by statements
such as the commitment in Woodrow Wilson's 14 Points
to self-determination for the non-Turkish nationalities of
the Ottoman Empire. As this chapter shows, however,
the Kurds were able to establish a separate state for only
a year.

More recently, Kurdish nationalist aspirations have
focused on developing an autonomous status with Iraq short
of complete independence. The precise enunciation of
goals has changed over time, apparently in response to
assessments both of resources and environmental con-
straints.

The Kurds received aid from nation-states, in particular Iran. This aid was given apparently because of
Iranian-Iraqi conflicts rather than because of a strong
identity of Iranian and Kurdish interests. The upshot is
that the Kurds remain a group seeking national autonomy
but constrained severely by the international environment.
The Iranian-U.S. aid, while providing resources, was
essentially an environmental factor, in that the Kurds
themselves could not control its continuity.

Major Kurdish activity has taken place within Iraq,
whose recent governments have shown an ambivalent vacillation between expressing support for and then withdrawing
support from Kurdish aspirations. The Kurds stand as an
example of an NSN that has sought independence but has

cut back its aspirations, in light of the nation-state environment. The Kurds have tried to achieve the delicate
balance of durability and audibility in an environment of
nation-states whose perceived interests do not seem to
overlap extensively with Kurdish interests.

—Judy S. Bertelsen

This chapter focuses on and applies the NSN framework to a
group of people known as the Kurds. Kurdistan is not recognized as
a nation-state by any other nation-states or by any international organizations. However, various Kurdish groups have, in this century,
organized themselves and behaved suspiciously like nation-states.
Kurdish leaders have explicitly asserted claims to national sovereignty: They have claimed territory; they have raised Kurdish armies
to fight the armies of internationally recognized nation-states; they
have asserted international treaty rights; and they have received economic and military aid (some of it covert) from nation-states. By
definition, therefore, there is a Kurdish nonstate nation.

Although the Kurds have a long history and a distinct culture,
this will not be detailed in the present chapter. However, enough historical background will be provided to facilitate the analysis of the
Kurdish nonstate nation. Indeed, the nonstate nation framework should
force the analyst to ask the types of questions that can cut through
and organize the mass of detail that one has to deal with in case studies. The emphasis of this chapter is on the attempts, since 1958, by
the Kurds of Iraq, under the leadership of Mulla Mustafa Barzani, to
gain autonomy and control over Kurdish areas within Iraq. These
Kurds have been the most audible and durable in recent times and, at
least to outside observers, have appeared likely to attain their goals.

HISTORICAL BACKGROUND

The Kurds are located in the mountainous area that forms the
mutual borders of Turkey, the Soviet Union, Iran, Iraq, and Syria.
Estimates of the total population of the Kurds vary as do the estimates
of the Kurdish populations within these nations. For example, Schmidt
(1974) estimates that there are somewhat less than 2 million Kurds
in Iraq, 3-4 million in Iran, more than 5 million in Turkey, a little
more than 300,000 in Syria, and approximately 175,000 in the Soviet
Union. His total population estimate, therefore, comes to more than
10 million. Another recent estimate by Head (1974) puts the individual
populations at 1.5 million in Iraq, 1.8 million in Iran, 3.2 million in

Turkey, 320,000 in Syria, and 80,000 in the Soviet Union, for a total population of 7 million. Smaller numbers of Kurds can also be found in Pakistan and Afghanistan (Edmonds 1957).

Throughout their history the Kurds have been an unfortunate victim of the interaction of the nation-states which surround them. As early as 1639, when the Turks and Persians demarcated their frontier, they did so by cutting through the center of Kurdish territory. Although the Kurds were nominally under the rule of Russians, Persians, and Ottomans, they were left pretty much to themselves, and Kurdish areas were actually ruled by various local chiefs or sheikhs.

The first stirrings of Kurdish political nationalism occurred in 1880 when a Kurdish sheikh named Ubeidullah (living in the Kurdish region nominally controlled by Turkey), with Turkish encouragement, invaded the Kurdish area nominally controlled by Persia. His intent was to create a Kurdish state loyal to Turkey. Although Sheikh Ubeidullah was unsuccessful and eventually died in exile in Mecca, he was the first Kurdish nationalist leader of any note in modern history (O'Ballance 1973, p. 16).

Kurds have been recruited into the armies of the various powers who nominally control Kurdish territory. For example, in 1871 the Turks raised an irregular unit of Kurdish cavalry, known as the Hamidiye Regiments, who were used primarily to police Kurdish areas in Turkey. During the Young Turks Revolution of 1908, a Kurdish sheikh with 1,500 Kurdish irregulars occupied and held Damascus for the sultan. During World War I the Hamidiye Regiments fought for the sultan, at one time numbering as many as 30 units on the eastern Turkish front. The Kurds, sponsored by the Turks, also engaged in a series of mutual massacres against the Christian Armenians and Assyrians, who were sponsored by the Czar of Russia.

The Collapse of the Ottoman Empire
and the Interwar Period

The end of World War I saw the dismantling of the Ottoman Empire, and Kurdish territory was divided among five nations: Turkey, Persia, what is now the Soviet Union, Syria, and the new country of Iraq (formed from the three former Turkish vilayets of Mosul, Baghdad, and Basra), which was now under British control.

A mild Kurdish nationalist organization had existed in Turkey since 1909, and during World War I the Russians tried to encourage the idea of a Kurdish nation-state. In 1918 the aspirations of the minorities of the Ottoman Empire (including the Kurds) were recognized in Point 12 of Woodrow Wilson's "Program of the World's Peace," which stipulated that the non-Turkish nationalities of the empire would be "assured of an absolute unmolested opportunity of autonomous development." The means for such development were provided by Article 22 of the Covenant of the League of Nations setting up the system of Mandates.

These conceptions were given concrete form in the Treaty of Sèvres, imposed by the victorious allies on the Turkish Sultan in 1920. The treaty provided for the recognition or creation of the three Arab states of Kijaz, Syria, and Iraq, and, in what is now eastern Turkey, of an Armenia and a Kurdistan, to which the Kurds of the Mosul vilayet were to be free to adhere. However, with the rise of Mustafa Kemal Ataturk the treaty was never ratified. The Treaty of Lausanne signed in 1923 between the Allies and Turkey made no mention of an Armenia or a Kurdistan. The ownership of the Mosul vilayet was excluded from the settlement and was left for future negotiations between Turkey on the one side and Great Britain (as the Mandatory power for Iraq) on the other.

When negotiations between Great Britain and Turkey broke down the dispute was referred to the League of Nations. The league awarded the vilayet to Iraq on the condition that regard should be made to the desires expressed by the Kurds that officials of Kurdish race be appointed for the administration of their country, the dispensation of justice, and teaching in the schools, and that Kurdish should be the official language of all these services. In 1931 the British government sponsored the application of Iraq to the League of Nations. As a way of confirming its acceptance of the league's conditions the government enacted a "Local Languages Law" which specified the administrative units to which the stipulations should apply. In 1932, when the British Mandate came to an end and Iraq was admitted to the league, a fresh statement of the Iraqi government's undertakings toward the Kurds was embodied in a declaration, which was to rank as an entrenched part of the Constitution and to be a matter of international concern (Edmonds 1967, p. 11).

During the 1920s and 1930s there were several Kurdish uprisings against the governments which had nominal control over the Kurdish areas. The British fought the Kurds in Iraq from 1919 until their Mandate expired in 1932. The Kurds in the Soviet Union, in the area known as Azerbaijan, were completely suppressed during the consolidation of the Bolshevik Revolution. In Turkey, Kemal Ataturk had to send forces against Kurdish rebellions in 1924, 1927-30, and 1930-37. In Persia the Kurds revolted in 1920-23, 1930, and 1931. In all cases the Kurdish revolts were successfully put down so that by the end of 1937 the Turks and Persians could announce the end of their "Kurdish problems." In Turkey the word itself was banned and the Kurds were officially known as "Mountain Turks who had forgotten their mother tongue." Despite these revolts there was no unity among the Kurds and various Kurdish units were incorporated into the armies of Turkey and Iraq during the interwar period.

The advent of World War II brought a renewed British occupation of Iraq and a joint Anglo-Soviet occupation of Persia. The war also brought renewed opportunities for Kurdish rebellion. In 1943 Mulla Mustafa Barzani fought the Iraqis to a stalemate and by 1944 a Kurdish flag flew over parts of Kurdish areas in Turkey, Iraq, and Iran (Persia). As the end of the war approached the Kurds made vain attempts to gain recognition by the United States and the Soviet Union for an independent Kurdistan. However, before any action could be taken, combined elements of Iraqi troops and Kurdish tribesmen opposed to Mulla Mustafa successfully suppressed the revolt and the small Kurdish army hastily fled to the Kurdish area of Iran.

The Republic of Mahabad

In December 1945 the Kurdish Republic of Mahabad was established in the Kurdish area of northwestern Iran. Although the republic was short-lived (lasting only a year), it stands as a significant part of Kurdish history because it was the first outright attempt to establish an independent, sovereign Kurdish nation-state. The Republic of Mahabad deserves a separate NSN analysis because the decision makers, goals, components, resources, and environment were different from the period examined here. Suffice it to say here that the republic was set up under the leadership of Qazi Mohammed with extensive Soviet support, including the protection of Soviet occupation troops in northern Persia. When Soviet troops were withdrawn from Persia, Iranian troops moved in and crushed the republic, hanging Qazi Mohammed and many others in the process. Mulla Mustafa Barzani, who is to emerge as the primary decision maker in the period under analysis, was one of five generals leading the Kurdish armed resistance on behalf of the republic. When the republic collapsed (in the face of Iraqi, Turkish, and Persian reprisals against Kurds) Mulla Mustafa with 500 to 800 of his men retreated to the Soviet Union where he remained in exile for 12 years (Eagleton 1963; Roosevelt 1947). Although the Kurds, under his leadership in the time frame examined here, seem to be demanding autonomy and not independence (see the section, "Goals"), it is important to remember that Mulla Mustafa was a significant leader in the attempt to establish an independent Kurdistan. The experiences of the republic are also signifi-

cant in understanding Mulla Mustafa's distrust of foreign commitments to Kurdish causes.

Recent History

A few days after the Iraqi Revolution of July 15, 1958, which
overthrew the monarchy, the new head of state, General Abd al-Ka-
rim Qasim, promulgated a "Temporary Constitution" which, although
it described Iraq as part of the Arab world, went on (Article 3) to
refer specifically to the Kurds as copartners with the Arabs within
the framework of Iraqi unity and to guarantee their communal rights.
Mulla Mustafa was brought back from exile and became an all-Iraqi
figure, a champion of the struggle against "the imperialists and their
stooges." It was confidently assumed that the equality thus proclaimed would mean a considerable measure of administrative devolution,
a fairer share than before of development projects and social services, and enhanced status for the Kurdish language. On this assumption the various Kurdish organizations, in Iraq and abroad, rallied
to the support of the new regime.

There was never any serious attempt by the Qasim government
to implement the promises to the Kurds implicit in the Temporary
Constitution. In the autumn of 1960 the strongly left-wing Democratic
Party of Kurdistan (Iraqi Branch), of which Mulla Mustafa had been
elected president, was declared illegal. Some of its office holders
were arrested, and several newspapers were suppressed. Mulla
Mustafa himself returned from a visit to the Soviet Union to find the
house, car, and salary allotted to him after his return in 1958 withdrawn; he then retired to his native village of Barzan.

Fighting broke out in July 1961 and continued until a cease-fire
was agreed to following the overthrow and death of Qasim in February 1963 at the hands of a military junta associated with the extreme
pan-Arab Baath party led by General Tabir Yahya, who became chief
of the General Staff. General Abd as-Salam Arif, who had been Qasim's principal colleague in 1958, was brought back as president of
the republic, and General Ahmad Hasan al-Bakr became prime minister. In March, after a visit by Tahir Yahya to Mulla Mustafa, the
government issued a proclamation recognizing "the natural rights of
the Kurdish people on the basis of decentralization."

A Kurdish delegation was sent to Baghdad to negotiate the details of an agreement, and on April 24 it published a statement of
Kurdish claims for home rule, which was intended as the opening
move for further negotiations. The statement was never discussed.
On June 10 the Yahya government arrested the Kurdish representa-

tives, issued an ultimatum demanding the surrender of Mulla Mustafa
and his forces within 24 hours, and launched an offensive against
Kurdish positions.

In the middle of November 1963 the Baath regime was overthrown, President Arif assumed more direct control, and Tahir Yahya became prime minister. This change of government was followed
in February 1964 by a second cease-fire and negotiations between
Arif and Mulla Mustafa. No progress was made in these talks, and
the new Temporary Constitution promulgated by the Arif regime was
even less satisfactory to the Kurds than that of Qasim's Constitution.
Full-scale fighting broke out again in April 1965, and the Iraqi government committed even larger forces than before against the Kurds.

At the beginning of September 1965 Tahir Yahya resigned the
premiership and was succeeded by Abd ar-Rahman Bazzaz, the first
civilian to hold the office since 1958. The Arif Temporary Constitution was amended on September 9 to mention explicitly the national
rights of the Kurds. The change of prime minister was followed by
a lull in hostilities and assurances of the new government's good intentions. However, no serious discussions ensued, and the government demanded that the "rebels" lay down their arms. Fighting again
broke out.

On April 13, 1966, President Abd as-Salam died in a helicopter
crash and was succeeded by his elder brother Abd ar-Rahman. The
succession brought no change in the government's policy toward the
Kurds, and on May 1 the Iraqi army began another large-scale offensive against the Kurds. On May 12 the Iraqi army suffered its worst
defeat of the entire war when two battalions were nearly wiped out by
Kurdish forces on the heights of Handren above Rawandiz. After a
period of intensive retaliatory bombing, the third formal cease-fire
was agreed to in the middle of June on the initiative of the prime
minister. On June 29 the prime minister broadcast a 12-point program which was accepted by Mulla Mustafa as a starting point for
fresh negotiations. This pronouncement, known as the "Declaration
(or Agreement) of June 29, 1966," has been adopted by subsequent
Iraqi administrations as the basis for their promises of a "just and
peaceable settlement" (see the section, "Goals").

A settlement on the basis of the June 29 agreements was ob-
structed by frequent changes of regime or cabinet within the Iraqi
government. Bazzaz resigned on August 6, 1966, and was succeeded
eventually by Tahir Yahya in July 1967. Yahya lasted only a year,
until July 17, 1968. The Arif regime was then overthrown by a junta
of army officers known as the Revolutionary Command Council (RCC),
and General Ahmad Hasan al-Bakr emerged as president. On July
30 al-Bakr dismissed the prime minister, and the minister of De-

fense and assumed the office of the prime minister in addition to his other duties.

Although the Kurds expected the worst from an al-Bakr government composed of the same officers who were responsible for the genocidal policies of 1963, the initial relations between the government and the Kurds remained relatively peaceful for a short time. The Iraqi army garrisoned the towns and some of the larger villages in Kurdistan, but Kurdish forces dominated most of the countryside and collected taxes for the "Free Kurdish" organization. Visits to Mulla Mustafa by Iraqi officials were frequent (including one visit by the Iraqi president), and Kurdish negotiating teams spent long periods in Baghdad. Al-Bakr emphatically announced his determination to bring about a just and peaceful solution on the basis of the 1966 agreements. He issued two decrees, one indicating his intention to implement Article 6 of the declaration by the formation of a Kurdish Cultural Academy and the nomination of a committee to draft a law for a University of Sulaymani, and the second (based on parts of Articles 9 and 10) proclaiming a general amnesty and directing the restoration of dismissed civil servants as far as possible to their posts.

The al-Bakr government did nothing to implement its promises and grant the Kurds a measure of self-government. Neither was any attempt made to rebuild Kurdish districts that were leveled during the fighting. Furthermore, the government took the Kurdish group headed by Mulla Mustafa's rivals Jelal el-Talbani and Ibrahim Ahmed under its protection, equipped it with arms, and even used it later in the fighting against Mulla Mustafa's troops.

By November 1968 limited fighting had broken out and in February 1969 the Iraqi forces mounted a general offensive against the Kurds, putting 60,000 men into the field supported by aircraft, armor, and heavy artillery. Despite the size of the Iraqi commitment and the destruction of some 200 Kurdish villages (far exceeding past destruction), the Kurdish forces scored sizable victories. By November 1969 the al-Bakr government started contacts and negotiations with Mulla Mustafa's representatives, which eventually led to the signing of an agreement on March 11, 1970. The agreement left Mulla Mustafa in control of most of Kurdistan and acknowledged his de facto authority in areas previously under Iraqi military control. There was to be a four-year interim period before the provisions of the agreement came into effect. March 1974 was the end of that four-year period, and negotiations between the Kurds and the Iraqi government broke down in the beginning of that month. By mid-April the Iraqis launched another offensive sending seven Iraqi divisions, including two armored divisions, supported by 200 bombers and fighter bombers, into Kurdish territory along three fronts (Head 1974).

ANALYSIS OF THE KURDS AS A NONSTATE NATION

Decision Maker: Mulla Mustafa Barzani

There is little doubt that Mulla Mustafa Barzani is the primary decision maker of the Kurdish nonstate nation. As previously described, he has a 50-year history of fighting and negotiating with British, Turkish, Persian, Iraqi, and opposing Kurdish forces. The last major opposition to his leadership from within the Kurdish political infrastructure occurred in March of 1964 (Arfa 1966, pp. 147-52) following a cease-fire which Mulla Mustafa negotiated with the Arif government. Mulla Mustafa, as military commander of all Kurdish forces, had decided that the continuation of the war against Iraq could not be sustained (at that time). The whole Kurdish region had been ruined by Iraqi Air Force bombing. The crops vital for the continuation of the rebellion had been destroyed, the population had been increased by the influx of refugees without shelter or means of livelihood, and the ammunition stocks were exhausted. Furthermore, with the collapse of the Baath government in Iraq, Nasser had withdrawn his support for the Kurds.

Mulla Mustafa had always faced a certain amount of resistance to his leadership from elements of the Kurdish intelligentsia (who considered him too tribally oriented and politically conservative) and from other tribal leaders (who resented his overlordship over their previously autonomous tribes). Mulla Mustafa's opposition in the Kurdish Democratic party (PDK) were obliged to accept him, however, as the uncontested military chief of the rebellion and the only person having the confidence of a majority of the warring tribes. Now that he had himself initiated the cease-fire negotiations on lines widely differing from the claims which had been made by the chiefs of the rebellion, they considered him no longer indispensable. They presented him with a memorandum disagreeing with the terms of the cease-fire and declaring that the Iraqi government did not intend to make any appreciable concessions to the Kurds and was only trying to buy time to consolidate its position in the country. The memorandum touched off a split in the PDK and in the army, resulting in a portion of Kurdish leaders and soldiers fleeing to Iran. In mid-September a congress of Iraqi Kurds summoned by Mulla Mustafa, at Ranya, gave him full powers to administer the Kurdish rebellion, but at the same time invited him to recall the PDK dissidents from Iran. Eventually this congress granted leadership of both the military and civilian affairs of the Kurds to Mulla Mustafa. Mulla Mustafa pledged to resume hostilities against the Iraqis if autonomy should not be granted after a reasonable length of time. Mulla Mustafa further consolidated his position at a conference of Kurdish notables held at Ranya on October 4, 1964. It was decided at this conference that three assemblies should be formed and charged with looking after Kurdish affairs: (1) the Senate, under the chairmanship of Sheikh Latif Hafidzadeh (son of the late Sheikh Mahmud of Suleymaniyah); (2) a Consultative Assembly presided over by Mamand Abbas Aqa (chief of the Aku tribe, a faithful friend of Mulla Mustafa); (3) a Revolutionary Council, in charge of warlike operations, presided over by Mulla Mustafa himself. Each of these assemblies would consist of 16 members: 4 representating the tribes, 4 selected by the PDK, 4 representing the intellectuals and townspeople, and 4 nominated by Mulla Mustafa.

In this way Mulla Mustafa gained control over two of the three assemblies, and by choosing Sheikh Latif to preside over the Senate he ensured the collaboration of the conservative and religious elements who favored an early reconciliation with the Arif government. These arrangements were later followed by the appointment of a Council of Ministers, presided over by Mulla Mustafa.

Thus Mulla Mustafa consolidated in himself the decision-making function of the Kurdish nonstate nation. Since the unsuccessful coup against him in 1964 (described above), most of Mulla Mustafa's opposition within the Kurdish political infrastructure has either been reconciled or exiled or has defected to the Iraqis. The most notable example of the latter is Jalal Talabani, the former ambassador at large for the Kurds and the person largely responsible for negotiating with the Egyptian government. Talabani, a leader in the 1964 Kurdish opposition to Mulla Mustafa, has led what little remained of (Iraqi supported) Kurdish opposition to Mulla Mustafa.

The decision of when and where to fight the Iraqis has been made by Mulla Mustafa as have been the decisions to cease fire and come to an agreement (however temporary) with the Iraqi government. The final decision to cease the struggle against the Iraqis (at least temporarily) came from Mulla Mustafa on March 18, 1975, in line with the shah of Iran's demand of the Kurds as part of the Iranian settlement with Iraq (Kimche 1975, p. 19).

Goals

In order to understand the goals of the Kurdish nonstate nation it is useful to examine not only what the Kurds say they want but to also look at the provisions made on behalf of the Kurds in international treaties and by international organizations as well as the de-

tails of the various agreements that the Kurds have signed with a succession of Iraqi governments.

Post-World War I Recognition. With the collapse of the Ottoman Empire at the end of World War I, the proposed Treaty of Sèvres (August 1920) included the following provisions for the recognition of a
Kurdistan:

> Article 62. A Commission sitting at Constantinople
> and composed of three members appointed by the British,
> French and Italian Governments respectively shall draft
> within six months from the coming into force of the pre-
> sent Treaty a scheme of local autonomy for the predom-
> inantly Kurdish areas lying east of the Euphrates, south
> of the southern boundary of Armenia as it may be here-
> after determined, and north of the frontier of Turkey
> with Syria and Mesopotamia. . . .
>
> Article 63. The Turkish Government hereby agrees
> to accept and execute the decisions of both the Commis-
> sions mentioned in Article 62 within three months from
> their communication to the said Government.
>
> Article 64. If within one year the Kurdish peoples
> within the areas defined in Article 62 shall . . . show that
> the majority of the population of those areas desires inde-
> pendence from Turkey, and if the Council [of the League
> of Nations] then considers that these peoples are capable
> of such independence and recommends that it should be
> granted to them, Turkey hereby agrees to execute such a
> recommendation and to renounce all rights and title over
> these areas (Eagleton 1963, pp. 11-12).

With the rise to power of Kemal Ataturk the Treaty of Sèvres
was never signed (see p. 72 for a description of this period).

The Agreement with Qasim. With the Iraqi Revolution of July 1958,
which overthrew the monarchy, General Qasim promulgated a "Temporary Constitution." Although the Constitution described Iraq as
part of the Arab world, it went on to refer specifically, in Article 3,
to the Kurds as copartners with the Arabs within the framework of
Iraqi unity, and to guarantee the Kurds communal rights (Edmonds
1968).

The Agreement with Yahya. Of course Qasim's promises were never
kept and the Iraqi army fought the Kurds from July 1961 until the

overthrow and death of Qasim in February 1963 in a revolt led by General Tahir Yahya. The subsequent cease-fire with the Kurds and a visit by Yahya to Mulla Mustafa were followed by a proclamation recognizing "the natural rights of the Kurdish people on the basis of decentralization." The three major provisions of the Iraqi scheme of decentralization were that: (1) the country should be divided into six regions to be named after the cities of Mosul, Kirkuk, Sulaymani, Baghdad, Hille, and Basra, each (with the exception of the first two) comprising two or more liwas;* (2) that the Sulaymani region should include the liwas of Arbil, Sulaymani (plus one qada transferred from Kirkuk), and a new liwa of Dihole to consist of five Kurdish qadas detached from the Mosul liwa; and (3) that in the Sulaymani region Kurdish should rank as an official language together with Arabic and that the language of public instruction should be Kurdish in the primary and intermediate classes of schools, Arabic in the secondary classes. The new regions of Mosul and Kirkuk would each consist of what remained of the present liwa of the same name.

Although the partition of the large heterogeneous liwa of Mosul into an all-Kurdish liwa of Dihok would have been a gain for the Kurds, the Kurds objected because they claimed the scheme ignored the presence of larger homogeneous Kurdish majorities in the greater part of Kirkuk liwa and in a large part of Dryala (Edmonds 1968). The exclusion of Kirkuk was particularly significant because it is the center of a large pool of proven oil reserves. At any rate, the scheme was never put into operation. With the arrest on June 10 of the Kurdish negotiating team and the demand for the surrender of Mulla Mustafa and his forces, the Yahya regime launched an offensive against the Kurds which exceeded even the efforts of Qasim to suppress the Kurds.

The Agreement with Arif. The Baath regime of Tahir Yahya was overthrown in November 1963 and Abd as-Salam Arif, the new president, negotiated a cease-fire with the Kurds in February 1964 and shortly thereafter opened negotiations with Mulla Mustafa.

Part of the reason for again opening negotiations with the Kurds was the continuation of disastrous military defeats that the Iraqis were suffering at the hands of Mulla Mustafa's forces. The Kurdish

---

*For purposes of administration, Iraq is divided into 14 liwas, each subdivided into two or more qadas, further subdivided into nahiyas. The great majority of the Kurds are established in the former vilayet of Mosul, now the liwas of Mosul, Arbil, Sulaymani, and Kirkuk, but they spill over into the former vilayet of Baghdad at its eastern end, now the liwa of Diyala (Edmonds 1968, p. 515).

demands in a settlement with the Iraqi government grew with their
successes on the battlefield. Under Qasim the Kurds had confined
themselves to demands for administrative and cultural autonomy within the framework of the Iraqi state. With the advent of the Baaths,
and continued military success against ever larger Iraqi forces, the
Kurds began insisting on obtaining not only administrative and cultural autonomy, but also political autonomy. The main points of the
Kurdish demands put forward to the Arif regime were that:

   • Full autonomy be granted to the Kurdish regions of northern
Iraq, whose geographical boundaries should be defined and recognized
in the Iraqi constitution;

   • The Kurdish language be the official language of the autonomous region and the second official language of Iraq, and that it be
taught in Kurdish and mixed schools;

   • The political setup of Iraq and the Kurdish autonomous region
be organized on the following basis: (1) The regime in Iraq would be
a democratic one, with political activity permitted; (2) The vice-president and deputy minister of Iraq would be Kurds; (3) besides the central Parliament in Baghdad, a local assembly would be elected in
Iraqi Kurdistan; (4) an autonomous government would be set up in the
Kurdish provinces; (5) the Kurds would be represented in proportion
to their percentage of the total Iraqi population—in Parliament, in the
government, and in the central administration; (6) foreign affairs,
defense, and finances would remain under the province of the central
government; all other matters would be transferred to the competence
of the autonomous government; (7) Kurdish army units would remain
under Kurdish command, and would be placed at the disposal of the
autonomy; (8) the budget of the autonomous regime would be derived
from taxes levied in the Kurdish region plus a just share of the revenue derived from oil royalties, which would not be less than one-
third of those revenues (in negotiations the Kurds demanded that
Kirkuk, the oil production center, be included in the autonomous region [Salomon 1967, p. 19]); (9) any questions arising in the future
concerning the status of the Kurds would be solved democratically
through mutual agreement and absolute equality between the Kurds
and the Arabs (Salomon 1967).

   Arif's representatives began negotiations in February 1964
with Mulla Mustafa's representatives. The Kurds insisted on their
demands for autonomy, while the Iraqis were not prepared to make
any concessions on this point, claiming that Kurdish autonomy would
inevitably lead to the secession of the northern region of Iraq. Arif
proposed that the Kurds waive their demand for autonomy, in exchange
for which he revived proposals for the decentralization of the Iraqi

provinces, the same proposal that the Kurds had rejected when put forward by the Baaths.

While Iraqi-Kurdish relations deteriorated throughout 1964, the Kurds announced the establishment of Kurdish institutions of representation and government. In October 1964 the Kurds established a kind of parliament and legislative council called the Supreme Revolutionary Council, with 43 members representing all sections of the population in the Kurdish north. Under Mulla Mustafa's leadership a Kurdish cabinet was also established as well as a judicial authority, a tax-collecting apparatus, and various committees to deal with local government and the drafting of a constitution.

These developments caused a great deal of concern within Arif's government, which was under increasing pressure to prevent the loss of the oil-rich districts of northern Iraq. Another offensive against the Kurds was launched in April 1965.

The Agreement with Bazzaz. Despite the Iraqi's concentrated military effort and some initial setbacks, the Kurds gradually assumed the initiative toward the end of 1965 and the beginning of 1966. The death of Abd as-Salam Arif in a helicopter crash on April 13, 1966, and the succession of his elder brother Abd ar-Rahman Arif brought no change in policy. However, the most serious battle defeat of the Iraqi army by the Kurds to date on May 12 brought a new cease-fire. On May 29 the new civilian prime minister, Abd ar-Rahman Bazzaz, broadcast a 12-point program which was accepted by Mulla Mustafa as a starting point for fresh negotiations. This "Declaration of June 29, 1966" is important because it has since been adopted by subsequent Iraqi administrations as the basis for "a just and peaceable settlement." The main points of the agreement are: (1) recognition of "Kurdish nationality" to be confirmed in the Permanent Constitution; (2) enactment of a Provisional Administration Law providing for decentralization and the transfer of wide powers to locally elected councils; (3) use of Kurdish for administration and public instruction; (4) early Parliamentary elections; (5) representation of the Kurds in the National Assembly and all branches of the public service in proportion to their numbers in the total population; (6) generous grants for study abroad at all levels, establishment of a faculty of Kurdish studies in Baghdad University and, eventually, of branches of the University of "the north"; (7) appointment of Kurdish officials to Kurdish districts; (8) permission for political association and for literary and political publications; (9) a general amnesty "when violence ends" to include all persons already convicted and deserters reporting with their arms, plus disbandment of the Cavaliers (the Iraqi-sponsored anti-Barzani forces led by Jalal Talabini); (10) reappointment of ab-

sentee officials as far as possible to their previous posts; (11) formation of a special ministry to supervise reconstruction and compensation for sufferers "in the north" and to coordinate administration in the various Kurdish districts; (12) resettlement of persons
evicted from their homes, or compensation in lieu.

Edmonds (1968) also reports that the Baghdad press has mentioned three supplementary "unpublished articles," which were presumably added at some point during subsequent negotiations. These
promised: (1) release of all political prisoners; (2) specific permission for the Democratic party of Kurdistan to function publicly; (3)
formation of all Kurdish districts of the Mosul liwa into a new liwa
of Dihok.

The Agreement with al-Bakr. As we have seen, the frequent changes
of government within Iraq from June 1966 prevented implementation
of the June 1966 Agreements. On July 17, 1969, Ahmed Hasan al-
Bakr undertook a coup which brought the Baaths back to power. Immediately after taking over, the al-Bakr government announced that
it intended to solve the Kurdish problem peacefully according to the
12-point program which the Bazzaz government had drawn up and presented to the Kurds in June 1966. Nothing ever came of these promises, and fighting broke out again in November 1968. By February
1969 the Iraqis had launched another, even larger, full-scale offensive. By the end of 1969 it was evident that the Iraqi army had again
failed to suppress the Kurds and in November and December of that
year peace talks began.

Again the Kurds demanded full political autonomy within their
district. However, the al-Bakr government regarded the concession
to such demands as constituting a major step toward Kurdish secession from Iraq. They were not prepared to allow the creation of what
they called "a second Israel" at the other end of the Middle East
(Salomon 1970b). The Iraqis proposed to negotiate on the basis of the
old Bazzaz 12-point plan of June 1966. However, the Kurds now pres-
sed new demands, these being: (1) the inclusion of Kirkuk among the
regions which were to form the new Kurdish district that would be
administered by Kurdish Barzani appointees; (2) special foreign loans
to be obtained for the Kurdish Northern District which was to be established under the decentralization scheme, through the Ministry
for the North which was to be established and which was, as had already been agreed, to be headed by a Kurdish minister; (3) proportional representation of the Kurds on the Iraqi Revolutionary Council;
(4) the grant of full legislative powers to the Revolutionary Council in
a form to be determined by Mulla Mustafa; (5) parliamentary elections
after a two-year transition period.

Despite the fact that the Iraqis rejected all of these demands Mulla Mustafa was able to convince Kurdish "hardliners" to sign a treaty. The March 11, 1970, peace treaty between the Kurds and the Iraqi government has not been published, but its main points were included in a special proclamation by Iraqi President al-Bakr, which was broadcast over Baghdad Radio and in an Iraqi television program (Salomon 1970b, pp. 34-38).

The agreement included 15 points and is similar in substance and spirit to the 12-point Bazzaz plan of June 1966. Its main provisions are:

1. Recognition of the Kurdish nation. To this end the provisional constitution of Iraq was to be amended by a section stating that the Republic of Iraq consists of two main nations, Arabs and Kurds.

2. Recognition of the Kurdish language, in the form of a constitutional amendment laying down that both Kurdish and Arabic will serve as official languages in those districts in Northern Iraq in which the Kurds are in the majority.

3. The legal powers of the districts are to be increased by legal amendment. A new Kurdish district named "Dahuk District" will be formed, with the same enlarged administrative powers and a Kurdish governor.

4. A Kurdish vice-president will be appointed, and the Kurds will enjoy proportional representation on all executive and administrative bodies, including the government and the army.

5. Administration officials in districts with a Kurdish majority must be Kurds or at least speak Kurdish.

6. The national right of the Kurds to the development of Kurdish culture is recognized in every aspect, including the establishment of a Kurdish university in the Suleimania District, the publication of Kurdish books and newspapers, Kurdish-language broadcasts and telecasts, and the recognition of Kurdish customs and holidays.

7. All Kurdish students will be permitted to return to their studies and their educational standards will be improved.

8. The Kurds will be permitted to establish youth and adult organizations (ostensibly nonpolitical), as customary in all parts of Iraq.

9. A general amnesty would be proclaimed for all who have taken part in the Kurdish rebellion, and Kurdish public servants and soldiers would be reinstated in office.

10. All Kurds who have left their villages would be permitted to return, and for those unable to return for different reasons, new housing would be provided.

11. Kurdish soldiers would be granted pensions, and dependents of fallen Kurds would be compensated.

12. A Committee for the Rehabilitation of the Northern Districts and Compensation of War Damage would be established and an economic development plan for the Kurdish region would be drawn up and implemented with all possible speed.

13. Steps would be taken to assure the speedy implementation of land reform in the Kurdish regions in Northern Iraq, under which the holdings of the Agawar (landlords) would be expropriated and distributed among the tenants cultivating them. Also, all land debts of Kurdish farmers for the last nine years would be canceled.

14. The arms held by the Kurdish fighters would be surrendered to the Iraqi government during the final stages of the implementation of the treaty. The same applies to the secret Kurdish broadcasting station "Free Kurdistan."

15. A high commission consisting of representatives of the central Iraqi authorities and of the Kurds would be established to supervise the implementation of the treaty.

Al-Bakr's broadcast announcement referred to Mullah Mustafa as "the leader of the Kurdish Democratic party." This clearly implied official recognition of the legality of what was now the single most important political body of the Kurds in Iraq, and of Mulla Mustafa as leader of the party and of the Iraqi Kurds — a meaningful step which the Iraqis had thus far refused to take.

The announcement also stated that the exploitation of the country's natural resources (meaning the Kirkuk oil fields) would continue to be within the domain and under the control of the Baghdad government. Mulla Mustafa's statement, broadcast after that of al-Bakr, also referred to the "oil fields in Kurdistan" as "the property of the entire people of Iraq" (Salomon 1970b, p. 36).

There was to be a four-year interim period during which the provisions of the agreement were to be implemented. In practice the ensuing four years became an armed truce. The Iraqi government carried out few of the terms of the agreement. Some economic development in Kurdistan was begun; a Kurdish university was opened in Suleimaniya; however, the essential Kurdish demands—political autonomy in Kurdistan and a Kurdish share of power in Baghdad—remained unfulfilled.

In December 1973 the Kurds published a draft of their constitutional demands. These included an elected legislative council and an independent executive, their own armed force, and participation not just in the cabinet but in the Revolutionary Command Council of Iraq. They also wanted national elections in a democratic Iraq and they wanted their capital in Kirkuk, center of the oil fields.

The Iraqi government came back with its proposal. Although it offered little of what they really wanted, the Kurds accepted it as a basis of negotiation. Mulla Mustafa sent his son Idriss to Baghdad but the Baathists did not really want to negotiate. They proclaimed their constitution and said they would impose it unilaterally. As a prelude to the outbreak of fighting in April 1974 the Iraqi government executed 11 prominent Kurds who were moved from Baghdad to Arbil at the edge of Kurdish territory to make the occasion more demonstrative. Shortly thereafter the Kurds executed 17 Iraqi officers (Schmidt 1974, p. 57).

Summary of Goals. When interviewed by American journalists Mulla Mustafa denies claims to independence for the Kurds. He claims that the Kurds are demanding autonomy and a share of national spending proportional to their population, which he estimates should amount to 20 to 25 percent of the Iraqi budget (Roberts 1974).

Mulla Mustafa has also denied any desire to keep the oil revenues derived from Kurdish oil fields. He has said that the oil revenues should go to the central Iraqi government and that Kurdistan should receive a percentage of all Iraqi revenues, not just oil revenues.

Although Mulla Mustafa made claims only for Kurdish autonomy within Iraq, Kurdish demands for a say in revenue sharing according to their population were unacceptable to the Iraqis. (These demands can be seen as similar to demands made by states and provinces in the federal structure of the United States and Canada.) Even more disturbing to Iraqi authorities were Kurdish nation-statelike activities in the international environment. Essentially a third of the country (of Iraq) was operating in its own network of international interactions. At various times Mulla Mustafa sent representatives (or himself) to Cairo, Damascus, and Tehran in order to gather support for Kurdish "anti-Iraqi" activities. Al-Bakr's 1967 reference to Kurdistan as "a second Israel at the other end of the Middle East," was a thinly vieled attempt to invoke Arab unity against the Kurdish cause. Finally, the Iraqi governments were simply unwilling (for obvious reasons) to give in to Kurdish claims to the oil-rich Kirkuk area.

Components

The components of the nonstate nation are the separate missions or projects designed to achieve the NSN's goals. In order to achieve the goals of the Kurdish nonstate nation, Mulla Mustafa has employed two major components, one military and the other political.

The Military Component. The military component consists of two elements. One is the tribal fighters who constituted, at the beginning,
the chief fighting force of the Kurds. These acted in the traditional
way of tribal guerrillas, assembling at a certain point at a given time
to deliver an attack or raid a locality, then returning to their homes
in a village or an encampment. They kept their rifles and ammunition
concealed somewhere underground or in a cave to prevent being dis-
armed by Iraqi troops. In this way the Barzanis and the other tribes
fought against the Turks in the 1920s and 1930s, against the Iraqis
before 1961, and against the Iranians in 1945 (Arfa 1966, p. 138).
One of the lessons learned from the ill-fated Republic of Mahabad
was the unreliability of tribal fighters. When fighting broke out between the Kurds and Qasim's government in 1961, the PDK Central
Committee convinced Mulla Mustafa of the necessity for a permanent
Kurdish army which became the second, and most important, element of the military component.

The permanent force of the Kurdish insurgents is called Lach-
gar-i-Shoreshi-ye-Kord; the soldiers are Pishmargeh and the officers Sarmargeh (which mean, respectively, "Facing Death" and
"Heading Death"). They are armed with rifles of different makes although their chief purveyor has been the Iraqi army itself, as many
arms fell into the hands of the Kurds during the fighting and many
others had been brought to them by Kurdish deserters from the Iraqi
army. In the later phases of the conflict the Kurds were receiving
rifles, medium-range artillery, antiaircraft guns, and ammunition
from Iran (Clarity 1974a).

The Kurdish military strategy has been to keep fluid front lines
while taking advantage of the lofty hills of northern Iraq. These hills
offer inaccessible refuges where the Kurdish detachments can retreat for a time and then launch again a lightning attack on an ill-pro-
tected column progressing or camping in a valley or on the slopes of
the mountains.

The Political Component. The political component of the Kurdish
NSN is also split into two elements, both of which operate through
the PDK. One of the elements is the domestic component dealing with
the Iraqi government in Baghdad. Mulla Mustafa has controlled Kurdish dealings with Iraq as we have seen in the section, "Decision Maker." The Kurds, however, have also operated in the international
environment, interacting with nation-states and international organizations in order to garner support. "Kurdish questions" were relevant to Iraq's application for membership to the League of Nations
(see the section, "Historical Background"). Although the Kurds have
at various times appealed to the United Nations, they have been, for

the most part, politely ignored. On November 16, 1961, the Central Committee of the PDK sent a message to UN Secretary General U Thant accusing the Iraqi army of genocide and asking for an international commission to investigate on the spot, but the Kurds received only the vaguest of replies (O'Ballance 1973, p. 80). In 1963 Mulla Mustafa had not yet gained predominance over the PDK and some of the members of its Central Committee had communist sympathies. The Kurds were at that time fighting the Arif government, and the Soviet Union was at least supporting the Kurds verbally. In May of 1963, on Soviet instigation, the Mongolian People's Republic asked the United Nations to put the Kurdish question before the General Assembly, but this request was later withdrawn in September (O'Ballance 1973, p. 101). On February 18, 1966, Mulla Mustafa, after the start of a January winter offensive by the Bazzaz government, sent a memorandum to the Secretary General asking for a UN Commission of Inquiry to be sent to northern Iraq. Mulla Mustafa alleged that the Iraqi government was conducting a scorched-earth policy and deporting thousands of Kurds from their homes after bombing their villages in an attempt to exterminate the Kurdish people. Mulla Mustafa, once again, failed to raise any UN interest (O'Ballance 1973, p. 134). In October 1968 intense political and military fighting was taking place between Mulla Mustafa and Jalal Talabani and his followers. As it was becoming evident that Talabani and his followers were getting the worst of their encounters with Mulla Mustafa, the al-Bakr government stepped in and sent troops to Talabani's aid. In support of Talabani, aircraft of the Iraqi Air Force bombed Kurdish villages, causing Mulla Mustafa, on November 18, to present another memorandum to the United Nations alleging that the Iraqi government was attempting genocide of the Kurds and asking for a UN mediator to be appointed (O'Ballance 1973, p. 151). Final appeals were made by the Kurds to the United Nations from June to December 1974; however, a subcommission of minorities of the Human Rights Commission, to which Secretary General Kurt Waldheim sent the appeals, repeatedly shelved them (New York Times, March 15, 1975, p. 26).

The Kurds had somewhat better luck obtaining support from nation-states who at various times and for reasons of their own opposed whatever Iraqi regime was in power at the time. When hostilities broke out between the Kurds and the Qasim regime in 1961, there was a great deal of indifference toward the Kurdish demands, and spasmodic interest was shown only when it was thought it might serve some selfish nationalist purpose. During the period of the union of Egypt and Syria between 1958 and 1961, President Nasser consistently refused to recognize the Syrian Kurds as a cultural minority and severely repressed any symptoms of nationalist tendencies.

Later, after the dissolution of the union, and during his period of enmity with the Syrian government, Radio Cairo supported the Kurdish national cause, as did Radio Damascus at times (O'Ballance 1973, p. 80). We have seen how in 1963 the Soviet Union, hoping to gain influence over the PDK, instigated a Mongolian request to put the Kurdish question before the United Nations. In June 1963 the Syrian Baathist government sent a brigade of 5,000 Syrian troops to take part in the second offensive against the Kurds. On June 30 it was widely reported that Syrian aircraft were flying with the Iraqi Air Force against Kurdish positions. By November 1963 the composition of the Iraqi government had changed with the widespread purging of hardline Baathists, and the Syrian brigade left Iraq (O'Ballance 1973, pp. 107-8). On October 22, 1965, the Arif government was able to get President Nasser to issue a communiqué stating that the UAR fully supported all efforts of the Iraqi government against the Kurdish rebels, and four days later the Kurdish representative in Cairo was ordered to leave Egypt (O'Ballance 1973, p. 132).

Although it was often alleged that the Soviet Union supplied arms to the Kurdish rebels and did its best to stir up dissidence, there is little evidence to support such charges. Soviet weapons appeared in Kurdish hands, but they had been bought on the black markets of the Middle East and smuggled in through Iran (O'Ballance 1973, p. 167). Indeed, by 1968 the Iraqis, failing in their efforts to obtain weapons from the French, had turned to the Soviet Union. Although weapons were supplied only reluctantly at first, by April 1974 (the start of the latest round of Iraqi-Kurdish fighting) Iraq had become the Soviet Union's principal ally in the Persian Gulf area (see section, "Environment"). By May 1974 the Soviet Union had supplied Iraq with 1,035 tanks, 188 combat aircraft, 1,300 artillery guns, and 20 small naval ships (New York Times, April 5, 1974).

One of Mulla Mustafa's more notable successes in the international arena occured in February 1968. The Iraqi government's efforts to obtain arms from France were seemingly about to be successful when the Kurds put a damper on the negotiations. A French military mission had visited Iraq in January 1968, and on February 7 President Arif paid an official visit to France where presumably he hoped to be able to conclude a satisfactory arms agreement. Mulla Mustafa, apprehensive at the possibility of French weapons being used against the Kurds, sent a letter to President de Gaulle asking him not to supply military material to the Iraqis until the Kurdish problem had been solved. A wave of French sympathy for the Kurds resulted in a statement, signed by a number of prominent Frenchmen, which urged that French arms be supplied to the Iraqi government only on the condition that they not be used against the Kurds. As a result, the communique issued at the close of Arif's visit on February 10 made no mention of the possible supply of arms. On February 14 it was stated in the French National Assembly that the question of arms for Iraq did not arise at the moment, although the following day it was reported that the French government had agreed to supply Iraq with 70 armored cars (O'Ballance 1973, p. 146).

Mulla Mustafa's greatest success in obtaining outside aid for the Kurds came in his dealings with the shah of Iran (see the section, "Environment"). His biggest failure was his attempt to obtain large-scale support from the United States. Mulla Mustafa, although (and possibly because of) spending 12 years in the Soviet Union, was a fervent anticommunist (which accounted for some of his differences with the procommunist elements of the PDK), and he tried to sell himself and Kurdistan as a possible ally of the United States in the Persian Gulf area. As Mulla Mustafa explained it, Kurdistan's location in an area adjacent to the southern border of the Soviet Union, lying roughly between the Soviet Union and the Persian Gulf, made the fate of the Kurds vitally important to the United States. As one journalist who interviewed Mulla Mustafa wrote:

> His appeal to me, the first American journalist to visit him, and to a succession of other journalists who have followed, is always the same: "Let the Americans give us military help, openly or secretly, so that we can become truly autonomous, and we will become your loyal partners in the Middle East" (Schmidt 1974, p. 56).

Besides their strategic/geographical location, Mulla Mustafa attempted to entice the U.S. government with the oil wealth of Kurdistan. Unlike the rest of Iraq, Mulla Mustafa promised not to nationalize the oil reserves of Kurdistan. He said that he would be willing to allow foreign oil concerns into Kurdistan to exploit its oil reserves (Roberts 1974).

In November 1975 the Intelligence Committee of the U.S. House of Representatives released information which indicated that President Nixon, acting at the request of the shah of Iran, in 1972 ordered the CIA to serve as an arms supplier to the Kurds (see the section, "Environment"). This is the first publicly available evidence of direct U.S. aid to the Kurds.

Resources

The resources of the decision makers are defined as things which are goal-relevant and that can be controlled by the decision maker.

Certainly, one of the resources of the Kurdish NSN is the leadership of Mulla Mustafa. Although opposed by some "detribalized" Kurds, Mulla Mustafa is the first Kurdish leader to achieve any success in uniting the various Kurdish tribes.

Other resources include the military component of the NSN. Estimates of the number of soldiers in the Kurdish permanent army in 1974 varied from 5,000 to 10,000 (Holden 1974) to over 20,000 (Schmidt 1974) to 50,000 (Smith 1974). This does not include a considerably larger number of tribal fighters. The light, mobile Kurdish guerrilla units with their training in mountain warfare, in familiar terrain, were faced by the clumsy regular Iraqi army, which had been trained in regular warfare on the plains and found it difficult to handle its heavy weapons and vehicles in an environment of high, inaccessible mountains. Furthermore, the Kurdish army had made enormous progress since the revolt of 1961 in numbers, organization and training, and arms and equipment (Salomon 1970a, p. 36).

Also included as resources are some 100,000 Kurds who had come from Baghdad and other cities to join Mulla Mustafa. Many of these people were doctors, engineers, students, university professors, and former Iraqi army and police officers (Roberts 1974).

The geography and climate of the Kurdish areas also can be considered a resource. The mountainous regions, particularly during the winter, provide difficult terrain for an Iraqi offensive involving tanks or other vehicles. Cave hideouts within the mountains also provide cover against Iraqi air attacks.

Environment

The environment of the nonstate nation includes anything that is goal-relevant that cannot be influenced or controlled by the decision maker. The Kurdish nonstate nation finds itself in an environment in which its cause is somewhat lost amid the larger games being played in the Middle East. However, the Kurds are affected in indirect ways from these larger games.

The Arab-Israeli conflict has had the effect of producing some support from Israel. As long as a major portion of the Iraqi army was occupied trying to suppress the Kurds, the Iraqis could not join other Arab states in attacks on Israel. A limited amount of financial aid was apparently given to the Kurds by Israel through intermediary organizations in Europe (Roberts 1974). One Western journalist has reported that Israel had also supplied the Kurds with several medium-range artillery pieces (Clarity 1974b). Similarly, Kuwait was anxious to see the Iraqis preoccupied with the Kurds, with less opportunity for Iraq to pursue its irredentist claims against Kuwaiti territory (Kimche 1975, p. 21).

The Kurds have also been beneficiaries of Iranian-Iraqi hostility. During the time frame we have been examining, Iran emerged as the largest supplier of outside aid to the Kurds. The shah of Iran permitted Mulla Mustafa's forces a limited amount of refuge in the Iranian border area adjacent to Iraq. Humanitarian relief was supplied to Kurdish refugees fleeing from the fighting in Iraqi Kurdistan, and medical facilities were provided for wounded Kurdish soldiers. The Kurds also received military supplies from Iran, including rifles, medium-range artillery, antiaircraft guns, and ammunition, but no airplanes or tanks (Clarity 1974a; O'Ballance 1974, p. 568). Kurdish officers, however, complained to Western journalists that requests for more artillery had not been forthcoming from Iran (Clarity 1974b).

The shah was anxious that Kurdish enthusiasm for an independent or autonomous Kurdish state did not spill over to affect the nearly 2 million Kurds in Iran. After all, the Kurdish Republic of Mahabad had once existed on territory claimed by Iran. The shah, however, did want to see the Iraqi army occupied with the Kurds for as long as possible, primarily in order to prevent challenges to Iranian hegemony in the Persian Gulf. Therefore, the shah was willing to supply the Kurds with enough arms to prevent the Iraqi army from winning a decisive victory over the Kurds, but not enough to enable the Kurds to win a decisive victory over Iraqi forces.

The biggest game of all is that being played by the United States and the Soviet Union for strategic advantage in the Middle East and for control of the Persian Gulf area where two-thirds of the world's oil reserves are located (Kimche 1975, p. 20). A huge pool of oil has recently been discovered west of Baghdad which would make Iraqi reserves second only to Saudi Arabia's. Iraq currently has proven reserves of 31.5 billion barrels and production of 2 billion barrels per day (Los Angeles Times, February 9, 1975, Part I, p. 5). The area which the Kurds occupy provides about 70 percent of Iraq's current crude oil exports (Holden 1974).

At the start of the last offensive against the Kurds in April 1974, encouragement for the Iraqi government came from the Soviet Union, which was already supplying arms in quantity to Iraq. At that time there was a Soviet Military Advisory and a Military Training Mission in Iraq. In March, Soviet Defense Minister Marshall Grechko visited Iraq, and on March 24 he openly condemned the Kurdish "revolt." On March 28 Soviet Minister of the Interior Nikolas Sholohov began a five-day visit to Baghdad. Iraqi oil is vital to Eastern Europe, especially to Hungary, Czechoslovakia, and Bulgaria, and the relation between the Soviet Union and Iraq was a reversal of previous alliances,

when Mulla Mustafa gave refuge to the communists. Now, as the
Iraqi government had a treaty with the Soviet Union, the Iraq Communist party had joined the Baath party to form the Progressive National Front, which the PDK had declined to enter. Only a small pro-
Chinese splinter of the Iraq Communist party supported Mulla Mustafa this time (Kimche 1975, p. 20).

On the other side, Iran is the primary alliance partner of the
United States in the Persian Gulf. The close relationship between the
U.S. government and the shah of Iran extends back to the CIA-spon-
sored coup of the Mossadegh regime and the installation of the present shah in 1953 (Gurtov 1974, pp. 17-23). Over the last few years
the shah has used Iran's oil revenues to buy large amounts of sophisticated weaponry from the United States and has served as Israel's
primary supplier of petroleum.

In May 1972 President Nixon visited Tehran. The Select Committee on Intelligence of the U.S. House of Representatives (under
the chairmanship of Otis Pike) disclosed, on November 1, 1975, that
the shah had been able to convince Nixon during the visit that the
United States should provide covert aid to the Kurds. After the visit
Nixon ordered the CIA to deliver millions of dollars worth of Soviet
and Chinese arms and ammunition (some of which were collected in
Cambodia) to the Kurds. Both the CIA and the State Department are
understood to have opposed U.S. involvement, but Nixon, reportedly
confiding only in Henry Kissinger rather than the National Security
Council, insisted that the CIA supply the arms. Former Treasury
Secretary John Connally was said to have been instructed by Nixon to
tell the shah, on Connally's visit to Iran in July 1972, that the weapons would be forthcoming. Connally had by that time left the Treasury Department and was serving as a "special representative of the
president." Allegations have been made that Nixon took this action
in return for money given to the Nixon reelection campaign by the
shah (Lardner 1975).

The Pike Committee Report, at the instigation of Gerald Ford,
was suppressed by the House. However the Village Voice has published the most important section of the report, which includes a description of the decision making in the U.S. government which led
Richard Nixon to authorize a $16 million program of covert aid to the
Kurds.* The Pike Committee Report charges that:

---

*"The CIA Report the President Doesn't Want You to Read,"
Special Supplement to the Village Voice, February 16, 1976 (on the
West Coast), pp. 70-92. See especially p. 71 of Aaron Latham's "Introduction to the Pike Papers," p. 85 of the Committee Report, and
the footnotes on pp. 87 and 88.

The President, Dr. Kissinger and the Foreign head of
state [the shah] hoped our clients [the Kurds] would not
prevail. They preferred instead that the insurgents simply continue a level of hostilities sufficient to sap the
resources of our ally's neighboring country [Iraq]. This
policy was not imparted to our clients who were encouraged to continue fighting. Even in the context of covert
action, ours was a cynical enterprise.

Evaluation of Kurdish NSN's Efficiency

On March 6, 1975, the shah of Iran concluded the Pact of Algiers with the de facto ruler of Iraq, Sadam Husain Tikriti. Following his return from Algiers, the shah summoned Mulla Mustafa to
Tehran and told him that Iran was withdrawing all aid to the Kurdish
resistance and recalling all arms and supplies; the shah ordered Mulla Mustafa to halt all military operations against the Iraqis. On March
18 Mulla Mustafa gave the order to the Kurdish army to abandon the
struggle (Kimche 1975, p. 19). The shah, in return for withdrawing
support from the Kurds, had received a favorable settlement from
the Iraqis on Iranian navigational rights on the Shatt al Arab waterway (New York Times Index, March 16-31, 1975, p. 75).
    Once again, history repeats itself for the Kurds. In 1946, when
the Soviet Union withdrew its support for the Kurdish Republic of
Mahabad, the republic collapsed. Now the shah of Iran has withdrawn
his support of the Kurds and the 16-year Kurdish struggle for autonomy within Iraq has ended, at least for the time being.
    Why have the Kurds failed to reach their goals? The answer
may be found in the twin problems of audibility and durability facing
every nonstate nation. Audibility for the nonstate nation involves the
problem of pursuing goals in such a way that at least some nation-
states or international organizations perceive the nonstate nation's
status as something other than a "domestic problem." Although the
Kurds had some success in achieving this sort of recognition, they
certainly did not match the successes of the Palestinians or Bengalis.
The "Kurdish question" was never brought before the United Nations
as the "Palestinian question" has been. Nor has a neighboring power
been willing to launch an all-out offensive in order to secure the goals
of the Kurdish nonstate nation as India did for the Bengalis. Therefore, the related problem of durability was never solved by the Kurds.
The shah of Iran was never willing to go as far as he could have for
the Kurds, even in terms of weapons supplies. Kurdish nationalism
in Iraq was, in the long run, disadvantageous for Iran. The shah
could not really allow Mulla Mustafa to succeed because of the effects

such success might ultimately have on the Kurdish population living within Iran's borders. For Iran the Kurdish fight against the Iraqis was a convenient way of keeping Iran's chief rival off balance. When it became advantageous for Iran to come to an agreement with Iraq, the Kurds were abandoned.

Impact on the International Context

The Kurdish strategy for attaining their basic goal of autonomy within Iraq was to fight the Iraqi central government until the resulting stalemate might cause a change to a regime in Baghdad more favorable to an agreement with the Kurds. At the same time the Kurds tried to gain as much external support as possible from international organizations and from nation-states opposed to the Iraqis.

This strategy had several effects on the international context. First of all, the inability of the Iraqis to put an end to the "Kurdish problem" for 14 years contributed to the instability of the central Iraqi government in Baghdad. This instability, combined with the constant need to deploy a major segment of the Iraqi army against the Kurds, severely limited the Iraqi government's actions in the international arena and also diverted funds from Iraqi development projects.

The constant turnover in the Iraqi central administration resulted in a continual shifting of alliances in the Middle East/Persian Gulf area, depending upon the ideological strain of whatever Iraqi government was in power at any given time. For other nations, Iraq's "Kurdish problem" allowed them a certain amount of leverage in their dealings with the Iraqi government. If the Iraqi government acted in a belligerent fashion toward Israel, Kuwait, Syria, or Iran, then those national governments could retaliate by aiding the Kurds. The aid that the shah of Iran provided the Kurds was particularly difficult for the Iraqis to handle. In the end the Iraqis had to concede to Iran navigational rights on the Shatt al Arab waterway (a major point of contention in Iranian-Iraqi relations for years) in order to stop Iranian aid to the Kurds.

REFERENCES

Arfa, Hassan. 1966. The Kurds. London: Oxford University Press.

Clarity, James F. 1974a. "Iraqi Forces Seize Most Kurdish Towns." New York Times, September 27, p. 4.

_____. 1974b. "Kurds Say Iran Supplies Them and That Soviet Sends Advisors to Iraq." New York Times, September 29, p. 2.

Eagleton, William Jr. 1963. The Kurdish Republic of 1946. London: Oxford University Press.

Edmonds, C. J. 1957. "The Kurds of Iraq." Middle East Journal 2, no. 1 (Winter).

_____. 1967. "The Kurdish War in Iraq: A Plan for Peace." Royal Central Asian Journal 54 (February), Part I.

_____. 1968. "The Kurdish War in Iraq: The Constitutional Back-ground." The World Today 24, no. 12 (December).

Gurtov, Melvin. 1974. The United States Against the Third World. New York: Praeger.

Head, Simon. 1974. "The Kurdish Tragedy." New York Review of Books, July 18.

Holden, David. 1974. New York Times, September 22, p. 4.

Kimche, Jon. 1975. "Selling Out the Kurds." New Republic 172, no. 16 (April 19).

Lardner, George, Jr. 1975. "U.S. Aid to Kurd Rebels Reported." Los Angeles Times, November 27, Part 6, p. 1.

O'Ballance, Edgar. 1973. The Kurdish Revolt: 1961-1970. London: Faber and Faber.

_____. 1974. "The Kurdish Factor In The Gulf." Army Quarterly and Defence Journal 104, no. 5 (October).

Roberts, Gwynne. 1974. "Kurdish Leader, Facing Possible Civil War, Looks to West for Support." New York Times, April 1, p. 14.

Roosevelt, Archie, Jr. 1947. "The Kurdish Republic of Mahabad." Middle East Journal 1, no. 3.

Salomon, Gershon. 1967. "The Kurdish National Struggle in Iraq." New Outlook 10, no. 3 (March-April).

_____. 1970a. "Peace With the Kurds: Part I." New Outlook 14, no. 4
    (May).

_____. 1970b. "Peace With the Kurds: Part II." New Outlook 14, no. 5
    (June).

Schmidt, Dana Adams. 1974. "The Kurdish Insurgency." Strategic
    Review 2, no. 3 (Summer).

Village Voice. February 16, 1976. Special Supplement: "The CIA
    Report the President Doesn't Want You to Read," pp. 70-92.

THE BASQUES AS A NONSTATE NATION
Milton da Silva

Basque nationalists include those seeking autonomy
within the Spanish state, as well as persons aiming
toward complete independence for a Basque state
that would include both French and Spanish Basques.
Spanish Basques who seek autonomy within the
Spanish state have worked through the electoral
process and have pursued their goals by constitutional means. Dissidents have challenged the
effectiveness of this course and have pushed not only
for more radical goals (independence) but also by
more violent means.

Because Basque aspirations in Spain were
suppressed by Franco, they were forced to become,
for the most part, inaudible within Spain during his
regime. More recently a range of voices in both
Spain and France have been proposing a range of
alternatives including autonomy within the established states and special representation within the
Common Market, as well as complete independence
for a Basque state.

A minority in both Spain and France, Basque
nationalists have worked within nation-state electoral
institutions but have sought autonomy within their
traditional geographical regions. While the demand
for autonomy coincides with the ethnic-national character of the group, such a demand also is appropriate
strategy for a group that sees no hope of dominating
national politics by its electoral strength. Moving
demands to the constitutional, moral, and ethical

questions of self-determination and national rights, while
developing electoral strength within one's ethnic national
region, gives the Basque nonstate nation a strategy that
combines a number of its resources in an attempt to
maximize effectiveness.

The study that follows is not divided into time periods
but is presented in one broad sweep of time. Nothing in the
NSN systems framework requires division into time periods,
and the authors have been free to divide or not divide, as
suits their preferences. The author of this chapter suggests
a rough and overlapping temporal division by distinguishing
among three "transformations." No clear dates or explicit
events separate these three transformations, however, and
the author has chosen to present the material in one conti-
nous time frame.

—Judy S. Bertelsen

The increasing number of violent incidents in the Spanish Basque
region since the early 1960s once again emphasizes the challenge
which Basque nationalism is posing to the Spanish government. This
challenge was dramatically highlighted in December 1970 at the spectacular trial of 16 Basque nationalists in the military tribunal of
Burgos. Almost two years later, in January 1972, the ETA (Euzkadi
Ta Askatasuna—Basque Nation and Liberty) kidnapped Senor Zabala,
a leading industrialist of the area, and again on January 17, 1973,
kidnapped F. Huesta, another industrialist. In retaliation for the
execution of Basque nationalists by the Spanish government, ETA
claimed responsibility for the assassination of Carrero Blanco,
Spanish prime minister, on December 20, 1974. These events have
put the Basque region under almost a constant state of siege since 1970.

Basque nationalism is not a new problem in Spanish politics.
It is now over 100 years old. It is the legacy of a problem that began
in 1812 when the Spanish liberals made their first attempt to centralize
the Spanish state and abolish the traditional administrative divisions
of the Spanish monarchy.

Although a small portion of the Basque country is within the
French state, this study will concentrate on the Basques of Spain because this group has shown the greatest militancy on the issue of
autonomy. Only recently have the Basques of France become vocal
about Basque autonomy, making a change in the development of Basque
nationalism.

HISTORICAL OVERVIEW

The Basque country, known by the Basques as Euzkadi, consists of four provinces in Northeastern Spain (Alava, Guipuzcoa, Navarra, and Vizcaya) and a section of the French department of Basse-Pyrénées located in Southwestern France. The Basques refer to this area as Labourd, Basse-Navarre, and Soule. Geographically and demographically the Basque country is a relatively small area. It consists of approximately 20,000 square kilometers and has a population over 3 million people, most of whom live within the Spanish state.[1] One writer has estimated a population of 4,844 million.[2] But this figure apparently includes people who do not identify with the Basque country. Most of the land area of what is considered the Basque country is located within the Spanish border.

From an economic standpoint there are vast differences between the Spanish and French Basques. The French Basque region is considered an economically depressed area without any significant modern industries.[3] By contrast, the Spanish Basque provinces (particularly Guipuzcoa and Vizcaya) make up one of the more highly industrialized regions of Spain. This area has a long tradition of mining, steel, paper, and chemical industries. Illustrative of this prosperity is the fact that in 1967, out of the 50 Spanish provinces, the four Basque provinces were among the top six when ranked on a per capita income basis.[4] Vizcaya, Guipuzcoa, and Alava occupied second, third, and fourth places respectively, exceeded only by Madrid, which had the highest per capita income. The economic development of the region is also illustrated by the occupational distribution of the population, with 14 percent engaged in agriculture, 55 percent in industry, and 31 percent in services. This level of development is high in comparison with the Spanish (national) percentages of 36 in agriculture, 33 in industry, and 31 in services.[5]

Linguistically, the Basques are radically different from the Spanish and French populations that surround them. The Basque language, Euskera, now spoken only by a minority of the Basques, has no resemblance to Spanish or French.[6] A subject of great fascination to philologists and anthropologists, it remains an enigma with no apparent relationship to the Indo-European languages.[7] In this respect the Basques are quite unique among European groups. Undoubtedly this linguistic uniqueness has reinforced their identity as a national group.

Knowledge of their political and social organization before the formation of the political kingdoms of the Iberian Peninsula and the emergence of the French and English monarchies is rather meager.[8] There are many stories, however, about their legendary resistance

to several conquest attempts by the Romans, Visigoths, and the
Arabs. In contrast with other European groups, they were converted
to Christianity quite late. It was not until the twelfth century that
they became Christianized.

Aside from the kingdom of Sancho El Mayor (999-1035) which
encompassed nearly all the Basques, their political organiztion
was apparently fragmented into small counties and republics which
frequently made war on each other. [9] As the Spanish and French monarchies increased their territories and consolidated their power
through marriages and conquests, Basque autonomy was gradually
eroded to the point where the Basque provinces became appendages
of the French and Spanish states, although the provinces retained
considerable autonomy until the eighteenth century in France and
the ninteenth century in Spain. Prior to the modern organization of
the Spanish and French states, the Basques viewed the French and
Spanish crowns more as allies than political overlords. Local
autonomy was recognized in the form of fors in France, and fueros
(traditional laws, customs, and usages) in Spain. The affairs of
each province were regulated by the diputaciones forales (local
parliaments) chosen by local notables. The point of contact between
each province and the crown was a representative of the king sent
to attend the local assemblies. No order of the king was valid or
accepted in each province without the consent of the local assemblies.
In Spain this practice was known as the pase foral (foral pass). In
addition the Basques controlled their budgets and were exempt from
taxation by the crown and from conscription into the central army
to fight in areas outside of the Basque region. The army of the king
could not enter the Basque provinces without the consent of the local
legislatures. Persons from outside the provinces could not hold
public offices. The Basque provinces also had customhouses which
taxed incoming goods along the Ebro River (which separates the Basque
region from Castile). Because of this autonomy the Basque provinces
used to be known as the "exempted provinces." As late as 1841, for
example, Navarra allowed no judicial appeal beyond the borders of
that province. [10] The following excerpt, taken from a report made by
the Junta of Madrid at the request of the Spanish crown, on the "abuses
of the royal revenues in the Basque provinces," reflects the autonomy
of the Basque provinces and the frustration of the policy makers in
Madrid with the existing relationship between the Basques and the
Spanish monarchy:

> It would appear as if the permanent deputations of these
> provinces had been established to oppose the measures of
> the government. There is nothing in common with the rest
> of the provinces in Spain. The laws are distinct; the

commerce free; the contributions almost nothing; the custom-houses profitless; the officers opposed in the execution of their duty--are maintained at great expense, and almost useless; the nobility has become universal and self-created; and in fact they have taken the government into their own hands.

The Peninsula appears open to all their commerce, and negotiations; and without doubt they enjoy greater advantages than the rest of the kingdom, being exempted from the contributions of Castile, and the general tax of the Crown of Aragon, from provincial rents, and from contributions and donations which have been so heavy since the French revolution. And even in the tithes and ecclesiastical contributions, they have paid almost nothing to the State from which they receive protection. They have been free from conscription, militia, from providing military stores, barracks, enlistment for the marine service, and in fact from every other tax or service for war.[11]

The last vestiges of Basque autonomy under the French monarchy were swept away by the political and administrative changes spawned by the French revolution. The fors were abrogated and the Pays Basque (Basque country) incorporated into what later became known as the department of Basse-Pyrénées. This was not done without some armed resistance, however.

The historical relationship between the Basques of Spain and the Spanish state is far more complicated than that of the French Basques and the French state. The question of Basque autonomy and the policy of state centralization became a much more complex problem in Spain, lasting throughout the nineteenth century and including the participation of the Basques in three civil wars (Carlist wars).[12] By the end of the century, however, the Basque provinces were stripped of most of their traditional autonomy and left only with some degree of fiscal and administrative autonomy.[13] This new arrangement, known as the concierto economico, to be negotiated from time to time between each province and the central government in Madrid, obliged each province to contribute to the national treasury a fixed amount of revenue each year, but gave each province the freedom to decide how to apportion taxes among its inhabitants. This lasted until the 1930s for all the Basque provinces and still remains in effect, in some modified form, for the provinces of Alava and Navarra.[14] Because of the support given by Guipuzcoa and Vizcaya to the republic during the civil war of 1936-39, these two provinces lost all their autonomy at the conclusion of the war in 1939.

The issue of Basque autonomy has gone through three transformations. Initially it emerged as an issue in the Spanish Basque
provinces trying to regain the autonomy taken away by the centralizing policies of nineteenth-century liberals. This period was
known as fuerismo, because of the emphasis on the traditional
fueros, and lasted from 1839 to approximately the end of the nineteenth century. The fuerista view continued to have support down
to the 1930s and even under the Franco regime. The second transformation appears with the formation of the Partido Nacionalista
Vasco (PNV Basque Nationalist Party) which discarded some of the
concerns of the fueristas and justified Basque autonomy on the
grounds of nationality. Although initially the PNV also made reference to the French Basque provinces, it gradually concentrated
its attention only on the Spanish Basque provinces and was willing
to accept autonomy within the Spanish state, a position that the
party still holds. The third transformation appears in the early
1960s with the formation of new groups in Spain and France demanding independence for the entire Basque country with an eventual
federation in a Europe of nations.

Although the issue of Basque autonomy can be seen to fall into
three rough time periods corresponding to the three transformations
discussed above, the NSN analysis that follows will be presented as
a single time unit from 1839 through the present. I have found the
narrative simpler to maintain without breaking the analysis into
separate time periods. Each decision maker will be discussed in
chronological order of origin.

TIME I: 1839 TO PRESENT
Decision Maker A: The Fuerista Party

Fuerismo was really more of a rural movement supported by
the local notables and the clergy than a formal political party. Initially fuerismo was associated with Carlismo,* which sought to reestablish the traditional conception of an absolutist and Catholic, but
decentralized, monarchy. The main support for the Carlist movement came from rural areas of the Basque region and Catalonia, another region with autonomist parties. [16]

---

*This term refers to a political ideology that emerged in Spain
in reaction to the liberal reforms of early nineteenth century. This
movement became tied to the cause of Don Carlos VI, (brother of
Ferdinand, the Spanish king), hence the name Carlismo. The defense
of the Basque fueros became linked to the fight of Don Carlos to
gain the Spanish throne. [15]

Goals

The primary goal was to preserve the Basque fueros and support the cause of Don Carlos VI, who accepted the conception of the medieval Spanish monarchy, limited by the fueros and the people.

Projects: Armed Resistance and Electoral Politics

The loss of the Basque fueros did not take place all at once, but by a piecemeal process. Although the monarchy of Ferdinand had already suggested to the Basque provinces that the fueros were not rights but privileges given by the crown, it was not until 1833 that the first major confrontation between the Basque government and the Basque provinces took place. The Basques became involved in a civil war, supporting the claim of Don Carlos to the Spanish throne. For six years the Basque region along with portions of Aragon and Catalonia confronted the Madrid government in a war that left the region nearly devastated. At the outbreak of the war religious concerns, not the fueros, seemed to be the motivating issue. As the war progressed, however, it became evident that Basque support for the cause of Don Carlos was based on the expectation that his regime would respect the traditional organization of the Basque region. In September 1834, for example, Don Carlos visited the historic city of Guernica, where in 1476 Ferdinand and Isabel had taken the oath to preserve the fueros, and also promised to protect the fueros. [17]

This war came to an end with the Peace of Vergara of August 1839, in which Don Baldomero Espartero, commander of the central armed forces in the northern provinces, promised to respect the Basque fueros. Espartero's promise, however, was not completely acceptable to the liberals who had majority in the Cortes (national legislature). They wanted to abolish the fueros once and for all. Instead a compromise was reached in which the central government recognized the fueros to the extent that they were not prejudicial to the constitutional unity of the monarchy. [18] This was not acceptable to the Basques because it recognized the fueros as mere privileges and not as rights. Modern Basque nationalists use this date as a watershed in the loss of Basque autonomy.

For the time being, however, the crown allowed the Basques to reconvene their local assemblies in a manner consistent with their fueros and set a later date for further reform.

A law passed by the Cortes on August 16, 1841, stripping Navarra of its fueros suggested to the other three provinces that the days of the fueros were numbered and that the promise of Espartero had not been kept. [19] Once again the Basque provinces supported an insurrection against the Madrid government led by General O'Donnell. As a punishment for their support of the insurrection, Espartero, now in charge of the government, issued a decree abolishing some of the most important aspects of the fueros; each province would have a jefe políticos and gave the local assemblies some autonomy on who would be the supreme political authority in each province; the traditional customhouses on the Castilian-Basque border were removed and placed at the Basque ports and the Spanish French border; and the Basques would be subject to military conscription. For the advocates of centralization this was considered a victory.

Another change of government in Madrid in July 1843 made some modifications on the decree of Espartero. It abolished the jefe políticos and gave the local assemblies some autonomy on matters dealing with local economic issues. By the 1850s some Basque notables had come to the conclusion that armed resistance was too costly and that it was not paying off. In a manifesto issued in 1850, expressing disappointment with the policies of the central government regarding the fueros, Basque political leaders decided to adopt political strategies rather than armed resistance:

> To negotiate, and negotiate with dexterity and foresight is the only rational course that the Basques must follow in order to salvage from ruin the sacred objects of their cult. It was in this manner that our forefathers, whose government consisted in a constant negotiation with the central power, worked on critical issues. Because our position is more critical, and the interest, whose fate shall be decided shortly, is far more transcendental and grave, it is incumbent upon us, their sons, to work with a double effort.
> Unity, and we shall be strong.[20]

In the Cortes the Basque deputies used techniques similar to the filibuster and opposed legislation critical to the Basque region in the form of amendments to change the intent of legislation. For example, during the debate on the Ley de Presupuestos (budget) in the Cortes of 1864, the Basque representatives proposed an amendment which would have the effect of restoring the pre-1839 fueros. This introduced a heated debate in the Cortes with both sides making use of extensive historical documentation to support or refute the source of the fueros. It seems that for the first time the Basque representatives referred to themselves as a nationality.[21]

The chaotic state of Spanish politics between 1868 and 1876 presented the Basques once again with the opportunity to place someone in Madrid government sympathetic to their cause. When the Carlists made their major effort to place their candidate,

Don Carlos VII, on the Spanish throne, the Basques took up arms in
support of the Carlist cause. This war (1872-76) brought defeat to
the Basques and the Carlists whose candidate left Spain for the last
time.

Although the war ended in defeat for the Basques, the fuerista
sentiment continued unabated. In the national elections for the Cortes
(January 20, 1876) the Basque candidates supporting the fueros
emerged triumphant. When the subject of the fueros was introduced
in the Cortes for discussion, a Basque deputy from Alava, Mateo
Benigno de Maraza, made a last appeal to the legislature imploring
it to spare the Basque fueros. Their abolition, he said, would mean
the "ruin and desolation of the unfortunate Basque country, so eminently Spanish and so eminently monarchic." "You are going to ruin,"
he said, "the country designated by Providence to be the impregnable
bulwark of the motherland and the progressive sentry of its independence which, in the fulfillment of these sacrosanct duties, has always been the model of pure loyalty to its kings."[22]

On July 21, 1876, the Cortes passed legislation defining the
relationship between the Basque provinces and the central government. The general laws of Spain would be applicable to the Basque
provinces also. Article IV of this legislation seemingly made a
concession to the Basques, leading some to believe that the traditional pase foral remained in force. It stated that the central government was authorized "to resolve with the consent of the provinces
of Alava, Guipuzcoa, and Vizcaya, whenever appropriate, all the
reforms that their traditional foral organization required, so that
the welfare of the Basques, good government, and the security of
the nation would be ensured."[23] The Basque deputaciones (deputies)
reacted negatively to this new legislation and maintained that their
"sacred rights remained intact as ever." The deputacion of Vizcaya
declared that it would not cooperate "directly or indirectly with the
government in the execution of the law."[24] The government threatened
to put them under martial law and in May 5, 1877, put Vizcaya
under the direct control of Madrid.

A final compromise was reached in the form of a concierto
economico to be negotiated from time to time between each province
and the central government. This gave each province some degree
of administrative and fiscal autonomy. For example, the taxation
system for each province would be decided by the local governments.

Although fuerista candidates continued to run for office during
the regime of the Restoration (1876-1923) and continued to make an
issue out of the fueros in the national legislature, and although
Carlismo continued to have supporters within the Basque region,
as the new regime established an accommodation with the Church
Carlismo lost some of its zeal, and some fueristas gradually divorced
themselves from the Carlist cause.

During the 1930s, however, Carlist and fuerista sentiment re-
appeared in national politics with the formation of the Comunion
Tradicionalista Carlista on June 6, 1932.[25] Because of some of the
anticlerical policies of the first governments of the Spanish Republic,
religious issues once again became fused with the defense of the
traditional Basque fueros. The stated objectives of the Comunion
were: defense of the Church and traditional Spain, restitution of the
fueros, and rejection of a single statute of Basque autonomy.[26] This
last point deserves some clarification. The inhabitants of the province of Navarra are also Basques; but because at one time Navarra
was an important kingdom of the Iberian Peninsula, the Navarrese
have traditionally looked upon themselves as more distinct than the
three other Basque provinces.[27] The Madrid government also
looked upon Navarra as somewhat different from the other Basque
provinces. In its official relationships with the Basque region, the
central government traditionally made reference to the Basque provinces (Alava, Guipuzoca, and Vizcava) and Navarra. While the inhabitants of Navarra identify as Basques, they also seem to have a
strong sense of provincial identity, a fact that the PNV tried to
change.

The Carlists, considered by the Spanish Left as the epitome
of reactionary ideology, eventually ended up fighting on the side of
General Franco against the forces of the republic. This situation
produced somewhat of a civil war within the Basque region, with
the Carlists, most of whom were from Navarra, fighting the troops
of the Basque government. For many Carlist Navarrese it appeared
that the PNV had sold out the interests of the church for the sake of
a statute of autonomy. The Basque clergy was also split on this
issue. Some, including members of the hierarchy, supported the
position of the PNV, while other groups, particularly in Navarra,
supported the position of the Carlists.

The relationship between the religious issue and the fueros was
not always clear. At times it seemed that religious issues took precedence over the fueros. But that the fueros were also an important
element of the Carlist ideology is evident from the fact that as soon
as the civil war began, the deputacion foral (provincial legislature)
of Navarra began to take steps to restore the traditional organization
of that province. On August 11, 1936, the Superior Committee on
Education of Navarra was established "to restore in its entirety the
foral regime insofar as it affected the organization of primary education in Navarra."[28] After the war, however, the Franco regime
accepted only the concierto economico which had existed since 1876
and would not entertain further suggestions to reinstitute the traditional fueros. It appears that the Carlists seriously entertained
the possibility that the Franco regime would reestablish the

traditional Spanish monarchy. The Carlist pretender, in exile since 1839, had also made some overtures to his followers in Spain in a manifesto issued in 1934 promising that the traditional monarchy would be federative and would restore "all the regions and their fueros, liberties, exemptions, usages, and customs and guarantee the pase foral. "[29] In effect a return to the pre-1839 relationship between the Spanish state and regions. The expectations of the Carlists were deflated, however, when Franco selected Juan Carlos as the future king of Spain.

In the late 1960s a new Carlist group appeared, the Grupo de Accion Carlista, [30] apparently a splinter group from the old Carlist movement. This group seems to be very small, and hardly anything has been heard from it.

Resources and Environment

The Fuerista party had limited resources. Its support came primarily from the rural population and the rural clergy which identified liberalism with secularism and anticlericalism. The cities of the Basque region did not support the fuerista cause because of its identification with Carlismo, instead they supported the liberal cause. Most important of all, the fueristas and the Carlists could not rely on the support of the national army. It remained loyal to the liberal policies of nation-building.

Evaluation of Decision Maker A

The Fuerista party did not succeed in preserving the traditional political organization of the Basque provinces. The provinces were successful, however, in retaining some degree of administrative autonomy.

The protracted conflict between the Basques and the central government had the effect, perhaps unintentional, of making Basque identity an issue in Spanish politics, and of reviving interest in Basque traditions, aspects of which had nearly been forgotten. It is from this period onward that a romantic literature defending the historical roots of Basque identity begins to appear.

In the 1930s fuerismo succeeded in frustrating the plans of the PNV to get the entire Basque region to speak with one voice.

PERIOD II: 1894 TO 1960
Decision Maker C:
The Partido Nacionalista Vasco (PNV)

Modern Basque nationalism appears with the formation of the
Partido Nacionalista Vasco (PNV, Basque Nationalist Party), founded
in 1894 by Sabino de Arana Goiri, who remained the leading ideological figure of Basque nationalism until his death in 1903.[31] Although
it never became the only political party of the Basque region, by the
1930s it had become a leading political force in the region and a
serious political group in Spanish national politics. The initial
membership of the party came primarily from some segments of
the urban middle class, students, workers, and from rural areas.
With very few exceptions, the industrial tycoons of the Basque region
did not support the party.

Goals

The objectives and philosophy of the party, written from the
point of view of Vizcaya, Arana's home province, were originally
stated in the following 13 articles:

Article 1--Bizkaya [Vizcaya] upon entering a
Republican confederacy, does so according to the acceptance of the political doctrine expounded by Aran
Goiri' tar Sabino [Sabion de Arana Goiri] in the slogan
of Jaun-Goikua eta Lagi Zarra ["God and the Old Laws],"
which is explained in the following articles.
Article 2--Jaun-Goikua-Bizkaya will be Catholic,
Apostolic, and Roman in all its aspects of its internal
affairs and its relations with other peoples.
Article 3--Lagi-Zarra-Bizkaya will be freely
reconstituted. It will be reestablished, with complete
integrity, the essence of its traditional laws, called
Fueros. It will restore the good practices and customs
of its predecessors. It will be constituted, if not
exclusively, then principally, of families of the Basque
race. It will establish Basque as its official language.
Article 4--ETA-Bizkaya will be established upon
perfect harmony and accord between the religious and
political orders, between the divine and the human.
Article 5--Distinction between Jaun-Goikua and
Lagi Zarra-Bizkaya will be established with a clear
and marked distinction between the religious and political orders, between the ecclesiastical and civil.

fundamentalist authoritarian theocracy.

loose Confederative

Article 6--Precedence of Jaun-Goikua over Lagi Zarra-Bizkaya will be established with a complete and unconditional subordination of the political to the religious of the State to the Church.

Article 7--Confederation--Since Bizkaya is by race, language, faith, character, and custom a sister of Alava, Benabarra [Basse-Navarre] ,* Guipuzcoa, Laburdi [Labourd] ,* Navarra, and Zuberoa [Soule] ,* it will become allied or confederated with these six peoples to form a whole called, Euskalerria, but without surrendering its particular autonomy. This doctrine will be expressed in the following principle: Bizkaya libre en Euskalerria libre [Free Bizkaya in a Free Basque Country] .

Article 8--The Basque confederation will be formed by all of the Basque states with each entering willingly and with all having the same rights in the formation of its confederation's foundations.

Article 9--The necessary basis for a solid and durable national unity are: unity of race as far as is possible, and Catholic unity.

Article 10--The essential bases to insure that the Basque states entering the union will retain equal autonomy and identical faculties are: freedom to secede, and equality of obligations and rights within the Confederation.

Article 11--Once the Confederation is established each member state will have the same rights and identical obligations.

Article 12--The Confederation will unite its members solely in terms of the social order and international relations, in all other respects each will maintain its traditional absolute independence.

Article 13--All of the articles in this document and political doctrine are irrevocable. [32]

These articles expressed the long-run goals of the party. The more immediate goals, expressed in Bizkaya por su independencia, also written by Arana, aimed at raising the ethnic awareness of the Basques who, he believed, had forgotten their history and their language. Although the extent of Basque autonomy demanded by the nationalists has varied from time to time, Arana called for outright independence

---

* These are the French Basque provinces.

for the Basques, coined the term Euzkadi to refer to the Basque
nation, argued against the marriage between Basques and non-
Basques, and advocated the expulsion of the non-Basques from the
Basque country.[33] He looked upon Spaniards as an inferior race
and viewed the Basques as the purest race of Europe.

Environment

From the point of view of the Basque nationalists, the most
important variable in the environment within which they had to operate was the attitudes and power of the Spanish government. The
central government did not recognize the Basques as a nation nor
was it willing to grant the autonomy demanded by the nationalists.
Second, the nationalists had to face the fact that large segments of
the Basque population did not perceive themselves and the Basque
region from the perspective of the nationalists. Although some
sentiment for the restitution of the traditional Basque autonomy had
long existed and was supported by many people, this segment of
opinion was linked to the Carlist cause and the fueros, the ideology
of which was not completely acceptable to the nationalists. A
potential resource to the nationalists, this group remained hostile
to the position of the PNV.

The nationalists also faced the fact of Basque assimilation, a
process which they probably would have to reverse, or at least stop.
It appeared that by the end of the nineteenth century the process of
Basque assimilation had become almost irreversible; the Basques
had lost their fueros, and their language and culture was receding
in their very homeland. The exclusive use of Castilian in the public
schools of the Basque region had relegated the speaking of Basque to
some fishing and farming villages. The attraction of large numbers
of non-Basque labor migrants to the industries of Vizcaya and
Guipuzcoa was making the Basques a minority in their own urban
centers, and thus further threatening the dissolution of the Basques
as distinct people. It has been estimated that by 1899 approximately
70 percent of the population of Bilbao, the capital city of Vizcaya,
was non-Basque.[34] The upper classes of the region had become
assimilated into Spanish culture and identified with the central
government and the crown.[35]

Another environmental variable of considerable importance is
the vact that the Basques were, and continue to be, a minority of the
total Spanish population. As of 1965, the population of the four
Spanish Basque provinces was approximately 6.5 percent of the
Spanish population. But one should exclude from this figure 1.2
percent born outside of the Basque region, thus bringing the

percentage of the Basque population to 5.3 percent.[36] In light of
this figure, even if the PNV became the dominant part of the Basque
region, it would remain a small minority in national politics.

The traditional economic importance of the Basque country to
the Spanish economy is also an environmental variable of no small
consequence. The Basque country continues to be one of the dynamic
centers of the Spanish economy.[37] Bilbao, for example, is a major
financial, industrial, and shipping center of Spain. At the turn of
the century 30 percent of the total Spanish investments were Basque,
thus making the Basque banks the single most important financial
center of Spain.[38] While the Basques constitute approximately 5
percent of the Spanish population, in terms of Spain's GNP their
importance to Spain outdistances that of their relative numbers.
This fact, undoubtedly, makes it very unattractive for the Spanish
government to consider seriously the idea of political independence
for the Basques.

Finally, the nationalists had to compete with the established
political groups of the region who did not seem to take the nationalist
cause very seriously.[39]

Resources

The PNV started its campaign of nationalism with two very
important resources. First, the Basques already perceived themselves as a distinct ethnic group and identified with a specific territory which they already occupied. The initial efforts of the party
were to make ethnic awareness more salient, eventually to break
the traditional provincial identifications within the Basque region,
and to get all of the Basque provinces, at least the Spanish provinces, to think in terms of a single unit. Second, the nationalists
could capitalize on the resentment of many people in the region
over the loss of the fueros. The Basques already had a long tradition of resistance to the central government over this issue.

Besides the nationalists, there were other groups in the Basque
region interested in cultural revival, although many of them did not
necessarily support or identify with the political objectives of the
PNV.[40] On the assumption that cultural activities would eventually
translate into political activities, a Basque cultural revival could be
a considerable resource to the nationalist cause.

One could also count as a resource some aspects of the Spanish
political system, particularly during the formative years of the PNV
and during the 1930s. During its initial stage the PNV operated in a
political environment that was relatively open and thus allowed the
party to canvass openly for public support and to run for public

office. The political regime of the Spanish Restoration (1876-1923) was one of the more democratic regimes in Spanish political history.[41] Parties were allowed to function and elections were relatively free. Thus, Basque nationalism emerged in a period which gave the PNV relatively democratic and almost "ideal" political conditions within which to function and proselytize followers. The same was true, for the most part, during the 1930s.

Projects

Project 1: Cultural Development. The initial strategy of the party was very simple. It relied on the written word and the use of publications such as books, newspapers, and pamphlets with the objective of reviving interest in the Basque language and culture. To achieve this end the party encouraged and supported folkloric activities, such as folk dancing, folk festivals, competition between bertsolarriaks (rural bards), and athletic competition involving traditional Basque sporting events.[42] The party also sponsored some serious scholarship in archeological excavations, the collection of folklore, Basque linguistics, the ethnology of rural life, and the sociology of urbanization. All these activities culminated in 1918 when the governments of the Basque provinces, with the help and support of the nationalists, organized the First Congress of Basque Studies.[43] Scholarly journals such as La Revista Internacional de Estudios Vascos and Eusko-Folklore were also founded. This strategy was eventually to be followed by electoral politics. Although in the formative years of the party some inroads were made in local and provincial politics, it was not until the 1930s that the PNV became a leading party of the Basque region and a serious political force in national politics.

Violence was not advocated or used by the party. Between 1894 and the 1930s Basque nationalism was devoid of violent conflict either in the form of political assassinations or riots. With the exception of some arrests, including Arana, closure of some clubs, and censure of some publications by the central government, the activities of Basque nationalism proceeded on a nonviolent course.

Project 2: Electoral Politics. The new climate of political freedom that swept Spain with the advent of the republic in 1931 allowed the party to surface on the national scene. If the first generation of Basque nationalists had laid groundwork for Basque cultural revival, and achieved some modest local political gains, the second generation, led by José Antonio de Aguirre y Lecube during the 1930s, was able to get the last government of the Spanish republic to grant autonomy to the Basques.[44]

Right after the proclamation of the Second Spanish Republic
(April 14, 1931) the nationalists mounted a campaign in order to make
an issue out of the question of Basque autonomy, which had not been '
publicly discussed since 1923 when General Primo de Rivera led a
successful coup d'état and dissolved all political parties except his
own, the Unión Patriotica.

Project 3: Gestures of Unity with the Carlists. One of the primary
targets of the PNV was the province of Navarra where Carlismo
still dominated public opinion on the issue of autonomy. Although the
Carlists continued to view the nationalists with some degree of suspicion, the fear that the new Spanish Cortes might be composed of a
Leftist majority, which within the context of Spanish politics would
mean an avalanche of anticlericalism, motivated the Carlists to join
the nationalists in an electoral alliance in order to block Leftist
candidates from the Basque elections. After this electoral agreement, the Society of Basque Studies was asked to write a proposal for
Basque autonomy which was later approved at an assembly of Basque
municipalities held in the Navarrese town of Estella, the old Carlist
capital.[45] This seemed a significant political event from the point
of view of the nationalists, because they had been able to get Navarra
to join them in a common cause. The Carlists, however, accepted
the proposal with less than rampant enthusiasm. Their motivation
was different from that of the nationalists. While the nationalists
viewed the coming elections for the Cortes as a plebescite for or
against the formation of a Basque state, the Carlists looked at them
as a vote for a "Catholic-fuerista coalition for the defense of the
high interests of the Church, full restitution of the fueros," and
finally the proposal of autonomy.[46] For the Carlists it seemed that
religious issues, particularly the position of the Catholic Church in
Spanish society, had greater urgency than the issue of Basque
autonomy. Furthermore, the Carlists continued to differ with the
nationalists on the extent of Basque political unity. The Carlists
continued to argue for the traditional provincial division of the
Basque country, while the nationalists preferred a single Basque state.
In order to allay the fears and gain the support of the more
doctrinaire Carlists, the nationalists accepted as part of the proposal
of autonomy an article stipulating that within the Basque region relations between church and state would be governed by a concordat
to be negotiated between the Basque provinces and the Vatican. This
aspect of the proposal, however, was going to alienate some of the
groups in national politics whose support the nationalists needed in
order to get their statute of autonomy. It immediately aroused the
anticlerical feelings of some Spanish socialists who felt that "Spain
could not tolerate the Basque country turning itself into a Vaticanist
Gibraltar."[47]

The general elections to the constituent Cortes (June 16, 1931) produced a republican-socialist majority. These elections were also a relative success for the PNV. The party wrested control of the electorate of Vizcaya and Guipuzcoa from the traditional Carlist party and captured 13 out of the 17 seats of the Basque region. The remaining four were split between republicans and socialists.

Among the first items to be discussed by the constituent Cortes, which started its first session on July 14, 1931, was an old and sensitive issue in Spanish politics, namely, the role of the Catholic Church in Spanish life. When Article 26 of the new constitution was brought to the floor for debate, the first fury within the Cortes took place. According to this article, the Catholic Church would lose all the privileges that it had enjoyed under the Spanish monarchy. The traditional government budget for the church would be eliminated within two years, religious orders would have to register as any other secular organizations, and the church would be allowed only as much property as required for its survival. Furthermore, church property would be taxed and its educational activities would come to an end.

This issue brought the Basque nationalists into their first conflict with the new government. Given the religiosity of the Basque population and the fact that significant elements of the Basque clergy were supportive of Basque nationalism, the nationalists had no choice but to make a strong proclerical stand on this issue. After some acrimonious debate they walked out of the Cortes and were labeled by their fellow deputies as "cavemen." [48] In the Basque region there were mass demonstrations against the government, and the press, most of which was in Catholic hands, launched a virulent attack on the new government.

By September 1931 the Basque delegation formally presented to the government its proposal for autonomy. But the religious clause of that document was not acceptable to the government, which appointed a committee to revise it. The revised proposal, ready by January of 1932, omitted the possibility of a Basque concordat with the Vatican and gave the central government greater control over the area of public education. As might have been expected, the Carlists immediately refused to accept the revised proposal which they labeled as "Godless." [49] While the nationalists were ready to accept the revised proposal, the Carlists decided to go their own way and on January 6, 1932 joined forces with members of an old Integralist party to form the Comunion Tradicionalista Carlista. [50]

Project 4: Municipal and Popular Referenda. Despite the opposition of the Carlists, a preliminary municipal referendum for autonomy took place on June 16, 1932. The results of this referendum indicated that Navarra was still wedded to the Carlist viewpoint. The municipalities of Navarra rejected the referendum by a vote of 123 to 109, while 35 municipalities abstained. But it was approved overwhelmingly by the municipalities of Vizcaya and Guipuzcoa and by 51 of the 77 municipalities of Alava.[51] The nationalists felt confident that they could carry these three provinces and decided to organize for a popular plebescite on the question, with or without the support of the Carlists. The Carlists reacted by launching a vituperative campaign against the nationalists and in August 1932 produced a document revealing an alleged Nationalist-Communist-Jewish-Masonic plot to destroy the Catholic Church.[52] This seemed to mark the end of the alliance between the nationalists and the Carlists. The PNV was able, however, to get the bishops of Vitoria (capital city of Alava) and Pamplona (capital city of Navarra) to express publicly that the document had no foundation.

Since they had lost the support of the Carlists, the nationalists now concentrated on maintaining good rapport with the government in Madrid. But the options available to the nationalists were decreasing due to the polarization taking place in the Cortes and the country at large. If the nationalists became too close to the Carlist position they would be labeled reactionaries by the central government in Madrid. On the other hand, if they became too supportive of the central government, the Carlists would accuse them of supporting the destruction of the Catholic Church. The political situation of the nationalists was further complicated when in May 1933 the Cortes passed the Law of Congregations in order to implement Article 26 of the Constitution dealing with the position of the Catholic Church. This law was a source of tremendous consternation among Catholic groups. Allegedly some bishops had threatened to excommunicate those deputies who voted for the law, but were dissuaded from such action by the Papal Nuncio, Bishop Tedeschini.[53] The Catholic deputies, including the Basque deputies, published a manifesto calling "all citizens of good faith" to oppose this law.[54] This was followed by a pastoral letter issued by the Spanish bishops to remind the faithful that attendance at lay schools was contrary to canon law. On June 3, 1933, Pope Pius XI issued an Encyclical, Dilectissimi Nobis, asking all the Catholics to oppose the law by "all the legitimate means which Natural Law and civil legislation allowed them" and exhorted them to support Catholic Action "for the defense of the Faith and to ward off the dangers which threatened civil society."[55] This placed the nationalists in a very difficult position. Willy-nilly, the course of events was forcing them to get involved with broad national (Spanish) issues which initially they had tried to avoid.

On this issue the Carlists were willing to work with the nationalists and approached them to form an electoral alliance for the
coming general elections. But the nationalists refused because of
their fear that such an alliance might dilute the question of political
autonomy.

Although the religious issue complicated the strategy of the
nationalists, and intensified their differences with the Carlists, it
also brought them some positive results. It apparently helped to
convince some elements of the Basque population of the need for
political autonomy, at least for religious reasons. For some
members of the Basque clergy, nationalism and political autonomy
for the Basque region became a means to preserve the religiosity
of the area.[56]

On November 5, 1933, the popular plebescite on autonomy was
held in the three provinces of Vizcaya, Guipuzcoa, and Alava. It
resulted in a victory for the nationalists. Out of a total electorate
of 489,887 voters, 411,756 approved the proposal for autonomy,
14,196 voted against it, and 63,935 abstained. The greatest degree
of support once again came from Vizcava and Guipuzcoa, where it
was approved by 88.5 and 89.7 percent of the voters. In Alava,
however, only 46 percent supported it, while 11 percent voted
against and 43 percent abstained.[57] The results of the November
19, 1933, general elections for the Cortes also suggested that the
PNV was the leading party of the Basque region. Although it lost
one seat, thus retaining 12 out of the 17 Basque seats, it captured
46 percent of the popular vote, making it the party with the largest
support in the region.

Project 5: Policy of Aloofness.   The confidence of the nationalists
was soon deflated, however, when the national results of this election
became apparent. The new majority in the Cortes was controlled
by CEDA (Confederacion Española de Derechas Autonomas), a right-
of-center group, led by Gil Robles, opposed to regionalist-nationalist
movements.[58] This new majority did not accept the results of the
Basque plebescite on the grounds that Alava's vote did not meet the
constitutional requirement of a two-thirds majority. The nationalists
opposed this interpretation on the grounds that Alava's abstentions
should be counted as approval.[59] The nationalists interpreted the
actions of the new government simply as another delay tactic. This
interpretation was confirmed when the government submitted the
proposal of Basque autonomy to a Cortes committee, with a Rightist
majority, which blocked further action on the issue.

Meanwhile, political life in Spain was increasingly becoming
polarized between Left and Right. The Left was disappointed over
the fact that it had lost its majority, and embittered at the actions

of the new government. The Law of Congregations passed by the
previous government was ignored and left unenforced. Some of the
property of the religious orders confiscated by the previous government was returned to the Church. [60]

Although ideologically closer to the new CEDA majority, the
political turn of events was forcing the nationalists to look to the
Left, which was now actively canvassing the support of the PNV.
Indalecio Prieto, the leader of the Socialists of Bilbao, who not
too long before had exhorted his socialist followers not to vote for
Basque autonomy, now became an avid supporter of Basque nationalism. [61] In return, Aguirre, the leader of the PNV, declared that
should the Right try to impose a dictatorship or to reinstitute the
monarchy, his party "would oppose those institutions with all its
strength; and if the occasion should arise, the party would take
measures to meet the circumstances of the moment." [62] The Left
was not satisfied with such an equivocal stand, however. While
some elements of the Left seemed ready to take up arms against
the government, the leadership of the PNV continued to advocate
a nonviolent course and would not commit itself to go beyond a
defense of the existing republic. But this position was not shared
by all members, some of whom were calling for the use of violent
means. There was also another segment of the party becoming
apprehensive about the association between the PNV and the Left.
This group, consisting primarily of Alavese, broke away from the
party in October 1934, and formed the Derecha Autonoma Vasca
(Basque Autonomous Right). This became the right wing of Basque
nationalism, strongly associated with the more traditional position
of the Carlists.

In order to steer a middle course and to avoid collision either
with the Right or the Left, the nationalists decided to stay aloof from
the great issues disturbing Spanish society. In the course of an
interview with ABC of Madrid on June 30, 1934, Aguirred declared
that the Basques were "neither with the Left nor the Right; they
were simply autonomists." And when in the fall of 1934 Spain was
afflicted with a series of violent strikes, Aguirre told the government that although his party would not encourage rebellion, "but
neither would it lift a finger to help the government." [63] It had now
become clear to the nationalists that a statute of autonomy granted
by the Right was out of the question. CEDA was now actively cam-
paigning in the Basque region, defending the concierto economico
and spreading the notion that a statute of autonomy would be disastrous to the Basque economy.

The results of the 1936 general elections for the Cortes suggested that the polarization of Spanish politics was eroding the
popular support of the PNV. Although the nationalists had run

independently of both the Left and Right, and had supported the
Popular Front which in its election campaign had promised autonomy
for the regions, their share of the popular vote went down in every
Basque province: in Vizcaya from 58 percent to 51 percent, in
Guipuzcoa from 46 percent to 37 percent, in Alava from 29 to 21
percent. CEDA carried Navarra. This resulted in the loss of two
seats. The party now had only ten seats in the Cortes.[64]

The national Right, which by 1936 had clearly become anti-PNV,
increased its percentage of the total vote of the Basque region from
25 percent in 1933 to 32 percent in 1936. But so did the national
Left. It increased its percentage from 29 percent in 1933 to 33
percent in 1936. The percentage of the PNV went down from 46
to 35 percent.[65]

The results of the 1936 elections produced another shift in the
Spanish government, this time to the Left. The Popular Front,
consisting of Socialists, the Republican Left, and Republican Union,
and the Communists, won a majority of the seats. Out of a total
of 435 seats, the Popular Front controlled 257, more than enough
to control the Cortes.[66] This new majority produced panic on the
Right. Among the first pieces of legislation was the repeal and
modification of some legislation passed by the previous government.
In addition, the new government began to take action against Right-
wing generals in the form of early retirements and transferals.

On July 18, 1936, the Right initiated an insurrection which led
to a civil war that lasted until 1939.

Although on July 19, 1936, Euzkadi, a publication of the nationalists, supported the republic in "la lucha entre la ciudadania y el
fascismo" (the struggle between freedom and fascism), there was
some disagreement among the nationalists as to the exact course
that the Basques should take and the nature of their support for the
republic. Some were of the opinion that they should take this opportunity to declare their independence, while others felt that there was
not enough public support for such a move, and that the government
would send troops to the area. Other elements of the party looked
upon the civil war as a Spanish problem and that the Basques should
concentrate in maintaining peace in their own area: "The others
should take care of themselves and the Basques should take care
of the Basques."[67]

As the war progressed it became increasingly difficult for the
nationalists to stay out of this conflict. First, as soon as the insurrection began, fighting broke out in the Basque region. Second,
there were many Basques who identified with the national Right and
supported the insurrection, such as the Carlists, and there were
also within the Basque region large numbers of non-Basque migrant
workers who identified with the national Left.

In order to ensure that the nationalists would continue to support the republic, Prime Minister Largo Caballero, supposedly approached Aguirre in September 1936 and offered him a cabinet post. It is reported that an agreement was reached whereby Aguirre would become Minister of Public Works in return for a statute of autonomy. But allegedly Aguirre refused the post on the grounds that he disapproved of communist participation in government.[68] Instead, Manuel de Irujo, a nationalist from Guipuzcoa, became minister without portfolio.

On October 1, 1936, two months after the insurrection had begun, the beleaguered Republican government granted autonomy to the three provinces of Alava, Vizcaya, and Guipuzcoa. By this time, however, a portion of the Basque country had fallen into insurgent hands. Navarra, where General Mola had planned the insurrection with the help of the Carlists, was now beyond the reach of the nationalists. In Alava the regiment of Vitoria had taken that city on July 19 with apparently little effort. By September, Guipuzcoa, in which extensive fighting took place, had fallen to the insurgents. The nationalists evacuated this area and retreated to Vizcaya where they fought until June 19, 1937.[69]

Project 6: Armed Resistance. After the statute of autonomy was granted, a General Council with representatives from the three provinces was formed and the first Basque government was organized with Aguirre as its first president (lendakari). It was a coalition government consisting of four members from the PNV, one from the Accion Nacionalista Vasca, three Socialists, one Left Republican, and a Communist. This government mobilized the population of Vizcaya, kept order in that province, and conducted a small war against the Franco forces in the north. The Basque Autonomous Government hastily improvised a small army, the Gudaris, and on November 30, 1936, it launched an offensive to take back Alava from the insurgents. Equipped with antiquated artillery bought from the Soviet Union, the Gudaris were no match for the forces of Franco supported by Italian troops and the German Condor Legion.[70] This, the only Basque offensive, ended in defeat.[71] The Basque troops retreated back to Vizcaya where they put up a resistance until June 19, 1937, when the Franco forces took over that area. With the fall of Vizcaya, the entire Basque region was now under the military control of the forces of General Franco. The Basque government moved to the neighboring province of Santander where it set up its own administration and continued to fight until August 1937, when they finally negotiated their surrender with the Italian troops under the command of General Mancini.[72] The Basque government went in to exile in France.

As the civil war came to an end, the provinces of Vizcaya and Guipuzcoa, the centers of Basque nationalism, were stripped of their concierto economico and put under the direct control of the central government in Madrid. Manifestations of Basque culture, particularly in Guipuzcoa and Vizcaya, were forbidden, including the speaking of Basque by the clergy at church services. The central government "embarked on a deliberate policy of imposing the Castilian language and banning or ostracizing the local language, outlawing its use in the administration, education, mass media, translations. . . as well as making impossible any association that directly would foster the national sentiment."[73] After 1939 many Basques looked upon themselves as a defeated nation under occupation, a view that the PNV holds to this day.

Project 7: Maintenance of Audibility and Durability. Since 1939 the PNV and the Basque government have operated from exile. The party and the government have maintained a relatively active propaganda campaign supported by many Basque centers that were formed overseas by exiled Basque political leaders. Two publishing houses, one in Buenos Aires and one in Caracas, were founded to deal exclusively with Basque nationalist literature and with cultural themes of the Basque country. Some of this literature has routinely been smuggled into Spain.

Evaluation of Decision Maker A

Among the stated objectives of the PNV were, first of all, to raise the awareness of the Basques as a people and, second, to form an autonomous state out of the four Spanish Basque provinces. In both of these efforts the party was partly successful. Although it was unable to persuade Navarra and a significant part of Alava to accept its political objectives, it succeeded in getting the support of Vizcaya and Guipuzcoa and finally wrested from the central government a statute of autonomy. While this autonomy was short-lived because of the events surrounding the Spanish Civil War, it nevertheless can be regarded as an accomplishment.

Probably of greater significance is the fact that the party and the Basque government in exile have been able to maintain the durability and audibility of Basque nationalism, despite their exiled status and the efforts of the Franco regime to stifle nationalist sentiment in the Basque region. Through its youth organization, Eusko Gastedi (Basque Youth), the party has been successful in recruiting a new generation of activists to carry the banner of Basque nationalism. It seems that today Basque nationalism is more intense than ever before, as measured by the recent activism and the number of recent organizations concerned with this issue. It also means that the PNV no longer is the major spokesman of Basque nationalism.

Decision Maker B: Accion Nacionalista Vasca
(ANV, Basque Nationalist Action)

ANV, formed in 1930, reflected a wing of Basque nationalism that did not support the confessionalism of the PNV. Although ANV is part of the Basque government in exile and one its members, Tomas Bilbao, participated in the government of the Spanish republic during the last months of the civil war, it never acquired a significant popular following. Little is known about the membership and extent of support for this organization within the Basque region.

Goals

In the Manifesto de San Andres published in 1930, ANV recognized the Basques as a nation, including the French Basques, and supported an autonomous Basque state within a federal-republican Spain. ANV also advocated an eventual European federation of nations. In its political ideology it favored social democracy and would give the state a predominant role in the conduct of economic life such as nationalization of basic resources. More recently, ANV has called for the formation of a Basque Socialist party.[74]

Projects

During the 1930s ANV sought alliances with the Center-Left in national politics and adhered to the Pact of San Sebastian (1930) which sought to establish a republic in Spain. In contrast to the PNV, ANV seemed much more concerned with the type of political regime that Spain should have. It seems that for the PNV it did not matter whether the regime should be a republic or a constitutional monarchy, so long as the Basques were given autonomy. Again, in contrast to the PNV, ANV participated in the Popular Front elections of 1936, an action which the PNV refused to take.[75]

Since 1939 ANV has operated from exile and publishes a weekly newspaper entitled Tierra Vasca (Basque Country).

Decision Maker D: Euzkadi Ta Askatasuna
(ETA, Basque Nation and Liberty)

During 1953-54 a group of students at the University of Deusto
in Bilbao, capital city of Vizcaya, founded a clandestine journal,
Elkin (Action). This group later became associated with EGI, the
youth wing of the PNV. But because of the moderate wait-and-see
approach of the PNV and EGI, the Elkin group left and established
itself in 1960 as ETA with a new journal, Zutik (Arise). Several
years later, in 1967, because of an ideological dispute, some of
the original members of ETA split from the party and became known
as ETA-zarra (old ETA). They apparently were unwilling to go
along with the radical Marxism of the rest of the membership. [76]
The arrests of ETA members by the Spanish police indicate
that the membership of this organization is quite young, between
the ages of 18 and 30, and from a middle-class background.

Goals

In 1967 ETA declared itself as a "Basque Socialist Movement of
National Liberation." Led by José Maria Escubi Larraz, considered
a Marxist, it established some contacts with international communist
groups. ETA foresees the creation of a Basque state out of the seven
Basque provinces to be federated in a Europe of nations. [77]

Projects

ETA has followed three approaches in its strategy: propaganda,
guerrilla tactics, and organization of workers in the Basque region.
The core of the organization have been the milis (direct action
squads), led by Juan José Echave Orobengoa. In 1968 they assassinated Meliton Manzanas, an official of the Spanish political police
and in 1974 had their most famous kill, the Spanish premier, Carrero
Blanco.
ETA apparently also has made some contacts with other groups,
such as the Catalans, the Palestinian Arab Black September, the
Irish Republican Army, the Kurds, and the Breton Liberation Movement. [78] Not very much is known, however, about the nature of
these contacts.
Although most of the activity of ETA has been within the Spanish
Basque region, the assassination of Carrero Blanco in Madrid
suggests that ETA may be willing to take its struggle to areas outside of the Basque region.

Decision Maker E: Enbata

As mentioned previously, Basque nationalism has been an issue primarily in the Spanish Basque region. But in 1960 some French Basques also established a political organization, Enbata (Ocean).

Goals

Enbata looks upon the Spanish-French border that splits the Basque country as a "crime against nature and a wall of shame, like the one dividing Berlin," and favors the unification of the Basque provinces, also to be federated with other European nations. It is their belief that Europe should be federated on the basis of ethnic groups. But for the moment Enbata seems willing to settle for the formation of a département (French administrative division) consisting exclusively of the three traditional French Basque provinces. [79]

Projects

Enbata has followed a moderate approach concentrating pri- marily on propaganda work and electoral politics. It is difficult to assess the extent of its popular support. But judging from the results of the 1967 French general elections, its support does not seem to be very substantial. It received only 5 percent of the vote in the French Basque region.

Other Decision Makers

There are a number of other organizations advocating varying degrees of autonomy for the Basque region. But because they have to operate underground, little is known about them or the extent of their membership and support. The Basque Nationalist Christian Socialists Movement advocates an independent democratic Basque state to be federated in a Europe of nations. [80] This is a recent group formed within the Basque region of Spain. There is an anar- chist group, Grupo Autonomo Askatasuna, formed recently, which supports an independent Basque nation with an anarchist political organization.[81] This group links the struggle for Basque indepen- dence with an international workers' revolution and is willing to participate with other Spanish anarchist groups. It is a member of the Confederacion Nacional del Trabajo (CNT-National Confed- eration of Work), an anarchosyndicalist trades union. It wants a

socialist socioeconomic organization based on a Basque confederation of free communes to be linked eventually with an international
confederation of anarchist communes. In addition, there is also the
Communist party of Euzkadi (Basque Communist party), affiliated
with the Spanish Communist party, which also favors some degree
of autonomy for the Basque region. It appears that by the 1960s the
Spanish Communist party was in favor of a "pluronational" state for
Spain with specific statutes for Catalonia, the Basque region, and
Galicia.[82]

Evaluation of Decision Makers

The resources of all the decision-making groups, with the exception of the PNV, are very limited. They seem to rely primarily
on the efforts of small numbers of individuals. All of them, with
the exception of Enbata, must operate underground, thus making
their activities difficult and risky. Despite this constraint, however, ETA with its form of urban guerrilla warfare has recently
done more than any of the existing groups in focusing attention on
the Basque problem.

Although the existence of these groups has made Basque nationalism a salient issue in Spanish politics, and more recently also in
French politics, none of them, with the exception of the PNV during
the 1930s, has achieved its primary goal, namely, Basque autonomy
or independence. This goal will depend largely on the direction of
political change within the Spanish political system. If the Spanish
political system moves in the direction of an open and democratic
system, the possibility of autonomy will be enhanced. But if the
regime remains authoritarian, it is unlikely that it will consider
autonomy for the regions. The use of force by the Basques to
achieve autonomy does not appear as a realistic possibility. First,
I do not think that such a move would enjoy popular support, and
second, the Madrid government would use its superior force to
put it down.

Impact on the International Context

The impact of the decision makers on the international context
has been, thus far, very insignificant. The earliest attempts by
the PNV to get international attention was done in the form of a
telegram sent by Arana to President Roosevelt to congratulate him
on the independence of Cuba. In this telegram he also made reference to the Basques as an oppressed nation. In 1916 the PNV

sent a delegation to the Conference des Nationalités (Conference on Nationalities) held in Lausanne, Switzerland, to canvass support for the Basque cause. In 1918 a telegram was sent to both President Wilson and Clemenceau in order to bring to their attention the existence of the Basque question. Throughout the 1930s the PNV also attempted to get the Vatican to recognize their cause, but without success. The PNV participates in European conferences on minorities, is one of the founding members of a recently formed European group on minorities, Bureau of Unrepresented European Nations, which also includes Plaid Cymru (Welsh Nationalist party), the Alsace National party, and Srollad ar Vro (Brittany). [83] Through its labor union, the Euzko Langillen Alkartasuna (ELA, Solidarity of Basque Workers), the PNV also participates in the International Confederation of Free Trades Unions. The party has also maintained a delegate in Washington and one in New York City to keep abreast of events at the United Nations.

NOTES

1. It is difficult to get an accurate account of the Basques for neither the French nor Spanish government makes ethnic distinctions in their population census. For population figures, see Banco de Bilbao, Renta Nacional de España y su Distribucion Provincial (Bilbao, 1967); José Domingo de Arana, Hombre, raza, nacionalidad, universalidad, presente y futuro del pueblo vasco (Bilbao, 1966).

2. F. Sarrailh, Vasconia (Buenos Aires, 1962).

3. Sergio Barzanti, The Underdeveloped Areas Within the Common Market (Princeton; Princeton University Press, 1965).

4. Camara Oficial de Industria de Guipuzcoa, Estructura económico-industrial de Guipuzcoa y su evolucion (Madrid, 1970) p. 212.

5. POESSA, Informe sociológico sobre la situacion social de España (Madrid, 1970), p. 172.

6. Manuel de Lecuona, Literatura oral vasca (San Sebastian, 1964), p. 8; Geografia historica de la lengua vasca (San Sebastian, 1960), p. 10.

7. Morton Levine, "The Basques," Natural History, 76 (April 1967): 145; see also Rodney Gallop, A Book of the Basques (London, 1930).

8. Morton Levine, "Basque Isolation: Fact or Problem?" Symposium on Community Studies in Anthropology, proceedings of the 1962 Annual Spring Meetings of the American Ethnological Society (Seattle: University of Washington Press, 1963), p. 21.

9. Anacleto Ortueta, Sancho El Mayor, Rey de los Vascos (Buenos Aires, 1963); Julio Caro Baroja, Los Vascos (Madrid, 1958); Vasconiana (Madrid, 1975).

10. A discussion of the traditional Basque fueros, the name by which their traditional liberties were known, is found in Bernardo Estornes Lasa, Historia del Pais Basko (Zarauz, Spain, 1933); Gregorio de Balparda, Historia critica de Vizcaya y de sus fueros (Madrid, 1962); Ramon Sainz de Varanda, La ley paccionada de Navarra y la vigencia de las normas forales sobre sucesion intestada (Pamplona, 1970).

11. Quoted in Francis Duncan, The English in Spain (London, 1877), pp. 167-70.

12. These were the nineteenth-century wars to defend the right of Don Carlos VI to the Spanish throne. Edgar Holt, The Carlist Wars in Spain (Chester Springs, Pa.: Dufour, 1967).

13. Jaime Ignacio del Burgo, Origen y fundamento del regimen foral de Navarra (Pamplona, 1968).

14. José Badia La-Calle, El concierto economico con Alava (Bilbao, 1965); Juan Plaza Prieto, "Conciertos Economicos," in Notas sobre política economica española (Madrid, 1954).

15. See Santiago Galindo Herrero, Breve historia del tradicionalismo español (Madrid, 1954); R. Oyarzun, Historia del carlismo (Madrid, 1930).

16. For a more detailed discussion of this movement, see Raymond Carr, Spain 1808-1939 (New York, 1966), pp. pp. 155-96.

17. Maximiano Garcia Venero, Historia del nacionalismo vasco (Madrid, 1945), p. 143.

18. Ibid., p. 180.

19. Ibid., p. 101.

20. Ibid., p. 201.

21. Ibid., p. 212.

22. Quoted in Ibid., p. 227.

23. Ibid., p. 228.

24. Ibid., pp. 230-31.

25. Santiago galindo de Herrero, Los partidos monarquicos bajo la segunda republica (Madrid, 1956), pp. 129-31.

26. Richard A. H. Robinson, The Origins of Franco's Spain (Pittsburgh, 1970), p. 92.

27. Maria Puy Huici Goni, Las cortes de Navarra durante la edad moderna (Madrid, 1963).

28. Jaime Ignacio del Burgo, Origen y fundamento del regimen foral de Navarra (Pamplona, 1965), p. 475.

29. Galindo de Herrero, op. cit., pp. 240-41.

30. Keesing's Contemporary Archives, January 1-11, 1968, p. 23112.

31. Pedro de Basaldua, El libertador vasco (Buenos Aires, 1953). For detailed treatment of the political origins of Basque nationalism, see Maximiano Garcia Venero, Historia del nacionalism vasco (Madrid, 1945) and Juan J. Linz, "Early State-Building and Late Peripheral Nationalism against the State: The Case of Spain," in Building States and Nations: Models Analyses and Data Across Three Worlds, ed. S. N. Eisenstadt and Stein Rokkan (London: Sage Press, 1973)."

32. Quoted in Garcia Venero, ibid., pp. 244-45. For more information on the general ideology of the movement, see Luis de Arana Goiri, Formulorio de los principios esenciales y basicos del primitive nacionalismo vasco contenidos en el lema Jaun-Goikua eta Lagi-Zarra (Bilbao, 1932).

33. Sabino de Arana Goiri, Bizkaya por su independencia (Bilbao, 1932), Obras Completas (Buenos Aires, 1965).

34. Pedro de Basaldua, op. cit., p. 127.

35. Sabino de Arana Goiri, Obras Completas, op. cit., p. 16.

36. J. J. Linz, "Opposition to and Under and Authoritarian Regime: The Case of Spain," in Regimes and Oppositions, ed. Robert A. Dahl (New Haven, 1973), p. 240.

37. Ramon Tamames, Los centros de gravedad de la economia española (Madrid, 1968); Andoni de Soraluze, Riqueza y economia del pais vasco (Buenos Aires, 1945).

38. Raymond Carr, Spain 1808-1933 (London, 1966), p. 406.

39. Janvier de Ybarra y Bergé, Political nacional de Vizcaya (Madrid, 1948).

40. For more detailed information on this, see Milton M. da Silva, "The Basque Nationalist Movement: A Case Study in Modernization and Ethnic Conflict," unpublished dissertation, pp. 99-102.

41. J. J. Linz, "The Party System of Spain: Past and Future," in Party Systems and Voter Alignments, ed. Seymour M. Lipset and Stein Rokkan (New York, 1967), pp. 197-282.

42. Garcia Venero, op. cit., pp. 395-404.

43. Primer Congreso de Estudios Vascos (Bilbao, 1919).

44. For some biographical material on Aguirre, see Pedro de Basalduna, En defensa de la verdad (Buenos Aires, 1956); and for Aguirre's views on Basque nationalism, see José Antonio de Aguirre, Entre la libertad y la revolucion (1930-1935 (Bilbao, 1935); La verdad de un lustro en el pais vasco (Bilbao, n.d.)

45. This proposal later became known as the Estatuto General del Estado Vasco.

46. Aguirre, Entre la libertad y la revolucion, op. cit.,
p. 92.

47. El Socialista, June 30, 1931.

48. Robinson, op. cit.

49. Aguirre, op. cit., p. 93.

50. Santiago Galindo Herrero, Los partidos monárquicos
bajo la segunda republica (Madrid, 1956), pp. 129-31.

51. F. Janvier de Landabura, La causa del pueblo vasco
(Paris, 1956), p. 13.

52. Robinson, op. cit., p. 146.

53. Gabriel Jackson, The Spanish Republic and The Civil
War 1931-1939 (Princeton, 1965), p. 106.

54. El Debate, June 4, 1933.

55. El Debate, July 1, 1933.

56. Juan de Iturralde, El catolicismo y la cruzada de
Franco, II (Bayonne, France, 1955), p. 424.

57. Basque Government, White Paper of the Basque
Government (Paris, 1955), p. 39.

58. Robinson, op. cit., p. 149; J. M. Gil Robles,
"The Spanish Republic and Basque Independence," The Tablet,
June 19, 1937, pp. 876-77.

59. Debates de Seciones de las Cortes Constituyentes,
February 8, 9, 1934.

60. For a discussion of the political issues that confronted
the Spanish Republic, see Stanley G. Payne, The Spanish
Revolution (New York, 1970).

61. Joaquín Arrarás Irribarren, Historia de la cruzada
española, II (Madrid, 1939), p. 401.

62. Ibid.

63. Robinson, op. cit., p. 191.

64. Linz, in Regimes and Oppositions, op. cit., p. 251.

65. Ibid.

66. For a discussion of the Popular Front election, see
Jackson, op. cit., pp. 184-95.

67. Garcia Venero, op. cit., p. 574.

68. Ibid., p. 591.

69. For an account of the civil war in the Basque region,
see George L. Steer, The Tree of Guernica (London, 1938).

70. On April 26, 1937, the German Air Force bombed the
old Basque town of Guernica, a symbol of Basque autonomy, and
machine-gunned the population. This incident was given extensive
international coverage and motivated Picasso to produce what
later became a famous painting, entitled "Guernica," dramatizing
the destruction of that town. As a result of this bombing, "The
Basque government in exile attempted to bring a case against

Germany at the Nuremberg War Crimes Tribunal. The attempt was unsuccessful, since no events which occurred before 1939 were taken into account at Nuremberg." Hugh Thomas, The Spanish Civil War (New York, 1961) p. 420.

71. Luis Maria de Lojendio, Operaciones militares de la guerra de España, 1936-1939 (Madrid, 1940), p. 244.

72. Aguirre had indicated in his writings that earlier in 1937 Mussolini had suggested that the Basques surrender to the Italian troops and that then a separate peace treaty would be negotiated between the Basque government and the Italians, with the possibility of making Euzkadi a protectorate of the Italian government. Aguirre refers to this in his book as the "picturesque proposal of an Italian protectorate over the Basques." José Antonio de Aguirre, Escape via Berlin (New York, 1944), p. 52.

73. Linz, in Regimes and Oppositions, op. cit., p. 243.

74. Tierra Vasca, November 1972.

75. Ibid., November 1971.

76. On the development of ETA and recent developments, see Stanley Payne, "The Problem of Basque and Catalan Nationalism," paper presented at the Conference on Modern Spain, Center for Strategic Studies, Georgetown Univeristy, Washington, D. C., June 12-13, 1973, pp. 19-22; Kenneth Medhurst, "The Basques," The Minority Rights Group, Report no. 9 (London).

77. Zutik, April 1965. (publication of ETA.)

78. International Herald Tribune, February 7, 1973, p. 5.

79. For a discussion of the French Basques, see Paul Sérant, La France des Minorités (Paris, 1965); J. P. Mogui, La Revolt des Basques (Paris, 1970).

80. Pedro Gonzales Blasco, "Modern Nationalism in Old Nations as a Consequence of Earlier State-Building: The Case of Basque-Spain," in Ethnicity and Nation-Building: Local and International Perspectives, ed. Wendell Bell and Walter E. Freeman (Cambridge, Mass., 1974).

81. Its platform was published in Tierra Vasca, October 1974.

82. Guy Hermet, Les Communistes en Espagne (Paris, 1971), p. 170; in Payne, op. cit., p. 22.

83. Welsh Nation, January 27, 1975.

6

THE WELSH AS A
NONSTATE NATION
Ray Corrado

This chapter traces in some detail the Welsh nation from
its existence in the thirteenth century as an independent
state through its conquest and anglicization to the present,
with a resurgence of national assertiveness. The
relative success of Welsh nationalism in the recent past
is discussed in terms both of British party politics and
also of European Economic Community politics.

The goals of the leaders of Plaid Cymru (Welsh
nationalist party) include direct Welsh participation in a
confederal European community and dominion status
within Britain, rather than complete sovereign independence. Wales provides an example of a nonstate nation
(NSN) with deep historical roots and with significant but
limited modern resources. Plaid Cymru strategy seems
carefully designed to make the most of opportunities
within both the British and the wider European contexts
and also to avoid the pitfalls of demanding more autonomy
than would be feasible currently to administer. The
party seeks greater control over domestic matters,
thus increasing the resistance to cultural anglicization.
Within the European Economic Community the party
seeks direct representation for itself and for other
ethnic nations of Europe. The group seeks a confederal
rather than federal structure for European union
apparently because it fears the domination of Europe
by the larger members. Plaid Cymru thus proposes a
complex status of intermediate sovereignty involving
national recognition and participation within the European

community but autonomy short of full independence from Britain.

—Judy S. Bertelsen

On July 2, 1975, Plaid Cymru (Welsh Nationalist party) presented a memorandum to the prime minister of Belgium, Leo M. Tindemans. Tindemans was in Wales in his official capacity as the secretary of the Council of Ministers of the European Economic Community (EEC). His visit was part of the EEC investigation of the feasibility of a European union. Tindemans sought the views of Plaid Cymru on the political structure of the European union. In their memorandum response, Plaid Cymru maintained that the European union should take the form of a confederation of nations in which Wales would be accorded "Full National Status to achieve a comparable representation for Wales--to that of Denmark and Ireland on the Council of Ministers, the EEC Commission, the European Assembly and the Economic and Social Committee."[1]

Tindemans' meeting with the leaders of Plaid Cymru and their memorandum to him reflect Wales' status as a nonstate nation. On the one hand, Wales is not recognized as a nation-state, yet on the other hand, it is difficult for any EEC statesman to ignore the moderate claims of the Plaid Cymru for formal representation in the EEC institutions and Plaid Cymru's position on the European union. Plaid Cymru has joined with other ethnic nationalist political parties of other EEC nation-states in organizing a pressure group, the Bureau of Unrepresented Nations in Brussels, to lobby for the recognition of the rights of nonstate nations in the EEC. Since nonstate nations exist in most of the countries in the EEC, the potential political power of such a pressure might increase substantially with time. In addition, the growth and effectiveness of terrorist organizations, which appear to involve individuals and groups from NSNs within the EEC, might be blunted if the more moderate goals of NSN groups such as Plaid Cymru are at least considered in the EEC policy-making institutions. The presence of ethnic nationalist political parties in many countries of the EEC raises the possibility that in the future some ethnic nationalist parties may come to represent the majority of the electorate in certain NSNs. The involvement of the leaders of the ethnic nationalist political parties even to a small extent in the decision-making process concerning the future of a European union, might reduce the possibility that ethnic nationalist

I would like to thank Phillip M. Rawkins for his comments on an earlier draft of this chapter.

leaders will seriously challenge a future European union. For their part, the leaders of Plaid Cymru were willing to consult with Tindemans, since the consultation involves recognition, however informal and minimal, of their claim that Wales is a nation with a right to participate in decision making in the international context.

Plaid Cymru is the most visible expression of the desire of individuals in Wales to have some form of national sovereignty. A substantial percentage of Plaid Cymru supporters desire total separation from Great Britain, but the current leaders and a majority of the supporters of Plaid Cymru do not. The Plaid Cymru policy of supporting dominion status for Wales is a position short of demanding total sovereignty. Dominion status would involve a cooperative process where any decision making in the international context would involve Welsh leaders as well as decision makers from other parts of the United Kingdom. There are other positions held by various segments of the Welsh population. There are those individuals who maintain that Welsh decision makers should only be involved in the decision-making process in a consultative capacity, especially in the international context. There are still others who maintain that the responsibility for decision making within Wales and in the international context should continue to be made by "British" decision makers, rather than through a cooperative effort of autonomous Welsh, Scottish, Ulster, and English decision makers. [2]

There are, then, different views held by the peoples of Wales and England concerning the status of Wales as a nonstate nation. In order to understand the reasons for this diversity of opinion and what view is likely to dominate in the near future, it is important to divide Welsh history into four periods. The profile of decision makers, goals, components, resources, and environment changes significantly in each period, as do the durability and audibility of Wales.

The first period comprises essentially the thirteenth century, during which Wales was an autonomous state. The second period spans the fourteenth to eighteenth centuries, during which Wales was conquered by England and ceased to be a political entity. The third period includes the nineteenth to mid-twentieth centuries, during which the majority of the people of Wales were anglicized through the industrial and educational revolutions, and the national political parties completely dominated the political environment in Wales. The fourth period is that of the last 15 years, during which the urban-industrialized British society produced the decision makers, resources, and environment that facilitated the restoration of the Welsh nation culturally and politically. For the first time since the fourteenth century Wales became directly involved in the international context.

PERIOD I: TENTH TO THIRTEENTH CENTURIES

It was during this period that the clans of northern Wales were briefly united into a distinctive political entity—the Principality of Wales. The Welsh culture was vibrant in poetry, song, and language. This period can be viewed as the "golden age" of the Welsh nation; a culturally and politically distinctive Welsh ethnic group existed with near sovereign control of a separate geographic region.

While the Welsh nation was a viable political entity for only a brief time, it provided the "sense of nation" that in later periods became a basis for political movements based on the ideology of nationalism.

Decision Maker A: The Welsh Princes

The Welsh princes were the leaders of various clans which inhabited and dominated the major geographic regions of Wales.

Goals

Most of the Welsh princes wanted to unite the various clans in Wales under their own singular leadership. The political unification of Wales would facilitate achievement of another goal, the presenting of a united front to a common enemy, the English.

Resources

The Welsh princes employed armies recruited from their clans in order to unify Wales through interclan wars. The appeal to a common culture and language was also important in seeking the unification of Wales. The unification of Wales in turn was a valuable resource in creating a united front in the face of the continual threats and invasions from England.

Environment

The geography and topography of Wales were a crucial part of the environment for the Welsh princes. Wales is an area of 8,000 square miles, located in the west central area of Great Britain. Wales is also a peninsula with the Irish Sea to the north and west and the Bristol Channel to the south. It is primarily a mountainous area with the exception of a coastal rim and large valleys in the southern region. The main military threats were from England to the east and the Norman Marcher lords in southern Wales. (The Marcher

Lords were descendants of Norman Barons who had occupied the
borderland estates of southern Wales and southwestern England.)
In the face of more powerful armies, the Welsh princes, especially
those from the northern region, would withdraw into mountain
redoubts. It was far easier to conquer and control the clans who
inhabited the coastal rim and the southern valleys. These topograph-
ical differences between the northern and southern regions were
paralleled to some extent by cultural differences between the clans
from the two regions. These differences were an obstacle that the
Welsh princes faced in unifying Wales. They continued to be a part
of the environment faced by decision makers throughout the remaining
three periods. This suggests the crucial role played by environmental
factors with regard to the efficiency of NSNs as a system.

Component

The political unification of Wales occurred on two occasions
during this period. Late in the tenth century Wales became an
integrated and united state, but it quickly disintegrated again into
warring factions led by various Welsh princes. In the mid-twelfth
century the Northern Welsh prince, Llewellyn the Great, united
most of Wales and secured its autonomy from the English. The Welsh
were received at the court of the French king, Louis VII, and Wales
was accorded the effective status of an independent state. A strong
cultural revival manifested in religion, language, and literature also
took place. [3]

Decision Maker B: English Kings

Goals

The attempt by one ethnic group to subject all of the other
ethnic groups that have inhabited the British Isles as members of
clans or kingdoms appears to be a constant throughout most of the
history of this region. Romans, Saxons, Danes, and Normans with
varying success had sought hegemony over the British Isles. No one
ethnic group was completely successful; still, the persistent attempts
often led to the evolution of new ethnic groups such as the English,
who were an amalgamation of previous ethnic groups who inhabited
the area. The English kings followed the tradition of invading Wales
to try to subjugate the Welsh people.

Resources

The army was the most important resource that the English
kings employed in defeating the Welsh princes. The feudal structure

of England was somewhat more elaborate than that of Wales. The
English kings could formulate and carry out a military strategy that
took advantage of the stronger logistical support base that English
society could provide. Edward I also relied on the military cooperation of the Norman Marcher lords, who controlled the border lands
of south Wales.

Environment

The Welsh princes and clans were often geographically isolated
from each other. They did not have a strong tradition of common
military strategy. This reflected, in part, the absence of a centralizing monarch or common political institutions. Differences in
culture and language dialect were also forming on a north-south
geographic basis. The valleys of the south were readily accessible
to invading English armies. Wales did not have any strong alliances
with continental kingdoms which might have offset the military power
of England.

Components

The English kings followed the strategy of isolating the Welsh
princes and their followers in the mountainous areas. This was
accomplished by conquering and occupying the coastal areas with a
network of castles (which to this day dot the Welsh coastline). The
English maintained strategic control of the valuable agricultural land
of less mountainous regions and kept open their lines of support to
England. It was extremely difficult to defeat the English in the long
run, given their strategy of occupation and the Welsh princes' strategy
of retreat.

Evaluation of the Welsh System,
Tenth to Thirteenth Centuries

The Welsh princes were able to appeal to the Welsh culture
and language as the basis for establishing the Welsh nation. Interclan
wars were the basis for the establishment of a Welsh state dominated
by a particular Welsh prince. The durability of the Welsh nation and
state was weakened by the absence of a tradition of political integration,
especially since the main military threat, England, had been a politically integrated feudal society for centuries. In addition, the
cultural and geographical differences between northern and southern
Wales were not bridged during the short periods that Wales was
united; consequently, it was difficult to sustain a united front toward
the English. The Welsh princes did not participate extensively in the

international context. This was in contrast to the English kings, who still exercised sovereignty over strategic regions on the continent and had, therefore, continually been involved in the international context. Thus the Welsh princes were faced with a formidable enemy in England and its kings, while Wales was far less durable and audible.

PERIOD II: FOURTEENTH TO NINETEENTH CENTURIES

This period begins with the successful invasion and defeat of the Welsh princes by England's Edward I. The Edwardian conquest was briefly interrupted by a successful rebellion led by the Welsh prince Owain Glyndor, who established a formal political union of Wales that lasted for nine years. With this sole exception, the English kings and later English parliamentary leaders became the major decision makers until the nineteenth century. Wales ceased to be a separate political entity, and the Welsh culture and society were further transformed by the forced integration of Wales and England.

Decision Maker A: English Kings

The Tudor monarchs were the most important decision makers during this long historical period. Henry VIII, in particular, established goals and components that severely weakened the durability and audibility of the Welsh nation. It was during his reign, however, that the environment was altered.

Goals

The centralization of political power under the monarchy was a major goal of the English kings up until the Glorious Revolution. Another goal was the desire to secure England defensively by reducing the ability of continental kingdoms to form alliances with any government in the British Isles other than England. The goal was for England to dominate the Celtic regions of Wales and Ireland. Also, English culture, including the Anglican religion, was to be the dominant culture throughout the British Isles. In effect, England would be the political and cultural center, and the seas would provide a common and natural defense barrier against the continental kingdoms such as France and Spain. [4]

Resources

The army was important initially in ensuring that the English monarchs would politically dominate Wales. The army was obviously important in defeating actual and potential rebellions. The monarchs, especially Henry VIII, played the central political role by sponsoring legislation that would force the political and legal integration of Wales and England. Until the civil war during the seventeenth century, the monarchs politically dominated Wales and England—institutions such as Parliament and the Court of Star Chamber were largely dominated by the monarchs. Monarchical power was also evident in the economic system, particularly since the rise of the empire and the mercantilist policy. The navy and sea ports were effectively controlled by the monarchs for most of this period, and business monopolies were granted by the king. The cultural center of England and Wales was the monarch's court; consequently, the aristocracy and the cultural elite catered to the desires of the reigning monarch. With Henery VIII, the Anglican Church became the established church of England and Wales, and the official head of the Anglican Church was the monarch. The dominance of the monarchy over Wales was symbolized by the hereditary title that the monarch's eldest son held—the Prince of Wales. The monarch could also rely on his leadership role in the international context to ensure or build the allegiance of the Welsh people. [5] Also, the legitimacy of the monarchy in Wales was enhanced, since the Tudor line had Welsh origin, and Henry Tudor had raised a Welsh army to defeat Richard III.

Environment

Europe consisted of a myriad of kingdoms which were continually involved in alliances often based on intermarriage. These alliances were vital in facilitating the ascendency of a particular kingdom in Europe and successful empire-building in the new world continents. The Protestant Reformation and the Catholic Counterreformation also contributed to the turbulent international context of this period. In effect, the main actors in the international context were kingdoms. Many of the decentralized feudal societies of the previous historical period of the Middle Ages were replaced by far more politically centralized monarchical systems. The rise of empires in the relatively underpopulated new world introduced a novel vehicle for the radical expansion of the power of kingdoms such as Spain, Britain, and Holland. Wars of succession and imperial dominance were numerous throughout this period.

Components

Component 1. In 1536, Henry VIII sponsored the Acts of Union, which stipulated that all legal proceedings were to be in English, and all holders of public office had to be English speakers. These acts ensured that the English language and culture would completely dominate the political and legal institutions in Wales. [6]

Component 2. The policy of centralizing political power in London, instigated in earnest by Henry VIII, was important in creating a sense of British nationalism. The introduction of a constitutional monarchy and the onset of parliamentary supremacy resulted in the continuation of this centralization policy.

Component 3. During the Tudor reign, especially that of Henry VIII, the English court was an important vehicle for co-opting the Welsh gentry, which in turn influenced the urban middle class. The end result, according to Sir Reginald Coupland, was that "the Welsh aristocracy and the urban middle class had adopted English speech and ways of life: only such pride as they took in the beauty of their country and in their family history, distinguished them from Englishmen across a frontier which had lost its meaning. "[7]

Component 4. The mercantile system could be manipulated to ensure that certain individuals from the Welsh gentry and middle class would direct their allegiance to the monarchy and England and Wales. Legal monopolies granted by the monarchy were a growing and essential part of business life.

Decision Maker B: The Welsh Trust

The only decision makers who supported the survival of the Welsh culture were the religious leaders identified with the Welsh Trust. Their effort to promote religion among the Welsh people directly contributed to the preservation of the Welsh language.

Goals

The members of the Welsh Trust sought "to combat the notorious ignorance and the consequent irreligion of the poor. "[8] The main and interdependent goals were educating the poor or "working class" Welsh people and instilling the Protestant faith in them.

Resources

The Welsh Trust employed schools and Welsh language training to obtain their religious goals.

Environment

The environment was favorable because education was only rudimentary and the English-dominated British government was not concerned with educating Welshmen. The Welsh Trust was able to fill this vacuum without governmental interference. The language of communication among the majority of common Welshmen was Welsh. Welsh language training was, therefore, the appropriate vehicle for education and religious instruction.

Component

Welsh language training was established in schools to facilitate religious instruction.

Evaluation of the Welsh System, Fourteenth to Nineteenth Centuries

The durability of the Welsh nonstate nation was considerably weakened for most of this long historical period. The early and intense co-optation of the Welsh aristocracy and urban middle class meant that the major source of potential leadership for the Welsh nonstate nation was not available. This co-optation affected its audibility as well. Participation in the international political context was largely limited to the anglicized elites, especially because of the absence of easily accessible communications. Both the durability and audibility of the Welsh nonstate nation depended on the Welsh language. It was the main symbol of cultural distinctiveness, yet it was somewhat demeaned by being the language of the uneducated and unpropertied. Still, most of the people of Wales spoke Welsh. The very limited audibility resulted from the use of languages in Wales, Scotland, and France (Brittany) that had Celtic origins. Politically and economically, however, Wales was overwhelmingly obscured by England in the international political context. The British Empire was becoming the most powerful in the world at the end of this period, so Wales was only barely audible.

PERIOD III: NINETEENTH CENTURY TO 1960

The efficiency of the Welsh nonstate nation had declined enormously during the previous period. This decline was consciously engineered by English decision makers, whose main goal was the integration of Wales and England. The political component of this goal was achieved completely; the economic component was not completely achieved. Wales was a rural, agrarian society with an economy dominated by subsistence farming. This agricultural sector did not require extensive cross-border transactions. Therefore, economic transactions between England and Wales did not affect the bulk of the Welsh people as directly as the Welsh urban middle class and the aristocracy. By remaining in a rural environment with few transactions with England, most Welshmen retained their Welsh culture and identity. Thus, economically and socially the majority of the people of the Welsh nonstate nation were not very thoroughly integrated into England. Beginning, however, with the Industrial Revolution and up to the last decade, the integration of the previous period was accelerated so rapidly that economic integration became virtually complete and social integration appeared to be following this direction as well. Part of the dramatic weakening of the durability of the Welsh nonstate nation appears to have occurred inadvertently. The industrialization and urbanization of Wales was not a conscious policy decision on the part of English decision makers to destroy what remained of the Welsh nonstate nation. In the social sphere, however, English decision makers did initiate and enforce a language policy that has nearly destroyed the major social and identity component of the Welsh nonstate nation—the Welsh language. It can be argued, however, that the seeds of a major paradox were planted during this period. On the one hand, the Industrial Revolution and related phenomena such as urbanization, nationalism, democracy, and mass communication and transportation networks nearly eradicated the Welsh nonstate nation. On the other hand, however, they produced the decision makers and resources that appear in the next period both to have strengthened enormously the durability of the Welsh nonstate nation and to have significantly increased its audibility in the international context.

The major decision makers during this period belonged to political parties whose growth and dominance over other political organizations resulted from the expansion of the franchise toward universal suffrage, the ascendancy of the popularly elected House of Commons, and the related decline in power of the hereditary bodies of the monarchy and House of Lords. There were clearly other important decision makers belonging to voluntary organizations, which mainly took the form of interest groups such as trade unions and business federations. The enormous increase in the number of voluntary organizations appears to have accentuated the crucial role of political parties in the political process in Great Britain. In the early decades of the nineteenth century there was a movement toward political parties; consequently, most attempts by interest groups to influence government were directed through political parties. The

Conservative, Liberal, and Labour parties all played important roles with regard to the durability and audibility of Wales. It is possible to isolate important decision makers within these parties, most obviously the party leaders. Yet given the complexity of this historical period, it would be more helpful to refer to the more general political party policies than to specific individuals.

Decision Maker A: The Conservative Party

While the Conservative party formally emerged after the mid-nineteenth century, it clearly represented a party philosophy whose origins were embedded in "Old Toryism." The Old Tory members of Parliament did not belong to a political party in the contemporary sense, yet these Old Tories did adhere to a common view on many issues that were important to the Welsh nonstate nation. Beginning with William Pitt the Younger and ending with Harold Macmillan, the Tory or Conservative policies toward Wales have been consistent— Wales is an integral part of Great Britain.

Goals

The Conservative party policy toward Wales reflects an organic view of British society which requires the complete integration of ethnic and class units into a common British culture and society. More particularly, England and Wales should share common social, economic, and political institutions. Common political institutions, especially, are the cornerstone of the organic view of British society. Nearly every Conservative party leader has opposed any attempt to alter the once-dominant positions of the monarchy (at a minimum, in a symbolic manner), the House of Lords, and the Anglican Church, and they have been equally adamant in maintaining the nearly exclusive political power of the British Parliament throughout Great Britain. [9]

Resources

Throughout this period the Conservative party leaders were either the prime ministers or shadow prime ministers. In the former situation, especially when it was combined with a Conservative party majority in the House of Commons and up until 1911 in the House of Lords, the Conservative party leader exercised considerable control over the passage of laws. In addition, the prime minister retained ultimate control over the rapidly expanding civil and military bureaucracies. Even in opposition, the Conservative party leaders remained influential, since upon regaining the prime ministership they could overturn previous laws by passing new laws.

The Conservative party policy with regard to economic, social, and political issues directly affected the people of Wales. More specifically, issues such as the Corn Laws, the enfranchisement of the urban middle class and rural inhabitants, free trade, the disestablishment of the Anglican Church in Wales, and the establishment and maintenance of the welfare state were all important to the people of Wales. Naturally, the Conservative party leaders usually attempted to employ the above issues to the advantage of their party in terms of electoral support.

Beginning in the second half of the nineteenth century, the national organizational structure of the Conservative party also became important in achieving its goals. At the parliamentary level, allegiance to party policy was usually required in order to remain a Conservative party M. P. It was therefore costly for a Member of Parliament to challenge official Conservative party policy. Through the National Union, the Conservative party apparatus reached down to the "grass roots" level by involving common supporters in the decision-making process, albeit usually in an insignificant manner.

The Conservative party retained throughout this period the support of the large landowners throughout Wales as well as general electoral support in the rural and more anglicized constituencies, such as Radonshire and Pembrokeshire. After World War I many of the middle-class constituencies in the major urban centers of Newport, Cardiff, and Swansea supported the Conservative party policies and candidates. The Conservative party also relied heavily on its usually dominant traditional strength among the majority of the English constituencies. [10]

The international environment was an important resource for the Conservative party. This period begins with a threat from Napoleonic France. The Napoleonic Wars, along with the expansion of the British Empire, were important in solidifying loyalty to Britain. The two world wars demonstrated the necessity for an integrated British Isles since a hostile or neutral Ireland appeared dangerous to the security of Great Britain. [11]

Another resource in the international environment was the negative image of many of the nationalist movements after World War I. These movements were either fascist, communist, or anti-colonial; therefore, they could be perceived as anti-British. This negative image of nationalist movements was further reinforced by the opposition of some Welsh Nationalists to participating in a "clearly patriotic" war against the invading armies of fascist Germany. [12] The political turmoil and violence associated with Irish nationalism further discredited ethnic nationalist movements for many British people.

The Conservative party, while not the dominant party in Wales during most of this period, had considerable resources in the national and international environment that were important in weakening the durability and audibility of Wales.

Environment

The Conservative party faced a largely unfavorable environment in Wales from the mid-nineteenth century onward. The most dramatic changes in Wales resulted from the impact of the Industrial Revolution and the enfranchisement reforms. The Industrial Revolution occurred in Wales, partially because of the accessible coal fields and ocean ports such as Cardiff. The immigration pattern within Wales followed the universal pattern of industrializing societies, which meant a dramatic increase in the population of the southeastern industrial area. In Glamorgan, for example, the population increased by 235 percent during the period from 1860 to 1911. By the end of this historical period, three-fourths of the population of Wales was located in the southeastern belt. In addition there was an influx of Irish workers and Englishmen of all classes who came to work as laborers, managers, and government bureaucrats. The national profile of Wales changed quickly:

> The Industrial Revolution had different results in north and in south Wales. And it was more than an economic difference: it directly affected the growth of Welsh nationhood. For already at the outset of the 19th century, the Industrial Revolution was deepening and confirming the trends which divided Wales since Norman times. The South was becoming steadily more industrial, more urban, more anglican, while the North remained pastoral, rustic, more purely Welsh. [13]

In much of rural Wales the dominant social institution was the Welsh Nonconformist chapel—the church organization that formed the basis for religious participation for most non-Anglican Protestants in Wales. The politicization of the chapels occurred because of the official discrimination against Nonconformists. They were excluded from government office and from Oxford and Cambridge universities. Welsh rural society became "dominated internally by the chapel; the priest had a monopoly of power and was unchallengeable given the importance of religion in the system of social values."[14] The Conservative party support in Wales depended largely on the landed aristocracy, who belonged to the Anglican Church and spoke English.

They represented rural Wales in the House of Commons, in part because they were unopposed by the tenantry. Without a secret ballot the tenantry were exposed to economic retaliation from the landowners who monitored their votes. In addition, the landlords were commanders of the county militia and acted as the local judiciaries. While the anglicized landlord class dominated rural Wales politically and economically, they remained aloof from the dominant Nonconformist social life.

The preeminent political position of landlords was undermined beginning in 1867 with changes in the franchise. The Reform Acts of 1867 and 1885, as well as laws involving secret ballots, local government, and tenants' rights, altered the legal structure such that much of the basis for electoral support of the Conservative party was lost. In addition, the Conservative party was intimately linked to the Anglican Church, which the Nonconformists were trying to disestablish as the Church of Wales. Thus, the Nonconformist majority, which was becoming the dominant political force in rural Wales, turned largely to the Liberal party. With the exception of the border constituencies such as Flintshire, the Conservatives faced a largely unfavorable environment in rural Wales. [15]

Throughout most of this period the Conservative party did not, for various reasons, have much support in the urban-industrial area of south Wales. The industrialists prevented the landowners from monopolizing political power in this region. Both the industrialists and the workers were dependent on the export trade and therefore favored a policy of free trade. The Conservative party protectionist policies were thus strongly opposed by many industrialists and workers whose interests coincided at least on this issue. There was also far less social distance between the industrial elite and the common man in South Wales than between the elite and common man in North Wales because "many of the later industrialists, especially coalowners and managers, were Welsh. Nonconformists and their employees preserved a close relationship as they would combine against the anglicized squires who ruled Welsh society."[16]

Economic and ideological issues, centering on wages and class conflict, characterized industrial and class relations in South Wales for most of the first half of the twentieth century. In 1889 the Miners' Federation of Great Britain was founded in England and it included the South Wales Miners Federation. When economic conditions deteriorated during the early years of the twentieth century, the workers responded militantly by engaging in bitter strikes. The Independent Labour party also came into existence during the late nineteenth century, and its socialist ideology clearly opposed the classic elitism of the Conservative party. Finally the Labour party provided a well-organized political organization that the working class had never had before.

While structural changes occurred with regard to the organization of the working class, parallel changes had also taken place among the industrialists. The ownership of industries had become concentrated among fewer industrialists; consequently, much of the formerly paternalistic environment between the owners and the workers no longer existed. In the face of the growing militancy of the workers, the precipitous decline in the national fortunes of the Liberal party, and the concomitant rise in the strength of the Labour party, many of the industrialists and managers, as well as other segments of the middle and upper classes in the urban south, began supporting the Conservative party. *

Thus, the Conservative party lost its political base in much of rural Wales during the late nineteenth century. It did, however, gain some support among the urban middle and upper classes, especially after World War I.

Throughout the nineteenth century, the British Empire was dominant in the international environment. As mentioned above, the empire was more "ideologically" important to the Conservative party than to any of the other political parties. [17] By and large, individuals associated with the glorification of the empire were Conservatives, such as Wellington, Disraeli, Kipling, and Winston Churchill. While there were incidents such as the Boer War and the Suez Crisis, which were generally detrimental to the proempire adherents, on balance most of the British people appeared to take pride in the successes of the British Empire. [18] The two world wars, the Cold War, and the turmoil in Ireland were all historical events which could be interpreted as demonstrating the importance of the Conservative party's organic view of British society.

Components

In such a broad historical time period there were naturally a considerable number of issues on which the Conservative party took specific policy positions; however, there are two general categories that appear most directly relevant to the fortunes of the Welsh nonstate nation.

Component 1: Electoral, Social, and Economic Reforms. The Conservative party had to deal with the legacy that resulted from the

---

*The social and economic changes that contributed to the decline of the Liberal party and the rise of the Labour party will be discussed later.

policies of the Old Tories during the first half of the nineteenth
century. Disraeli was "aware that the Conservatives were associated
in the popular mind with Tory reaction and exclusiveness."[19] The
Tory strategy on electoral reform centered on an attempt to maintain
its electoral support among the large landowners in Wales, England,
and Scotland. Conservatives generally opposed the extension of the
franchise to certain classes of city workers and tenant farmers.
Beginning with Disraeli, however, the Conservative party leadership
appeared to accept the inevitability of major electoral reform, and
the party was actually instrumental in expanding the franchise in
certain cases.

   In the area of social and economic reform, the Conservatives
were usually associated with opposition to free trade, to nascent
workers' organizations, to the reform of working conditions, and to
secondary and general strikes by unions. They were also opposed to
landowner-tenant reforms and the disestablishment of the Anglican
Church in Wales, as well as to the creation of the welfare state and
the nationalization of industry. All of these issues received considerable support among the people of Wales. The Conservative party
policies on these issues rarely remained doctrinaire. Once these
issues were settled by legislation which was unfavorable to Conservative party policies, the Conservative party leadership did not usually
seek any substantial repeal. Thus, the Conservative party remained
quite flexible throughout this period with regard to electoral and
social reform, since its successive leaders regularly appeared to
try to adapt party policy to the exigencies of electoral politics. This
flexibility accounts, in part, for the increase in its electoral support
among middle-class voters in urban Wales.

   The Conservative Party policy toward the massive legislation
passed by the Labour government effecting both the welfare state
and the nationalization of certain industries after World War II was
quite flexible. They favored, for example, the nationalization of the
coal industry while, at least temporarily, opposing the nationalization
of the steel industry. Welfare legislation acts, involving the national
insurance and national health services, were left largely intact by the
Conservative governments of the final decade of this historical
period.

Component 2: Welsh Nation and State. For most of this period, Conservative party policies were usually opposed to any bills which
appeared to favor Welsh culture at the expense of the Old Tory view
of the British culture. The major cultural issues were often interrelated and usually involved the Welsh language, the Nonconformist
religion, and the position of the Anglican Church in Wales. Successive
Conservative party policies were generally opposed to the preservation

and subsequent resurgence of the Welsh language. English was perceived to be central to the British culture, while Welsh was perceived
to be "a manifold barrier to the moral progress and commercial
prosperity of the [Welsh] people."[20] The rigid moral judgment
against the Welsh language was dropped in the twentieth century, but
its perceived negative economic and divisive cultural consequences
remained part of the Conservative party policy. In addition, the
Welsh language was nearly extinct in the border constituencies, in
certain areas of Pembrokshire, and in the two major areas of Cardiff
and Newport. There was little support, therefore, for the Welsh
language in the areas where there was substantial electoral support
for the Conservative party. [21]

The attempt to disestablish the Church of Wales in the late
nineteenth century was strongly opposed by members of the Conservative party. The Anglican Church was considered a basic British institution which was entitled to both the economic support and, at least,
the moral allegiance of all of the people of Wales. As late as 1886,
not one bishop in Wales was a Welsh-speaking Welshman. The position
of the Anglican Church toward the Welsh nation was revealed at the
time by the loyal Conservative party member and leader of the Church
of Wales, the bishop of St. David, who in 1886 maintained that "Wales
is at present nothing more than the Highlands of England without a
Highland line: it is a geographical expression."[22]

Most Conservatives opposed the education reforms which
involved, in part, the attempt to remove the control of the Anglican
and Nonconformist churches in the rapidly expanding mass-education
structures. As with other reforms, once the educational reform bills
were passed and the Disestablishment Bill was passed in 1922, the
Conservative policy did not include serious proposals to repeal the
legislation.

Home Rule for Wales was opposed by the Conservative party.
The attempt to establish a Welsh Parliament with control over the
domestic affairs of Wales was, in the Conservative view, a prelude
to the disintegration of Great Britain. The next inevitable step would
be the creation of an independent Welsh nation-state. Conservative
party members were instrumental in defeating and delaying Home
Rule for Ireland and in the bitter struggle to keep Ulster as part of
the United Kingdom. There is far less geographic and cultural
distance separating Wales and England than Ireland and England;
consequently, the Home Rule movement involving Wales stood little
chance of even "flexible" treatment at the hands of the Conservative
members of Parliament. In effect, the disestablishment of the
Church of Wales could be tolerated ex post facto, but to diminish
the political power of Parliament in Wales through Home Rule was
intolerable.

Overall, the Conservative party policies had an important impact on the Welsh nonstate nation by furthering the integration of Wales and England in a British society. Although the party opposed many of the enormous number of political, social, and economic reforms that took place between 1800 and 1960, the most important element of Conservative party policy was the acceptance of reform once it became law. This flexibility was hardly designed directly for Wales, but it appeared very successful, since the Conservative party goal of an organic British society excluding any effective Welsh NSN seemed by the end of the period to have become a reality. The dominant issues in Wales after World War II had nothing to do with the Welsh NSN. The Nonconformist and language issues were simply unimportant in comparison to the economic issues of inflation, unemployment, and trade union strife. [23] In effect, as long as the various reforms did not constitute an absolute challenge to the political integrity of Great Britain, the Conservative party leaders usually accepted reform. One consequence was that after World War I the Conservative party was able to appeal to the urban middle class in Wales; the social, economic, and political reforms which appealed to this class did not become entangled with issues directly involving the Welsh NSN. The two sets of issues remained largely independent, partly because Conservative party leaders were flexible with the former set of issues while being far less flexible with the latter. At the end of this historical period, however, Sir Anthony Eden and Harold Macmillan assented to the establishment of Cardiff as the capital of the Welsh nation. This was a tacit recognition of the existence of Wales as a distinctive cultural entity within Great Britain. The creation of a minister for Welsh Affairs in the cabinet did constitute a slight amount of administrative devolution. There was no flexibility concerning the absolute political dominance of Westminster over the Welsh nation, however.

Decision Maker B: The Liberal Party

Up to World War I the Liberal party was dominant throughout much of Wales. One of the major leaders of this party was the one-time Welsh nationalist, Lloyd George. In many ways the political career of this man exemplified the intensity of the historical and structural factors that prevented the strengthening of the durability and audibility of the Welsh NSN. Lloyd George, who was from northern rural Wales, tried unsuccessfully to influence the Liberal party toward Home Rule for Wales, but he failed to unite the Liberal M. P. s from Wales on this issue—they split partly on the traditional north-south basis. He eventually joined the Liberal cabinet and became the leader of the Liberal party in the midst of World War I. Given the exigencies of first directing the British war effort and then leading the Liberal party in British-wide elections, Lloyd George virtually ignored the Home Rule issue. The international environment and national political party environment thus effectively overwhelmed most issues involving the Welsh nonstate nation.

The rise and fall of the Liberal party in Wales reflected the dramatic structural changes in the economic and social configuration in Wales and Great Britain that occurred during this period.

Goals

The Liberal party policy emphasized the desire to transform Wales from a society dominated by an anglicized, landed elite to one in which self-made individuals of accomplishment would govern with the ascent of the average educated and moral Welshman. Individual rights were primary, while hereditary rights were clearly secondary. Opportunity, competition, and mobility were important. For much of this period Liberal party policy supported the status quo with regard to the political relationship between Wales and England. Some Welsh Liberal M. P. s, led by Lloyd George and Thomas E. Ellis, formed the Cymru Fydd organization within the Liberal party with the aim of including Home Rule for Wales as a goal of the Liberal party. After World War II the Liberal party policy did move more toward the goal of the preservation of the Welsh nation through the enhancement of the Welsh culture and language and the creation of an autonomous Welsh political entity. By this time, however, the Liberal party had declined precipitously, reaching the point of near extinction at the end of this period. In spite of this decline, its goals were instrumental in changing the course of the Welsh NSN.

Resources

The most important resource of the Liberal party was its ability to become the governing political party of the United Kingdom. Most of the governments of the second half of the nineteenth century and early twentieth century were derived primarily from the ranks of the Liberal party. As the party of government, the Liberal prime ministers and members of Parliament were able to translate many of its policies into law. Like the Conservative party, the Liberals developed a nationwide organization, the National Liberal Federation, which facilitated a link between the parliamentary members of the Liberal party, party activists at the constituent level, and the rank-and-file voters.

Another resource was the reform legacy that carried over from the Old Whig philosophy, which was the precursor of the Liberal party radical or populist image. Reform was central to both philosophies. This image intensified, beginning with the Old Whig Grey Reform Ministry in 1830. The expansion of the franchise to the middle class and other electoral reforms, the drive to repeal the Corn Laws, and the attempt to repeal the repressive Six Acts passed by the Old Tory government of Lord Liverpool laid the basis for the reform image that was passed on to the Liberal party. The great Liberal leader, William Gladstone, solidified this image with a continual series of reform legislation throughout his numerous ministries. Nearly all of these reforms had a direct impact in Wales, since they were designed to undercut the traditional dominance of the large landowner, the Anglican Church, and the Conservative party in most of Wales.

The Liberal party also provided the vehicle for the political ambitions of middle-class Nonconformist Welshmen. With an expanding middle class, this was an important resource in the Liberal party's electoral dominance in Wales during much of the nineteenth century and, in rural Wales, throughout most of the first half of the twentieth century, as well.

All of the above resources of the Liberal party were symbolized and expanded in the political career of Lloyd George. He was an emotional orator who railed against the vested interests which represented an anglicized and squire-dominated Wales. As a cabinet minister and then prime minister, Lloyd George continued the tradition of reform which was so popular in Wales through World War I.

Environment

The industrialization of Wales affected not only the urban south-eastern region but also the villages and towns. Industrial areas arose which were:

> populated predominately by Welsh-speaking immigrants from the rural hinterland. In each village, there was reproduced the pattern of institutions of Welsh life: the chapel, the debating and religious societies, voluntary associations and the Welsh language press. With their decentralized structure, lack of hierarchy and reliance upon local cooperation and support, the chapels favoured independence of outlook and the development of a radical perspective. [24]

This radical perspective benefited the Liberal party, since its policy was largely consistent with a populist view. As mentioned previously, many of the industrialists and managers also supported the Liberal party because of the importance of the export markets, especially for coal and steel. Free trade appeared essential to the economic viability of industrial Wales.

After World War I the depopulation of rural Wales accelerated, and many of those individuals who migrated to urban Wales and England belonged to the generations of children who had received their education in English. The Education Reform Act of 1870 required that all elementary education in Wales be in the English language. This reform act also removed the Anglican and Nonconformist Churches from the educational system. Other educational reform acts created universal education and established a Welsh university system. Most of these changes during this period contributed to the decline of the Nonconformist influence in Wales. In addition, many of the issues that linked the Liberal party and the Nonconformist element of the Welsh culture had been resolved through social and electoral reforms. By the beginning of World War I the major domestic issues had become economic ones.

The disruptive impact of World War I on the British economy was severe. The reintegration of millions of soldiers, the collapse of the German economy, war debts to the United States, and the loss of markets in the Dominion countries and to the United States and Japan all put a dangerous strain on the British pound sterling. The cycle of inflation, recession, and unemployment struck industrial Wales particularly hard. The attempts to nationalize British industries by removing competition among industries within Great Britain resulted in the centralization of industry and management. The trade union movement had expanded dramatically by World War I, and it too developed an extensive organizational infrastructure throughout Great Britain.

Economic issues polarized politics in Great Britain on a class basis and overshadowed the links between the traditional cultural issues (for example, religion) and special interest groups such as the Anglican Church and large landowners. The Liberal party philosophy and policies during this period were still based on laissez-faire economics and continued to emphasize issues of morality such as alcoholism and urban decadence. While these issues were still important in rural northern Wales, three-fourths of the people of Wales were living in the industrial southeast. [25]

The Liberal party was unable to cope with the bitter intraparty divisions involving the two dominant Liberal party leaders, Lloyd George and Herbert Asquith. The party disarray intensified in the

Great Depression. The legacy of free trade and laissez-faire appeared totally inappropriate in such a drastic economic crisis; consequently, the Liberal party faced a largely inhospitable environment in most of Wales and the rest of Great Britain throughout the middle decades of the twentieth century. [26]

Components

Component 1: Electoral, Social, and Economic Reforms. Beginning with the Grey Reform ministry and culminating with Lloyd George's ministries, the Liberal philosophy and policies supported the extensive expansion of the franchise. The destruction of electoral constituencies which were controlled by the numerically small landed aristocracy marked the beginning of serious electoral reform. The Liberals supported the successive expansion of the franchise, expecially since it struck at the hardcore support of the Conservative party. In addition, the final bastion of the Old Tory conception of estates or organic society, the House of Lords, became a target of Liberal party policy. The Liberal party Prime Minister Asquith led the bitter struggle to pass the Parliament Bill which effectively reduced the House of Lords to a debating and ratifying body.

     With regard to social reform, the Liberals were instrumental in passing legislation which diminished the influence of the Anglican Church in the educational process. The disestablishment of the Church of Wales was favored as was the creation of a Welsh university system. Economic reforms were supported in the area of child labor and working conditions, but there was considerable ambivalence toward trade-union rights. Certain Liberal party leaders, such as Asquith, did not favor trade unions, yet the Liberal party, beginning in the late nineteenth century, joined various coalitions which included the trade-union-supported Labour M. P. s. Cooperation with the socialist and urban-based Labour party was a difficult maneuver given the laissez-faire Liberal philosophy and the Liberal party's dependence on the rural electorate such as in northern Wales.

Component 2: Welsh Nation and State. Liberal party policy opposed Home Rule for Wales for most of this period. There was, however, a strong link between the Liberal party policies and the Nonconformist culture. The Liberal party was clearly an important vehicle for integrating much of the population of Wales into the British political system. [27] The inability of Plaid Cymru to gain any serious electoral support in rural Wales during this period can be attributed in part to the success of the Liberal party in representing the interests of most of the people of rural Wales. The co-optation of Lloyd George into

the Liberal party hierarchy and the concomitant decline in his support
for Welsh nationalism reflected the integrative pull of national political
parties and the weakening of the durability of the Welsh nonstate
nation.

The components of Liberal party policy were largely implemented
into law by the 1920s; however, the precipitous decline in Welsh
speakers and the urbanization and industrialization of Wales had
radically altered the environment in Wales. A new set of decision
makers took advantage of this new environment at the expense of the
Liberal party.

Decision Maker B: The Labour Party

Unlike the Conservative and Liberal parties which evolved from
political associations from within Parliament, the Labour party was
founded by extraparliamentary groups. The participants in the Trades
Union Congress (TUC) meeting in 1899 decided to organize in order
to help elect M. P. s who would represent the interests of the Labour
movement in the House of Commons. The Labour party from its incep-
tion has been intimately linked to British trade unions. Members of
the Social Democratic Federation, Independent Labour party, and
Fabians were involved, to a small degree, with the formation of the
Labour party; however, it was not a socialist party at this point. An
extensive national organization evolved quickly including a National
Executive Committee, members of Parliament, and constituency
organizations. While an elaborate structure unified the various elements of the Labour party, it was best characterized as a "coalition
of pressure groups."[28] There were many decision makers within
this party, but the party leader in the House of Commons was the key
decision maker, and the official party policy was usually an accurate
reflection of the key decision maker's position on the issues.

Goals

The most consistent goal of the Labour party has been to unite
the working class throughout Great Britain in order to improve their
standard of living. The creation of a socialist society also became a
major goal after World War I. Given the different values of the many
pressure groups that constitute the Labour party, it is difficult to
maintain that this was one of the main goals throughout the period.

With regard to Wales, the goal was the unification of the working class in Wales with the working classes of other regions of the
United Kingdom. The electoral strength of the Labour party, particularly since World War II, has depended on its predominant electoral

support in the Welsh and Scottish nonstate nations. While the Labour party did acknowledge the existence of the Welsh nation, its leaders did little to support the cultural and political ambitions of the Welsh NSN. The goal of Home Rule was rather ambiguously a part of the Labour party policy for the 1945 elections. Once Labour was the party of government, however, it ignored the issue, or as Labour Prime Minister Clement Attlee maintained,

> I have every sympathy with those who are enthusiastic for the just rights of nationalities . . . . I note the attempts of the Liberals and the Tories to angle for the Welsh nationalist vote. If they are in earnest, why did they do nothing during the years of their power?[29]

Resources

The Labour party was highly organized with extensive "grass roots" or constituent-level participation. The trade unions provided a solid financial base. The combination of individuals committed to the trade union movement and those committed to socialist ideology resulted in a highly motivated party organization. Beginning in 1924 the Labour party became the second strongest party in the House of Commons and its party leaders led or were involved in various coalition governments between the two world wars. Labour Prime Minister Ramsey MacDonald introduced essentially liberal, rather than socialist-oriented, legislation, thereby enhancing the Labour party's respectibility among the general electorate. The constructive participation of Labour party leaders in the national government coalitions during the Great Depression and World War II perpetuated this moderate image.[30]

The landslide Labour victory in 1945 and the subsequent creation of the welfare society was a critical resource. The enormous expansion of social services was dramatic, and it was accomplished in an orderly and largely successful manner. Also, the nationalization of various industries, with one or two major exceptions, was undertaken quite smoothly. The Labour government of Clement Atlee established a powerful legacy for this; the Labour party under his leadership developed a dynamic and practical plan of action with regard to alleviating the hardships of industrial society on the working class in Wales and throughout the rest of Great Britain. In addition, the strong link between the economically powerful trade unions and the Labour party were helpful to labour governments in obtaining the cooperation of the trade union members with government policies. This close association was particularly relevant in Wales where the trade union movement was strong and contained certain radical elements. One of the major figures in the Labour party, Aneurin Bevan, symbolized the link between the Welsh working class, socialism, and the Labour party. The image, therefore, of the Labour party as the party of the working class had been a definite resource in industrially dominated Wales. Labour won 27 of the 36 Welsh seats in the House of Commons in 1945. The role of the Labour party in the completion of the welfare state virtually institutionalized its image as the party of the working class in Wales, as in the rest of Great Britain.

Environment

The growth of trade unions during the mid-nineteenth century, the industrialization of southeastern Wales, and the subsequent rural-urban population shift, created a highly favorable environment for the Labour Party in Wales. Trade unions were opposed by the Conservative party. The Taff-Vale decision, handed down by the Conservative-dominated House of Lords in its role as the highest appeal court, reflected the severity of antiunion sentiment among elements of the traditional power structure. As a result of this decision, unions were held legally responsible for any damages caused by their union members; consequently, employers could financially weaken the unions through lawsuits. While the Liberal party did represent many of the interests of the unions, its party philosophy of laissez-faire and the possibility of favorably disposed party leaders, such as Asquith, were not a sound basis for trade union representation in Parliament. The political importance of the attitude of the parties toward trade unions increased with the growth of the trade-union movement, as reflected in the rise in membership of unions affiliated with the TUC from 1.25 million in 1900 to 6.50 million in 1920.[31]

By the 1930s, most of the electoral and social reforms begun early in the nineteenth century had run their course. The dominant issues of the new period were symbolized by the bitter strikes immediately preceding World War I and the General Strike in 1926. The inflation, recession, and unemployment cycles were particularly difficult on the working class. The distribution of income was highly skewed toward the numerically few upper class. The depression of the 1930s hit the Welsh working class in Wales more severely than in any other region and helped to accelerate the emigration of young people from Wales to England and abroad.[32] The war effort required further sacrifice; but it did indicate that massive government involvement in the British economy was hardly incompatible with productivity. Thus, the environment was quite favorable to the Labour party's policies creating extensive welfare reform and the nationalization of certain industries such as coal and transportation.

The implementation of the welfare reform and the nationalization policy, particularly with regard to coal and steel, solidified the Labour party's dominant position in Wales. The Labour party-working class link meant that the working class majority in Wales was directly integrated into the British political system. The Labour party provided the vehicle that effectively represented many of the Welsh working class' interests in the economic issues that had created considerable strife since the turn of the century. The fundamental change that many of the working class individuals in Wales had sought had largely been brought about by the Atlee Labour party government and left generally intact by subsequent Conservative party governments.

Components

Component 1: Economic and Welfare Reforms. Labour party policy under Ramsey MacDonald was based on socialist rhetoric, yet the exigencies of coalition governments and the complexity and gravity of the economic turmoil of the 1920s and 1930s transformed the actual policy into a basically Liberal party policy. No fundamental economic or welfare changes were introduced. The moderate policy positions of MacDonald split the Labour party, and orthodox Labourites, led by Arthur Henderson, kicked MacDonald out of the party.

The major economic and welfare reforms date from the Atlee government of the 1945-51 period. The list of welfare reforms is too long to present, but the National Insurance Act and the National Health Services Act both demonstrate the immensity of the change. The former act virtually insures individuals from complete financial destitution from birth until death. The latter act nationalizes all the health services and makes them available to all British citizens at a nominal cost.

The major economic reform occurred with the nationalization of the mining, railways, civil aviation, telecommunications, electricity, and gas industries and the Bank of England. The attempt to nationalize the steel industry was basically unsuccessful. These reforms reflected a basic tenet of the Labour party philosophy concerning the debilitating results of private ownership of the major means of production and competition. *

---

*The nationalization component of the Labour party policy during the 1950s created divisive factions within the party. While other issues were also involved, the primacy and extent of further nationalization of industries split the coalition of pressure groups and Labour M. P. s into the moderate Hugh Gaitskell faction and the orthodox, or fundamental socialist, Bevan faction.

Component 2: Welsh Nation and State. The electoral strength of the
Labour party was in the coal valleys and working-class sections of the
urban areas and towns, where the Welsh language and Home Rule
issues were not very important. Still, the Labour party was dominant
in Wales so its policy was indirectly favorable to the Welsh sentiments.
This policy position appeared to avoid the image of an insensitive
English-dominated Labour party. [33] The Atlee government did little
in this policy area, partly because internecine party divisions concerning other policies seemed to preoccupy the Labour party during its
years as the loyal opposition party at the end of this period.

Decision Maker C: Plaid Cymru
(Welsh Nationalist Party)

The defeat of several Home Rule bills, especially during Lloyd
George's tenure as prime minister, provided the impetus for various
supporters of the Welsh Home Rule Movement to form Plaid Cymru
(The Welsh Nationalist party) in 1925. The leading decision maker
in this movement was John Saunders Lewis, who authored the party's
manifesto. In addition to his tenure as the official leader of Plaid
Cymru, he became its spiritual leader in large part because of the
intensity of his commitment to the Welsh nonstate nation.

Goals

The general goal of Plaid Cymru was the preservation of the
Welsh nation. The related goals involved the rehabilitation of the
Welsh language in Wales and the creation of an autonomous Welsh
political entity.

Resources

Plaid Cymru had few resources in obtaining its goals. It
lacked an extensive political party structure such as those that
characterized the Labour and Conservative parties. There were few,
if any, interest groups that could ensure a solid financial base to
establish and maintain a political party organizational apparatus to
cover even Wales. The dramatic decline in the number of Welsh
speakers, depopulation, and high unemployment in Wales were all
issues that could have been manipulated as a resource, particularly
during electoral campaigns. Still, these issues simply were not put
together in an effective party policy package; consequently, Plaid
Cymru suffered from a one-goal party image. The supporters of
Plaid Cymru appeared to be romanticists who were preoccupied

with the Welsh language and a potential Welsh state, but who largely
ignored the more prominent and immediate economic issues. John
Saunders Lewis could be viewed as a resource because he was an
intense and potentially powerful political personality. However, his
participation in violence against the British state in a time of
increasing international peril during the interwar years diminished
his effectiveness and exacerbated Plaid Cymru's romantic image.
Violent acts carried out by Plaid Cymru supporters and the personal
opposition on the part of these and other party supporters toward
conscription and the British involvement in World War II also tainted
the party as unpatriotic. [34]

During the 1950s, however, Plaid Cymru began to lay the foundations for a mass-based political party. Its supporters started to
run for local offices and to organize at the grass-roots level. Also,
Saunders Lewis, although he had bitterly withdrawn from active
politics, became an important symbol of Welsh nationalism to postwar generations. In addition, the Welsh university system provided
the institutional basis for a new group of leaders for Plaid Cymru and
other organizations that supported the Welsh NSN. * The international
and domestic environments changed quite dramatically after World
War II; consequently, the socialization experience of the postwar
generations, which reached maturity during the 1960s and 1970s,
differed significantly from the socialization of Saunders Lewis and
his cohorts. In effect the Welsh university system and the post-
World War II socialization experience were important resources for
Plaid Cymru, particularly in terms of leadership recruitment.

Environment

At least until the post-World War II years, the environment
was extremely unfavorable for Plaid Cymru during this historical
period. The co-optation of the Welsh aristocracy into the dominant
Anglican culture left the Welsh NSN leaderless at the beginning of
the period.

The continuous expansion of the franchise to the middle class
and certain segments of the working class in the nineteenth and
early twentieth centuries coincided with the evolution of the Liberal,
Conservative, and Labour parties. The Liberal party was clearly
identified with the Nonconformist religious issues that were so vital

---

*The Welsh University Colleges are part of an integrated Wales-
English higher educational system; consequently, they are not a Welsh
nationalist "institution" which serves as an exclusive recruiting source
for Plaid Cymru.

to the preservation of the Welsh nation. By the time Plaid Cymru had come into existence, Nonconformism was no longer a critical political issue to the majority of the Welsh people, and where it remained important, Liberal party partisanship already was institutionalized. The Welsh language issue was intertwined with Nonconformism, so it was difficult for Plaid Cymru to make inroads in terms of electoral and financial support in much of rural Wales where Nonconformism and the Welsh language were still commonplace. [35]

By the post-World War I period, which most prominently included the demise of the Liberal party, the Conservative party had established itself as the party of the urban middle class. The anglicization of the upper class that occurred centuries before had now taken effect among many individuals of the urban middle class. In addition, class became the dominant factor in defining the basis of electoral support. Most of the expanding urban middle class in Wales was tied, therefore, to the Conservative party because of cultural and economic affinities. [36]

The dramatic electoral success of the Labour party during the interwar years was epitomized in Labour's complete domination of the working-class vote in Wales, particularly in the heavily unionized mining valleys and industrial centers.

In effect, the political environment was characterized by essentially class-based political parties. There were definite deviations from this pattern in regions such as Cardiganshire in Wales where the Nonconformist legacy remained politically important and where the Liberal party retained its traditional electoral support. The political environment during this period is most succinctly summarized by the statement that "class is the basis of British party politics; all else is embellishment and detail."[37]

Plaid Cymru, therefore, was faced with an incredibly unfavorable domestic environment. The international environment was equally bleak. Great Britain had just suffered the trauma and exhaustion of World War I and during the interwar years had to cope with the economic chaos of the 1920s, the Great Depression, and the fascist nationalisms of Germany, Italy, and Japan. Plaid Cymru philosophy and party policies clearly were not tied to a fascist conception of nationalism, yet a political party advocating any brand of nationalism would have faced an unfavorable environment in Great Britain during the interwar period. In particular, the turmoil associated with Irish nationalism and the military dangers posed by Ireland during both world wars tainted Welsh nationalism. The advent of the Cold War, with the chaos and violence associated with the dismantling of the British Empire, perpetuated the unfavorable environment to the end of this period.

Components

Component 1: Social and Economic Reforms. Under Saunders Lewis' leadership, Plaid Cymru policy in these areas was basically oriented toward the defense of an already-dying rural-based culture. Party policy took exception to the perceived colonial relationship that effectively existed because of England's domination of the Welsh economy. There was, however, very little specific policy emphasis on social and economic change, with the major exception of the desire to preserve and enhance the Welsh language. Toward the end of this period there were attempts to design a more sophisticated policy analysis concerning economic issues, yet the cultural and political issues were dominant in Plaid Cymru policy.

Component 2: The Welsh Nation and State. The major effort to obtain political autonomy for Wales centered on the electoral process. Plaid Cymru had neither sufficient financial resources nor extensive grass roots support, so it could only field a limited number of candidates during the campaigns that took place toward the final decades of this period. It was extremely difficult to arouse the electorate on issues such as the preservation of the Welsh language and the destruction of the Welsh culture. Plaid Cymru did not win any parliamentary seats and received only a negligible percentage of the popular vote in Wales. The electoral path simply was unsuccessful throughout this period.

Saunders Lewis, along with two other Plaid Cymru members, resorted to some limited violence to popularize their related goals of the preservation of the Welsh nation and the need for self-government in Wales. In 1936 Lewis helped set fire to the Royal Air Force Bombing School in South Caernervonshire. Upon being arrested, Lewis and his colleagues admitted to committing a political act on behalf of Wales because the site of the new bombing school was a valuable cultural property of Wales. They believed that it had been destroyed without the consent of Welshmen. During the criminal trial Lewis refused to use the English language. A Welsh jury refused to convict Lewis, so they were tried before an English jury in the Old Bailey in London and were convicted. The only immediate consequence of this violence was that "Saunders Lewis withdrew from public life a bitter man. His actions to draw attention to the RAF station, the legal position of the Welsh language, and the state of Wales generally, had, in his eyes, failed."[38]

Throughout the decade of the 1950s, Plaid Cymru concentrated on establishing its presence in local council governments within Wales and lending support to those individuals who tried to persuade the national parties toward Home Rule for Wales.

Evaluation of the Welsh System, 1800–1960

The efficiency of the Welsh nonstate nation was at its lowest point during the nineteenth century and the first six decades of the twentieth century. The durability of the Welsh nonstate nation in previous periods rested, primarily, on the pervasiveness of the Welsh language and the relative isolation of the majority of Welshmen from outside cultural influences. Industrialization, urbanization, mass communications, and the international political context radically altered the environment in Wales. Wales became primarily an industrial, urban society intricately tied to England through mass communications, mass transportation, centralized national political party structures, centralized business and union organizations, and a centralized educational structure. The international political context contributed to the pro–British environment because the British Empire reached its zenith during the nineteenth century, while during the first six decades of the twentieth century Britain faced continual threats by various ideological movements in Europe and in the empire. The British culture became secular and class–oriented. The standard of living and economic growth became paramount. Political power depended primarily on economic issues. The aforementioned paradox occurred because compulsory mass education and the rapid growth of universities helped to create a new elite. Wealth was no longer the exclusive criterion for entry into the elite. Mass-based political parties covering the entire spectrum of political issues sought political power. The modern political party structure facilitated the entry of broader-based elites. Although Plaid Cymru was not organized as a mass-based political party in Wales, its mere presence suggested that a nascent elite existed which favored the Welsh nonstate nation. The idea of nationalism was also pervasive during this period, becoming the relevant ideology of many nonstate nations. The two world wars and colonial wars of independence had involved various nationalist ideologies. Since Wales was once an independent state and was still culturally distinctive as well as a contiguous geographic entity, the appeal of nationalism could hardly be ignored by some of the new Welsh elite, especially university-educated individuals. While ethnic nationalism could not compete successfully with British nationalism during this period, the international context changed rather dramatically. The rise of the European Economic Community, the dissolving of the British Empire, and the diminishing intensity of the Cold War would eventually create a much more favorable environment for ethnic nationalism.

The Welsh nonstate nation was hardly audible during this period. Although there were a few decision makers who supported the Welsh nonstate nation, they simply did not have the organizational format

to participate in the international context. It is not difficult to see
why scholars failed to view Wales as a nonstate nation. Wales had a
few nationalist leaders, but unlike other periods, the Welsh nation
appeared on the verge of extinction. The key symbol of Welshness
was the Welsh language and only a relatively few people, primarily
those living in the rural northwest of Wales, spoke Welsh. The
anglicization of Wales appeared coterminous with the industrialization
of Wales. The Labour party became one of the two contenders of political power at the end of this period and it dominated the Welsh
political scene. These trends weakened the durability of the Welsh
nonstate nation to a point where it seemed inaccurate to refer to
Wales as a system. The rapidly declining importance of the Welsh
language and culture augured the potential end of the Welsh nonstate
nation. This very threat, however, helped to contribute to a weak
trend in the opposite direction during the end of this period. Cardiff
was recognized by Westminster as the official capital of Wales and a
secretary of state for Wales was appointed.

PERIOD IV: 1960 TO 1975

The sharp intensification of the political movement for the
devolution of power to Wales and the concerted efforts to enhance
the official position of the Welsh language distinguishes this period
from the previous one. The durability and audibility of the Welsh
nonstate nation increases substantially as a variety of critical resources become available to the decision makers who support the
Welsh NSN; both the domestic and international environments become
far more favorable in terms of providing resources for these decision
makers. The overwhelming importance of political parties in determining the fate of the Welsh NSN is evident since nearly all the key
decision makers in this period belong to these organizations.

Decision Maker A: The Conservative Party

Of the various leaders of the Conservative party between 1960
and 1975, Edward Heath played the most prominent role. The current
leader, Margaret Thatcher, will undoubtedly play a major role in
the following years primarily because of the introduction of various
Home Rule proposals in the House of Commons in November 1975.
Thatcher can in no way be the dominant Conservative party figure
that Heath was during this period, because party policy generally
reflected the goals of Heath and other important Conservative party
leaders. There were exceptions, such as the issue of the European

Common Market, which created divisions within the party elite, but on most issues there was considerable support of Heath's leadership at least until 1974. *

Goals

The primary goal of the Conservative party with regard to Wales remained the complete political and economic integration of Wales and England and the dominance of the British culture in Wales. All of the policy positions on the Welsh language issue and Welsh Home Rule were largely defined by the traditional Old Tory organic conception of British society.

Resources

The Conservative party was either the party of government or the loyal opposition party from 1960 to 1975. In the former role, the Conservative party was in the position to meet the major demands of the people of Wales. Conservative party policies involving social services, housing, cost of living, and unemployment became law. The British cabinet and bureaucracy were continuously and directly involved in the lives of nearly all the people of Wales. Local government was dependent on the national institutions as was the maintenance of transportation networks, education, and mass media. Cabinet decisions usually determined, for example, the costs of eye glasses, school lunches, train tickets, the language of instruction in schools, the closing of coal mines, and, for many families, rent increases. As the party of government, the Conservatives were perceived as being able to affect the dominant economic concerns of the people of Wales:

> . . . it is plain that our sample (2, 009 respondents) as a whole saw the Government as being of great significance for their economic condition. Even among those who gave personal reasons for their circumstances having improved or worsened, almost two-thirds were prepared

---

*The successive defeats of the Conservative party in the last two General Elections and Heath's subsequent bitter withdrawal as party leader revealed considerable disapproval of his leadership. It is difficult, however, to decide whether Heath's personality and leadership style or his policies, especially toward the trade unions, was the more critical factor in determining the dissatisfaction among Conservative party parliamentary members.

to say that the actions of government could affect how
well off they were. Some (7 percent) actually cited
the Government's fiscal or monetary policies as the
direct reason for their change in prosperity. [39]

The ability of Heath and the Conservative party to influence the
economic needs of the people of Wales was an important resource,
which is reflected in the strong empirical relationship between
economic issues, especially unemployment, and party popularity.
The unexpected Conservative party victory in the 1970 General Elections can be attributed in part to the perception among a certain segment of the electorate in Wales and, particularly England, that Heath
would be better able to hold down the rate of inflation that Wilson,
who obviously had failed. [40] Another related resource was the
Conservative party image, intensely cultivated by Heath, of resisting
the inflationary pressures and industrial turmoil created by the
trade unions and wildcat strikes. This image was especially important to the middle class in Wales because of the militancy of the
Welsh coal miners. *
The European Economic Community was also a resource for
the Conservatives. Heath maintained that the British economy and
the material standard of living would benefit from Britain's membership in the EEC. The economic dynamism and capital strength of
many of the EEC countries, such as West Germany and the Netherlands, were relevant to the Conservative party view that investment
capital and assured markets were needed to stimulate the stagnant
Welsh economy. The EEC is also a resource because it is likely that
other conservative political parties in the member countries would
form a coalition against the formal recognition of NSNs within the
EEC.
As in the previous period, the Conservative party had a powerful resource in the electoral dominance of the densely populated Midlands and southeastern regions in England.
Finally, with eight M. P. s from Wales the Conservative party
was the second strongest party in Wales in terms of electoral support.
In the last three General Elections the party received an average
29 percent of the vote in rural Wales and 24 percent in industrial

---

*The author surveyed a random sample of 300 individuals in
the rural Caernarvonshire electoral constituency and 300 individuals
in an urban Cardiff electoral constituency in 1970-71. Most of the
middle-class respondents maintained that trade union strikes and
inflation were the primary problems when asked what were the most
pressing issues facing British society.

south Wales.[41] The Conservative party has retained a significant foothold of support in Wales and, equally important, it was significantly stronger than the electoral support for either the Liberal party or Plaid Cymru. This was essential for the Conservative party goal of maintaining the integral political link between England and Wales, since the level of support in Wales in conjunction with the much higher level of electoral support for the Labour party meant that an overwhelming majority of the electorate in Wales remained within the national political parties. This maintenance of traditional party partisanship in Wales was not evident in Scotland where the Scottish Nationalist party received 30 percent of the vote and replaced the Conservatives as the second strongest party.[42] This difference between Scotland and Wales became a resource in that it helped substantiate the Conservative party claim that Wales should be treated differently than Scotland in the devolution question.

Environment

The Conservative party faced an increasingly unfavorable environment in Wales and the Scottish nonstate nation. The Old Tory view was strongly predicated on the primary identity being British. Survey data indicated the primary identity of the majority of the peoples in Wales and Scotland was with their respective NSN rather that the British nation-state. British identity remained primary only in England.[43]

In the previous period one of the three national political parties had dominated the political environment in Wales and Scotland to the near total exclusion of ethnic-based parties. The Scottish Nationalist party (SNP) and Plaid Cymru vitiated this traditional dominance of the national parties. In the last three General Elections both ethnic nationalist parties made significant inroads in terms of percentage of popular vote and in the election of M. P. s. The SNP is now the second strongest party with electoral support in Scotland, supplanting the Conservative party. Plaid Cymru has not made such dramatic gains, yet they are well represented at the local level in Wales and have three M. P. s. Equally important, Plaid Cymru is well organized and contests nearly all the parliamentary seats in Wales. It appears that Plaid Cymru is well on the way to being institutionalized in the Welsh political environment. Although Ireland has always had viable Irish nationalist organizations which threatened the Old Tory view of the United Kingdom, this was the only historical period since the fourteenth century that Wales has had such politically viable institutions.

Socially, organizations such as the Welsh Language Society have spearheaded the drive to establish a bilingual Wales.

The attempt to reintroduce Welsh as the language of instruction along with English has met with some success even in urban south Wales. The mass media in Wales includes a television network which employs Welsh language broadcasting in their schedules. Many government documents are bilingual.

The widespread presence of the Welsh identity and the viability of distinctively Welsh political and social institutions have been related to other changes in the domestic and international environment. By the early 1960s the first post-World War II generation had reached adulthood. This generation was socialized into a British society and international environment that was drastically different from those of the previous generations. The presence of an extensive welfare system and the expansion of the British economy clearly resulted in a substantial change in the standard of living. [44] The university system was expanded as was the distribution of government scholarships. In the international environment there were no major wars. The British Empire was virtually dismantled by the mid-1960s, and Great Britain was no longer a major world power. This enormous loss of prestige and power was revealed partly by Great Britain's entry into the EEC after the rather haughty manner in which the EEC was shunned by Great Britain in the 1950s.

For the first time since the Industrial Revolution, Great Britain is considerably worse off economically than other industrial nation-states. The momentum of the postwar economic recovery had dissipated by the beginning of the early 1960s, and the growth of the British economy lags behind many other countries. Inflation in Great Britain has reached over 25 percent per year. These growth and inflation problems appear to reflect certain structural flaws in the British economy. [45] It is unusually dependent on imports of basic raw materials and foodstuffs; therefore, export trade is extremely important for the British economy. Productivity is essential to the competitive international markets, yet productivity has not increased sufficiently for a variety of reasons. The physical plant of British industry requires extensive capital investment. Militant unions, extensive wildcat strikes, inefficient labor and management practices hamper productivity and the creation of investment capital. Investment instability and high taxes appear to have scared private investors. The drastic devaluation of the British pound sterling to a historical low suggest that investors, nationally and internationally, are not convinced that any immediate revitalization of the British economy will occur. [46] This pessimism appears to exist in spite of the initial flow of oil from the North Sea oil and gas discoveries. Even these newly discovered natural resources have created skepticism since there is uncertainty over the actual amount of oil and gas and there are unusually large capital costs in extracting and transporting the oil and gas to the British mainland. [47] This capital scarcity necessitated the entry of the Wilson governments into the capital investment market. Public capital has gone to private companies such as Chrysler in order to prevent probable closures. Any major closures would further hamper productivity and seriously exacerbate the highest rate of unemployment since World War II. It is possible, however, that the oil and gas resources and membership in the EEC may help eventually to create a more positive economic environment, domestically and internationally. If Britain becomes an oil exporter, it may obtain the necessary capital to increase productivity and employment and buttress the position of the pound as an international currency.

The Welsh economy has been directly and adversely affected by the slow economic growth and the high inflation levels of this period. The total work force in Wales has declined quite sharply in basic industries. [48] Rural Wales has been affected because it depends on government economic grants to depressed areas as an incentive for industry. In the midst of an inflationary spiral, Westminster has not wanted to exacerbate the inflationary pressure by substantially increasing grants to rural Wales. The lack of economic growth contributes to the constant emigration of younger people to English cities. Both in rural and urban Wales there is strong resentment over the need to emigrate from Wales to obtain employment. * There is a history of greater economic decline in Wales than in England during periods of economic stress partly because of the lack of diversity of industry in Wales. [49]

The inability of the various British governments to solve the civil strife in Ulster and the commitment of the Labour and Conservative party elites to the EEC has created a unique environment. The traditionally powerful institutions of the Westminster government have failed to maintain the internal integrity of the United Kingdom, and they have relinquished some of their sovereignty to a supranational entity. While the latter event is unusual in British history, the cumulative impact of these two events is highly unfavorable to the traditional philosophy of the Conservative party; the integrity of the United Kingdom and the total sovereignty of the British government were cornerstones of the Conservative party philosophy of an organic British society. Clearly, British identity and patriotism were based in part on the British Empire and Great Britain's dominant economic position. The fact that Great Britain is the "economic sickman" of Europe and that former colonies, such as Canada and Australia, have

---

*In the author's Welsh survey sample, 80 percent of the 420 respondents expressed unfavorable responses concerning the need to find employment outside of Wales.

considerably higher standards of living, contributes to the already
distinctively unfavorable environment for the Conservative party.
This overall unfavorable domestic and international environment is
detrimental to the Conservatives' goal of weakening the durability of
the Welsh nonstate nation.

Components

Component 1: Devolution. The Conservative party policy under Heath
involved general opposition to Home Rule for Wales. Yet Heath was
forced to deal with the momentum of this issue that had built up in
Wales, Scotland, and in Parliament.[50] The Kilbrandon Commission
had produced its report on the restructuring of British centralized
political institutions. The six-member majority of the commission
recommended directly elected Welsh and Scottish Assemblies. The
body would consist of 100 members, elected by proportional representation with the premier and cabinet chosen from the majority party
for four years. The Welsh Assembly, or Senate, would have complete
law-making powers with the ultimate veto in rare circumstances
resting with Westminster. An autonomous Welsh civil service would
exist. In addition, the number of Welsh Members of Parliament would
be reduced from 36 to 31. This would make the Welsh representation
in Parliament consistent with the population ratio of the other main
regions in the United Kingdom.

A three-member minority report favored an elected Assembly
with only executive functions. Three other members of this commission favored an elected Assembly with only advisory functions.[51]

Prime Minister Heath favored an elected Assembly for Scotland,
but opposed it for Wales. He favored administrative devolution
through the secretary of state for Wales. The Conservatives feared
that an elected assembly in Wales would be dominated by the Labour
party. Even worse, an elected assembly might eventually be dominated by Plaid Cymru which, according to some Conservative M. P. s,
would lead to the disintegration of the British state.[52]

Prime Minister Wilson did introduce a White Paper to com-
mence discussion and debate on the creation of Assemblies for Wales
and Scotland and Conservative party opposition was immediate. It is
likely that most Conservative M. P. s and many English Labour M. P. s
will stall the formulation of a bill as long as possible. It appears
that most Conservative M. P. s will oppose any bill that devolves
legislative functions to a Welsh Assembly.

Component 2: Potential Coalitions in the European Economic Community. It is too early to observe any distinctive coalition patterns
among the various political parties of the nine countries in the EEC.

A potential coalition would be based on the common goal of opposing the recognition the numerous NSNs in these nine countries. It is likely that the Conservative party might find natural allies among the centrist and conservative parties of Europe, such as the Christian Democrats in West Germany and Italy and the Gaullist party in France. All of these parties oppose the devolution of political power to existing or potential NSNs in their respective countries. The Gaullist party members, in particular, are vehement in their opposition to any formal recognition within the EEC or European Community of the Basque, Breton, or Alsatian NSNs. [53] This component will become more important to the Conservative party if the proposed direct elections of the European Parliament in Strasbourg become a reality in the near future. Even now the current British representation of the European Parliament includes a member of the Scottish Nationalist party. If either the SNP or Plaid Cymru representation increases, then the cross-country party coalitions will become an integral party of Conservative party policy, especially since these two ethnic nationalist parties are in the process of forming coalitions with parties from other NSNs in order to gain formal recognition as autonomous political entities in the European Community.

Decision Maker B: The Labour Party

The dominant figure in the Labour party during this period was Harold Wilson. While the Labour party remains a "coalition of interests," which includes a variety of important decision makers within the Labour party hierarchy, Wilson was easily the major decision maker. * With regard to Labour party policy on Wales, the Welsh Labour M. P. s also constitute an important decision-making bloc. The 23 Welsh Labour M. P. s are distinct yet also an integral part of the national Labour party, which in the October 1974 General Election included 314 M. P. s. The Welsh M. P. s have and will continue to have some influence over Wilson and the Labour party policy in the light of the exigencies of the Welsh political environment. [54]

---

*Given the recent resignation of Wilson as Prime Minister and leader of the Labour party, it is too early to assess whether his replacement, James Callaghan, will alter significantly Labour's policies toward Wales. Since Callaghan holds a Welsh seat in the House of Commons and played an important role in defining Labour policy toward Ulster as Home Secretary during the late 1960s, he will surely be extremely sensitive to ethnic nationalism in Wales.

Goals

The main goal of the Labour party with regard to the Welsh NSN is to maintain its political dominance in Wales. This goal allows for a distinctive and durable Welsh nation. In effect, the Labour party policy appears to be pragmatic on the Welsh language issue as well as the Home Rule issue in the sense that Wilson and the Welsh M. P. s have supported these issues to a limited extent. The limitation is that the Labour party remains the major decision maker for the Welsh NSN in both the domestic and international environment.

Resources

As the party of government throughout much of this period, the Labour party has had access to the entire formidable array of government institutions which included the ability to transform policy into legislation. As the party of opposition, the Labour party retained considerable influence simply by being the only viable alternative to the Conservative party. In any case the Labour party continued to dominate Welsh politics at both the local and national levels. In the last three General Elections in this period, the Labour party averaged close to 50 percent of the vote in Wales. [55] In addition to the intense partisan identity with the Labour party among much of the Welsh electorate, the British Trades Union Conference remains important financially and organizationally to this party.

As the party of government, the Labour party through the Exchequer controlled two-thirds of the revenue received by local government bodies in Wales. Also the economic influence of the Labour government in Wales is evident in the labour party-controlled Welsh Economic Council, which can directly affect the stability and growth of the big mining industry, for example. General-purpose loans and the Selective Employment Tax and Regional Employment Premium were also important economic resources since these financial incentives can attract new industry to Wales. [56]

The EEC has been another important resource. Although the Labour party was divided on the issue of whether to remain in the EEC, Callaghan and most of his cabinet are pro-EEC. Apparently, the overwhelming majority of the electorate in Wales also perceived the EEC as an economic resource, since in the referendum in 1975 the pro-EEC vote was more than 65 percent. Cardiff had the highest pro-EEC vote of any city of its size in the United Kingdom. As an economic resource the EEC is potentially a part of the solution to Great Britain's growth and inflation problems, since it has access to a protected market of nearly 260 million people and to extensive capital. Finally, Callaghan is relying heavily on the North Sea oil

and gas as critical resources in dealing with the severe economic
growth problems in Great Britain in general, and in Wales
specifically.[57]

A more direct political resource involves the overwhelming
majority coalition in the House of Commons that could be formed
between English Labour M. P. s and the Conservative M. P. s on the
Home Rule issue. In effect, any attempt on the part of the SNP, Plaid
Cymru, Scottish Labour party, and Welsh Labour party M. P. s to
propose more devolution of political power to Wales and Scotland (than
is included in the goals of the national Labour party) would most likely
be opposed overwelmingly by most of the English Labour and Conservative M. P. s.[58]

Thus, Callaghan has considerable resources, ranging from his
Labour party's entrenched and dominant position among much of the
Welsh electorate to the control of government revenues from the
North Sea oil and gas resources. When these two resources are
considered in conjunction with the other resources discussed above,
it all amounts to the Labour party being in the best position of all the
decision makers to realize its goals concerning the Welsh NSN during
this period and likely the future.

Environment

The environment in Wales is largely favorable for the Labour
party, but there are political and economic trends that are evident
in this period that might portend an increasingly unfavorable
environment.

Wales remains a predominantly industrial society with a population that is numerically skewed more toward the working class than
the other regions of Great Britain.[59] While the Labour party has
considerably less complete dominance in partisanship among the
working class throughout the United Kingdom in general, this is not
the case in Wales. The Labour party has dominated most of the
working class electorate in Wales and has done better among its
middle-class voters than in other regions.[60] It is not intended here
to discuss systematically the relationship between the Labour party
and working-class vote, but it does appear that the social and economic
environment in Wales since World War I has contributed to a political environment, most importantly involving the dynamics of partisanship, that strongly favors the Labour party.

The economic environment in Wales does appear to be changing,
but in a manner that might alter the close relationship between the
Labour party and the working class. There has been a rapid decline
in the traditional Welsh industries of agriculture, forestry, mining,
and quarrying.[61] The mining industry has been particularly

important for the Labour party, yet mine closings continue in the Welsh coal valleys. There is considerable concern not only over the immediate loss of jobs but also over the migration of young people to England in search of employment. [62]

The impact of declining employment possibilities in Wales may be partly related to the difficulty of the Labour party to recruit members among the younger adults. In addition, support for Plaid Cymru is highest among the younger age groups. [63] It further may be possible to infer that the post-World War II generation has witnessed Labour party policies that, generally, have been unable to create sufficient employment opportunities in Wales. It will be increasingly difficult to develop the deep partisan Labour identity that formerly characterized the war and immediate post-World War II periods. Most of the major Labour party policies involving the creation of the welfare state and the nationalization of certain industries had become a permanent part of the Welsh environment by the end of the last period. The traditional alignment between class and party is in the process of decline since the "aging of class alignment" is now evident. [64]

Since 1951 most of the Labour party policies concerning the economy have not been notably different from Conservative party policies. According to the Gallup polls taken during this period, the decline in differences between the two dominant political parties is perceived by the public. [65] The impact of these trends is particularly vital to Labour's position in Wales because there has been a significant decline in electoral turnout in the traditional Labour strongholds in Wales. In commenting on this phenomenon throughout Great Britain, David Butler and Donald Stokes in their classic study, Political Change in Britain, noted that,

> the fall in the mining seats is more notable because participation there has been so high since the rise of the Labour Party and the realignment of electoral support on a class basis. For voters deeply involved with a belief in working class interests, a movement by Labour away from these goals does not increase the reasons for supporting the opposite party (the Conservatives) so much as it removes the motive to vote at all, since the parties are thought to differ less and less in class terms.
> The weakening of the class alignment is also consistent with the emergence of rival bases of enduring party support. [66]

In the last sentence of the above quote, Butler and Stokes are making the link between the decline of class alignment and the rise of the SNP and Plaid Cymru during this period.

Politics in the "collectivist age" in Wales involves few of the dramatic ideological issues that were evident in the previous period. Between 1960 and 1975 the economic environment appears to be increasingly unfavorable for the Labour party. On the one hand, the Labour party is ideologically committed to increasing the standard of living for the working class, yet, on the other hand, the electoral exigencies require that the Labour party cater to significant numbers of middle-class voters. In effect, the Labour party policies must emphasize policies that essentially can appeal to the general electorate. The political environment in Wales may, therefore, become increasingly neutral in the sense that the traditional extensive Labour party partisanship will be replaced by a more "floating electorate." Economic issues involving inflation, unemployment, and growth would dominate in such an environment.

The political environment has been disturbed by the civil strife in Ulster and the spreading terrorism in England. A political solution does not appear imminent, and the employment of troops and police continues to require considerable resources from the Callaghan government in the midst of a difficult economic environment. The internal civil strife is further complicated by the links between the terrorism in the U. K. and the international environment. Former Prime Minister Wilson, for example, angrily denounced the considerable financial support that the Provisional Irish Republican Army is receiving from Irish-Americans. [67] Callaghan appears to be facing a genuine dilemma in trying to resolve the problems of establishing the appropriate political settlement in Northern Ireland. If he continues the present course, the turmoil and violence will likely continue at its present terrorist pace. If he withdraws the British soldiers, a mass civil war is a likely possibility. The longer the bloody stalemate persists, the more likely that Wales may be affected. This proposition has to be strongly qualified; if Callaghan can successively resolve or mitigate Britain's economic woes as well as the Home Rule issue, then it is unlikely that terrorism will become a significant part of the environment in Wales in the late 1960s and its potential role is more than a very remote possibility. *

With the popular referendum in the spring of 1975 ratifying Britain's membership in the EEC, this organization becomes eminently important to Wales and the Labour party. The EEC's Regional Economic Development Fund may be directly and immediately important in the Welsh economic picture. This organization functions as a capital and expertise for those regions of member EEC nation-states

---

*The role of terrorism in Wales will be examined more closely in the discussion of Plaid Cymru decision makers.

that have basic economic problems. Wales appears to qualify because of its lack of diversity of industry and poor transportation infrastructure. It has yet to be seen whether this aspect of the international economic environment can be turned into a resource for the Labour party in the near future in arresting the relative economic decline of Wales compared to the more prosperous regions in Great Britain, such as the Midlands and Southeastern England.

The international political environment involving the EEC should be increasingly important to Wales. In December 1975, Wilson somewhat ambiguously agreed with the leaders of the other EEC nation-states to have eventually direct elections to the European Parliament. This institution has largely been ineffectual as a legislative body since the primary legislative function rests with the Council of Ministers. The latter institution is totally dominated by the national governments which jealously guard their sovereignty, so little has been accomplished in creating a political union among the EEC countries. [68] An elected parliamentary body will likely involve certain legislative functions which may establish the foundations for a political union. The Labour party already has traditional ties to the other socialist political parties of the EEC countries so their common ideology would probably be the basis for coalition-formation within the European Parliament.

Components

Component 1: Devolution. In late 1975 Prime Minister Wilson proposed in a White Paper that Wales be given an elected, 72-member Assembly with only executive functions. [69] This Assembly would not make primary law, but it would interpret and administer Westminster statutes in the areas of local government, health and social services, education, housing, private and criminal law, physical planning, the environment, and roads. No separate executive would exist; instead committees would be formed within the Welsh assembly to administer each devolved subject. A central coordinating committee, including all the committee leaders, would direct the allocation of the resources and services to the appropriate committees. Westminster would retain ultimate control over financial arrangements as well as reserve power to abrogate the actions of the Welsh assembly. The Welsh secretary of state would remain in the Westminster cabinet and would be particularly important in regard to Westminster's review power.

In the White Paper Wilson proposed that Scotland be given a 142-member Assembly with limited legislative and executive functions. An annual block grant from Westminster to the Scottish assembly would cover the expenditure of the same devolved fields that would be granted to the Welsh assembly. As a member of the Westminster cabinet, the secretary of state for Scotland would be able to effectively veto any legislation that was deemed "seriously harmful" to the general good of the United Kingdom or to specific nondevolved subjects such as policy concerning the North Sea oil and gas. Unlike the Welsh Assembly, the Scottish Assembly could legislate on devolved subjects; however, it would also be subject to the potentially strict reserve power of the Westminster government and parliamentary majority.

The strategy of discriminating between Scotland and Wales is based partly on the argument that Scotland has always had its own legal, religious, and educational system, while Wales has been an "integral" part of England since the sixteenth century. According to this argument, the historical institutional differences between England and Scotland warrant an assembly with executive and legislative functions for Scotland. In the absence of traditional institutional differences between Wales and England, administrative devolution should be sufficient for Wales.

The discrimination between Wales and Scotland is based further on the electoral strengths of Plaid Cymru and the Scottish Nationalist party in their respective regions. Callaghan and the Scottish Labour party are extremely worried about the growing electoral strength of the SNP; it is only 6 percent behind the Labour party in terms of the popular vote in the last General Election. Wilson had to devise a strategy that would appease the apparent intense devolution momentum that had built up in the Scottish electorate without fanning separatist sentiments or reducing Westminster's control of the North Sea oil and gas resources. According to Richard Rose, most English M. P. s from both the Labour and Conservative parties view the revenue from the North Sea oil and gas as a means of resolving Britain's economic problems, and they want, therefore, to keep total control over these revenues. [70] The Scottish Nationalists, in turn, maintain that the North Sea oil and gas revenues are solely Scottish natural resources. A combination of Wilson's position of limited legislative devolution for Scotland and his procrastination in submitting an actual devolution bill may provide at least part of the necessary time lag needed to repair the British economy. One week after the White Paper on devolution was made public, the Scottish Labour party suffered two devastating losses to the SNP in regional council by-elections. While another General Election is still four years away, there may ultimately be sufficient time, in Rose's words, "for the nationalist bubble to burst. "[71] Other observers of the British political scene disagree. In the assessment of The Economist, "popular reaction in Scotland to the white paper on devolution suggested an instant, decisive and politically significant hands down . . . reaction.

The SNP is well on the way to capturing a majority of the Scottish vote." Wilson's strategy with regard to the Scottish NSN may be doomed since "in Scotland, if not in Westminster, there is much private confusion where Labour goes now. There is even the genuine fear that the political game . . . could be slipping away beyond recall. "[72]

It is too early to assess exactly how the Welsh electorate will react to both the Labour government's policy of discrimination between Wales and Scotland and the apparent dissatisfaction that the White Paper has evoked among the Scottish electorate. Wilson put the Welsh Labour party in somewhat of a dilemma since it supports a legislative assembly, yet the official British Labour party position includes only an executive assembly. It is not clear how committed the Welsh Labour party is to the legislative assembly since it is too difficult to gauge how much devolution is sufficient to avoid serious defections to Plaid Cymru and whether the Wilson policy of discrimination between Wales and England will affect any such potential defections. [73]

Prime Minister Wilson's strategy on devolution for Wales clearly involves the Scottish NSN and England. The Labour party is in a particularly strong position with regard to Wales, yet the party's policy involving Scotland may seriously weaken its policy for Wales; a legislative assembly in Scotland is a clear precedent of the British government's willingness, given sufficient political pressure, to devolve legislative power away from Westminster. The Labour party appears to have staked the middle ground between Plaid Cymru—which favors, at a minimum, legislative devolution—and the Conservative party—which favors, at most, some slight administrative devolution. Within the House of Commons a likely Labour-Conservative coalition on the devolution issue would be formidable; this coalition would most likely support a strategy of procrastination and limited executive devolution for Wales.

Component 2: Coalitions in the European Community. As long as the Labour party continues to dominate the Welsh political environment, it appears that Callaghan and the Welsh Labour party do not have to be unduly concerned about the recently proposed direct elections to the European Parliament. Callaghan will likely strongly oppose any formal recognition of Wales as an autonomous political entity within the EEC. Representation to the European Parliament will likely be on a United Kingdom basis; consequently, the Labour party will be in a dominant position in terms of representation. Any formal recognition of Wales as a distinctive political entity within the EEC might alter the Labour party's position, especially if Plaid Cymru increases its electoral support to the level of the SNP in Scotland.

Callaghan appears to be in a very strong position on the issue of the recognition of Wales because of the traditional ideological ties to the socialist political parties in the other EEC countries.* With similar potential difficulties with the NSNs in their own countries, the socialist political parties, along with the more conservative parties such as the Christian Democrats, would form a formidable coalition with the Labour party against the ethnic nationalist political parties in the EEC. It is unlikely that Callaghan will facilitate a move to recognize Wales as a distinctive political entity. While the Labour party dominates Wales and will most likely continue to do so, Scotland poses a more critical threat. With Scotland as an autonomous political entity, the SNP would surely insist on control of natural resources in Scotland and a voice in matters such as the EEC's Regional Economic Development Fund. It is simply unlikely that Callaghan would accept any such serious dilution of the authority of Whitehall and Westminster in the international environment.

Decision Maker C: Plaid Cymru

The leading decision maker for this political party during this period was Gwynfor Evans, the first Plaid Cymru member of Parliament. He made the decision in 1975 to step down as the leader of Plaid Cymru, but he more recently appears to be reconsidering this decision, at least temporarily. During most of Evans' tenure in Plaid Cymru, the decision-making process was shared. The party chairman, general secretary, and, more recently, the elected Plaid Cymru M. P. s are all important decision makers in terms of policy formation and, equally important, the daily operations of the political party organization. [74]

Goals

The traditional main goal of Plaid Cymru is the preservation of the Welsh nation, involving preservation of its culture and language. This goal also necessitates a politically autonomous but not separate Welsh state which totally controls the domestic environment in Wales and shares the decision making with Westminster and the British government in the international environment on all issues involving Wales. [75]

----

*Many of the socialist political parties of EEC countries exchange delegates to annual party meetings, such as the British Labour Conference held in Blackpool, England, as well as regularly held conferences of all those socialist parties.

Resources

Unlike the previous period, Plaid Cymru now has an extensive
political party organization throughout Wales. The formal party
apparatus has constituency-level operations and is geared toward
both general elections and local government elections. Plaid Cymru
has therefore a fairly high profile among the Welsh electorate and
can recruit individuals as party activists. There is considerable
ideological diversity among Plaid Cymru membership. This diversity
is evident in Plaid Cymru M. P. s: Dafydd Thomas is "explicitly
socialist in the Welsh nationalist context" while Dafydd Wigley has
a "solid business background."[76] In addition, Plaid Cymru is no
longer a one-issue party since it directs its policies toward the
majority of the electorate in Wales. Plaid Cymru policy has been
deeply oriented to the predominantly economic concerns of the Welsh
electorate; well-researched economic position papers have been
formulated and publicized as an integral element of the party program.
Cultural and local issues are emphasized in those electoral constituencies where they are likely to make a difference. The development
of an extensive political party organization and a multiissue policy
orientation constitutes an important set of resources for Plaid Cymru.

It became evident through surveys taken during this period that
the majority of the people of Wales supported devolution.[77] This is
a likely resource in that once an individual is in favor of some
devolution he would probably be more susceptible to Plaid Cymru
persuasion on the devolution issue.

Plaid Cymru represents a political organization that is committed to constitutional means to achieve its goals. This constitutional
commitment is a resource since it is in line with the notion that it
is better to cooperate with a moderate ethnic nationalist organization
now when the political environment allows it than to allow for the
possibility that an extremist ethnic nationalist organization may
become a significant part of the political environment. There appears
to be little need for Plaid Cymru to publicize this resource, given the
continuing tragedy of Northern Ireland, as well as the terrorist
bombings in Wales in the 1960s and more recently in Scotland.

Plaid Cymru initially opposed British membership in the EEC
because many, but not all, of its members believed that Wales would
be shunted further to the geographic periphery of the economic and
political power centers. Specifically, Plaid Cymru leadership feared
the loss of Welsh industries and the dilution of the Welsh culture due
to the more extensive EEC industrial base and culture.[78] Plaid
Cymru, however, was very flexible or obviously pragmatic on the
EEC membership issue since its policy quickly changed in the face
of the overwhelming support revealed in the Welsh vote. Plaid

Cymru leaders joined the representatives of the Breton, Basque, and Alsatian political parties in forming the Bureau of Unrepresented Nations in Brussels. This organization will attempt to gain formal recognition by the EEC institutions of the representation rights of the Welsh and other NSNs in the European Community.[79] Plaid Cymru leaders are then officially forging a political coalition within the EEC. It is too early to tell whether they can expand the coalition to include ethnic nationalist organizations in Belgium and the Netherlands. If this coalition is expanded to other NSNs and can enlist the support of the smaller countries such as Ireland, Denmark, Belgium, and Luxemburg, then the coalition policy represented by the formation of the Bureau of Unrepresented Nations may prove to be an important resource for Plaid Cymru. In any case this organization explicitly establishes the formation of an interest group, representing the Welsh NSN within the European Community political system.

Environment

The political environment in Wales has become significantly more favorable for Plaid Cymru during this period than the last one. In the last three elections Plaid Cymru has consistently polled approximately 11 percent of the popular vote in Wales.[80] It has three M. P. s in the House of Commons. There are also trends in the electoral process that indicate that the traditionally strong relationship between class and the Labour party vote is beginning to weaken.[81] This trend may be critical since Plaid Cymru cannot substantially improve its electoral position in Wales without the electoral support of the working-class voters in the industrial south Wales region. This trend may accelerate if the economic environment in Wales deteriorates, causing more unemployment and emigration. There is also some evidence that support for Plaid Cymru goals is stronger among the younger age groups. If this relationship holds in the future, then Plaid Cymru support should automatically increase.

The electoral success of the Scottish Nationalist party has contributed to the decline of the traditionally dominant and nearly exclusive control of the Labour and Conservative parties throughout Great Britain. It appears that the electoral success of the SNP has forced the Labour party to seriously consider the devolution of political power to Wales and Scotland.[82] Despite the considerable differences in the electoral strengths of the SNP and Plaid Cymru, it will be difficult for Prime Minister Callaghan to discriminate between Wales and Scotland. According to Lord Chalfont, an astute observer of the political environment in Wales, any discrimination between the two NSNs "will play straight into the hands of the Plaid Cymru."[83]

While Plaid Cymru is not yet an immediate electoral threat to the
Labour party, Chalfont maintains that some decision makers in the
Labour government believe that members of Plaid Cymru are "bigger
enemies of ours than the Tories."[84] The political environment in
Wales, therefore, continues to be dominated by the Labour party,
yet there are definite indications that Plaid Cymru is an integral and
important part of this environment.

A decidely unfavorable environment exists, however, in
England. There is some survey evidence which suggests that the
majority of the English population oppose Plaid Cymru goals.[85]
The reaction to Wilson's proposal of an executive assembly for
Wales has been largely negative. The belief persists among some
of the English that Wales, along with Scotland, is overrepresented
in Westminster while England is underrepresented. There is the
further belief that sufficient devolution has taken place in these
NSNs; the existence of Welsh and Scottish secretaries of state, civil
service, and standing committees in the House of Commons amount
to administrative devolution.* A majority of the English M. P. s
appear to hold this view; therefore, it is doubtful that Plaid Cymru
conception of the Welsh NSN will be achieved through legislation in
the near future.

The international environment is considerably more favorable
for Plaid Cymru than during the previous period. In the dismantling
of the empire, many British decision makers agreed, implicitly or
explicitly, that colonialism is an inappropriate form of relationship
between the more politically and economically powerful nations and
weaker nations. It is debatable whether Wales has been treated as
a colony by England since the annexation of Wales by statute in 1284.
Michael Hechtor concluded after an empirical study based on longitu-
dinal aggregate data analysis employing certain economic and political
indicators of the relationship between Wales and England, that the
concept "internal colonialism" described the relationship between
these two nations.[86] An ethnic nationalist movement which is based
partly on the anticolonialist rationale and employs constitutional and
nonviolent means in seeking the goal of autonomy and not independence
is no longer automatically suspect. Plaid Cymru is the embodiment
of just such an ethnic nationalist movement and, therefore, it no
longer faces a directly hostile international and national political

---

*The belief that Wales and Scotland are already overrepresented
was voiced immediately by certain M. P. s in letters to The Times
November 27, 1975, in response to Wilson's apparent position that
some devolution is in order for Scotland and Wales but not for
England.

environment. Clearly, Belgian Prime Minister Leo Tindemans, for example, in his capacity as secretary of the Council of Ministers of the EEC, would not have sought the views of Plaid Cymru leaders if moderate ethnic nationalist movements were still viewed in a completely negative manner.

The creation of the EEC, Great Britain's membership in this regional community, and the attempt to forge a European union also signifies another fundamental change in the international environment. All member nation-states have had to relinquish some, albeit small, degree of sovereignty to the EEC institutions. If the European Parliament edges toward legislative power, then a further and more significant shift in sovereignty away from the nation-state will have occurred. It is plausible that such shifts in sovereignty from the nation-state toward a larger political entity may facilitate by precedent a similar movement toward NSNs.

It is further conceivable that "segmented pluralist" nation-states such as Belgium, the Netherlands, as well as Ulster may eventually devolve political power to ethnically homogeneous political units to resolve potential and actual ethnic tensions in their countries. A European union would provide the larger focus of integration for such multiethnic societies; a common set of economic and political institutions in a federal or confederal European community would maintain a different type of unity for multiethnic societies such as Belgium. It is exceedingly difficult to engage in conjecture concerning the relationship of the Welsh NSN to the British nation-state in a European union since the latter body will be the focus of considerable dispute in the process of becoming a reality. [87] It does seem certain that NSNs in the European Community will attempt to influence the eventual structuring of the European union in a manner that allows for their formal representation in its institutions.

Another element in the domestic and international environment during this period is the terrorist organizations. In the late 1960s members of the Free Wales Army (FWA) and the Movement for the Defence of Wales (MDW) were involved with terrorist bombings of public buildings and pipelines in Wales. While the terrorism was real, and some individuals were killed in the process, it does not appear that these organizations are still viable. John Jenkins, the MDW leader, maintained that violence was necessary because the constitutional means employed by Plaid Cymru would take too long and Wales would be completely anglicized. [88] This impatience and frustration may flare up again if Callaghan or any Westminster government procrastinates in devolving substantial political power to Wales. The international context might provide the necessary resources to make terrorist organizations more viable in Wales. While the FWA and MDW leaders have turned to the Irish Republican Army for assistance, the international context now includes far more favorable resources to potential decision makers of terrorist organizations. The French police uncovered an extremely sophisticated and well-financed international terrorist organization in Paris with links to ethnic nationalist movements in Canada and Great Britain. While it is difficult to determine whether these links include any Welsh terrorists, a delegation from Wales did attend a secret conference in Trieste: "Western intelligence sources say that most of the discussion was on a purely theoretical level, but they believe that terrorist organizations sent representatives to forge a more extensive conspiracy."[89] Whatever the actual circumstances involving terrorist organizations in the international context, it does appear that financial and other organizational resources exist and can be "successfully" employed.

Plaid Cymru leaders strongly oppose terrorism on moral and practical grounds, viewing it as a negative element of the environment. In the absence of a tradition of violence, or even serious bitterness, between the peoples of Wales and England, terrorism would anger the majority of the Welsh people[90] and turn them against any means of attaining a Welsh state.

Another significant change in the domestic environment which appeared generally favorable to Plaid Cymru involved the status of the Welsh language. The Language Act of 1967 established the principle of equal validity for the Welsh and English languages legally. This meant that any form or document written in Welsh would have the same validity as if it had been written in English. In the same year the Gittins Report on Primary Education in Wales recommended a noncompulsory bilingual education. This report provided the impetus for the development and funding of bilingual education in anglicized areas. The relationship between the language issue and support for Plaid Cymru and Welsh nationalism is complex. On the one hand, there is a link between those who support the enhancement of the Welsh language and those who support Plaid Cymru. On the other hand, the Welsh language and nationalism issues are not highly interdependent. Plaid Cymru has to avoid alienating those voters who see these issues as unrelated; in effect there are other mainly economic issues that are more important with regard to support for Welsh nationalism. The distinction between the Welsh language and nationalist issues is particularly important in urban South Wales.[91] Thus the increased support for the Welsh language in the environment is a delicate political issue which on balance is a resource for Plaid Cymru.

Major changes occurred in the domestic and international environment between 1960 and 1975. Many of these changes are clearly favorable to Plaid Cymru in terms of its goals of the Welsh NSN.

Components

Component 1: Devolution. Plaid Cymru's official position on devolution is that they favor an elected assembly with legislative functions for the domestic affairs in Wales. Plaid Cymru leaders see this type of Welsh assembly as a step toward "dominion status" for Wales. Dominion status would entail a virtually autonomous Welsh state with complete control of Welsh domestic affairs and a partnership between Wales and England in international affairs that involve the interests of Wales. There would be common external tariffs and no internal tariffs. There would be a common currency, uniform tax system, free movement of people and capital, and integrated investment planning.

The major emphasis is on obtaining the more limited devolution that is entailed in the legislative Welsh Assembly, or Senate, called for by the Kilbrandon Commission's Majority Report. Plaid Cymru M. P. s will likely join efforts with the SNP, Liberal party, and Welsh Labour party M. P. s to obtain such an assembly. It is not definite that the Welsh Labour M. P. s and even the Liberal party M. P. s are completely committed to a legislative assembly. If the support of these M. P. s is not forthcoming during the parliamentary debates and possible voting on the devolution issue in 1976, then Plaid Cymru will obviously make this "desertion" a major election issue in the next General Election.

The gradualist strategy of the devolution issue appears based on the belief that once the principle of devolution is established, then many of the resources and trends discussed above will facilitate the further devolution of political power to an eventual Dominion of Wales. [92]

Component 2: Coalitions in the European Community. The participation of Plaid Cymru leaders in political coalitions is not extensive. The most explicit step is the recent formation of the Bureau of Unrepresented Nations (BUN). This organization includes only Plaid Cymru, Scollard or Vro Sau party in Brittany, the Basque National party, and the Alsace National party. Plaid Cymru leaders will likely expand this coalition to include the remaining NSNs in the European Community. The BUN will attempt to represent the interests of its members in the key institutions of the EEC, particularly the commission. This institution is enormously important in aggregating interests throughout the European Community on key economic issues.

On the issue of the structure of the European Union, Plaid Cymru policy favors a confederation. They oppose a federation because they believe that Wales would be overwhelmed by the far more populous nation-states such as England and France. Plaid

Cymru policy is directed toward avoiding the substitution of an English-dominated Westminster Parliament with an English, French, German, and Italian-dominated Strasbourg Parliament. [93]

Decision Maker D: The Liberal Party

Not since Lloyd George has the Liberal party had any major decision makers in Wales. Yet as a political party it consistently commands 12 percent of the electoral vote in Wales. When this vote is considered in conjunction with an approximately similar level of electoral support for Plaid Cymru, the Liberal party remains a significant decision maker in Wales.

Goal

The Liberal party's main goal is to maximize the devolution of political power to Wales without increasing the probability of separatism.

Resources

The Liberal party can still rely on the electoral support of many of the Welsh constituencies where the Nonconformist religion predominates. The Liberal party has been slightly ahead of Plaid Cymru in the popular vote in Wales, but with two M. P. s from Wales it has one less than the Plaid Cymru. The Liberal party members in Wales also have the financial and electoral support of the small party organization throughout Great Britain.

Environment

The environment in Wales continues to be unfavorable for the Liberal party. Just as the Labour party made enormous inroads into the electoral support of the Liberal party after World War I, Plaid Cymru has made far less but still significant inroads into Liberal party constituencies in rural Wales since 1960. Also the general trend involving the decline in the importance of Nonconformism and political party vote continued largely unabetted during the last 15 years. [94] The Liberal party philosophy of individualism also seems quite inconsistent with an institutionalized welfare state and an extensively nationalized industrial economy. The Conservative party has effectively co-opted much of the middle-class vote in Great Britain that would likely vote Liberal. It is extremely difficult to overcome the legacy of the interwar years when the Liberal party suffered its precipitous decline from power. [95]

Component: Devolution

The Liberal party policy officially maintains that a federal system should be the form that devolution takes in not only in Wales and Scotland but also in England. Certain functions such as education would be controlled by Wales, while other functions such as defense would be controlled by Westminster.

It appears likely that in the absence of very much support for their federal plan that the Liberal party M. P. s would likely support a legislative assembly for Wales.

An Evaluation of the Welsh System, 1960 to 1975

Both the audibility and durability of the Welsh NSN increased substantially during this period. While the key sets of decision makers all disagree on their goals with regard to Wales, only the Conservative party is opposed to some form of increased political power for Wales in its domestic affairs. Even the Conservatives support greater administrative decentralization to the secretary of state for Wales and the Welsh Civil Service.

The emergence of Plaid Cymru as a well-organized and multi-issue political party that is visible at the local government level as well as the national level is one of the most important factors in the increased efficiency of the Welsh system. The political culture in Wales inescapably is a part of British democratic traditions. In order to appeal to the people of Wales, on the issues of the preservation of the Welsh nation and the creation of a Welsh state, it seems imperative that the approach be consistent with the political party culture that began in the nineteenth century as well as the postindustrial culture which evolved during the last three decades. Plaid Cymru directed its appeal on just such a basis; it is a constitutional political party that presents sophisticated policy positions on the complex economic issues that predominate in Wales.

The major decision maker in Wales, the Labour party, has responded to the presence of Plaid Cymru by taking moderate positions on the devolution and language issues. Political party competition in a pluralistic democratic society such as Great Britain clearly is central to the future of the NSNs. While cultural issues in Wales involving the Welsh language and Nonconformism are important in this political party competition, economic issues will most likely affect the relative strength of Plaid Cymru versus the Labour and

Conservative parties. The emergence of the deep economic problems
in the British economy has more sharply focused the relative economic
positions of Wales and England. The process of relative deprivation
will directly affect any movement toward or away from a Welsh
state. This relative deprivation process includes Scotland as well
as England; any political or economic powers given to Scotland and
not to Wales would likely intensify the perceptions of relative deprivation among the Welsh people.

For the first time since the thirteenth century there are Welsh
decision makers who are attempting to organize and institutionalize
the representation of Wales in the international environment. The
institutions of the European Economic Community are clearly important vehicles for the participation of Wales in the international
environment. This participation increases the audibility of the Welsh
NSN and also its durability, because it enhances the possibility of
some type of recognition of Wales as a political entity. Since Plaid
Cymru has been the main force behind the entry of Wales into the
international environment, the entry has been nonviolent.

Political and social organizations and institutions exist now
in Wales and in the EEC that will very likely increase the durability
and audibility of the Welsh NSN in the forseeable future. After nearly
seven centuries of the steady decline of the Welsh nation, this
dramatic turnabout is an indication of the complexity of variables
involved in the creation and destruction of nations.

NOTES

1. Welsh Nation 47, no. 40 (July 1975): 2.

2. For a discussion of the various positions of the devolution
issue in Wales as depicted in the numerous news columns of the
national newspaper of Wales, see Devolution: The Great Debate
1964-74 (Llandybie Amman Ford Dyfed: Salisbury Press, 1974).

3. For a discussion of the history of this period, see Sir
Reginald Coupland, Welsh and Scottish Nationalism (London: Collins,
1954).

4. John Bowie, The English Experience (New York: Capricorn
Books, 1972), pp. 236-57.

5. Ibid. , pp. 364-93.

6. P. Berresford Ellis, Wales A Nation Again! (London:
Tandem Books, 1968), p. 41.

7. Coupland, op. cit. , p. 116.

8. Ibid.

9. For an excellent history of the goals of the Old Tory Faction
and the Conservative party during most of the nineteenth and early

twentieth centuries, see Goldwin Smith, A History of England, 2d ed. (New York: Scribner, 1957), pp. 543–692. For a classic study of Old Toryism and the Conservative party, see Samuel H. Beer, British Politics in the Collectivist Age (New York: Vintage Books, 1969).

10. Richard Rose, ed. , Electoral Behavior (New York: The Free Press, 1974), p. 515.

11. Bowie, op. cit. , p. 395, and David Thompson, Europe Since Napoleon (New York: Knopf, 1962), pp. 542–43.

12. Ellis, op. cit. , p. 107.

13. Coupland, op. cit. , p. 131.

14. Kevin R. Cox, "Geography, Social Contexts and Voting Behavior in Wales" in Mass Politics, ed. Erik Allardt and Stein Rokkan (New York: The Free Press, 1970), p. 132. For a discussion of the historical relationship between Nonconformity and Politics in Wales, see David Williams, A History of Modern Wales (London: John Murray, 1950), pp. 246–68.

15. Cox, op. cit. , pp. 138–43.

16. It should be noted that there is disagreement concerning the characterization of the relationship between workers and employers in Wales during the nineteenth century. While Cox maintains that relationships were generally harmonious, David Williams argues that there was considerable strife or conflict, op. cit. , Chapters 14 and 15. See also Cox, op. cit. , p. 136.

17. Smith, op. cit. , p. 641.

18. Ibid. , p. 649.

19. Ibid. , p. 632.

20. Ellis, op. cit. , p. 61.

21. Cox, op. cit. , pp. 120–27.

22. Coupland, op. cit. , p. 217.

23. Cox, op. cit. , pp. 145, 149–56.

24. Phillip M. Rawkins, "Rich Welsh or Poor British," a paper presented at the Annual Meetings of the American Political Science Association, Chicago, September 1974, p. 8.

25. Cox, op. cit. , pp. 145, 149–56.

26. See J. A. Thompson, ed. , The Collapse of the British Liberal Party; Fate or Self-destruction (Lexington, Mass. : Heath, 1969) and Trevor Wilson, The Downfall of the Liberal Party, 1914–1935 (Ithaca, N. Y. : Cornell University Press, 1966).

27. Cox, op. cit. , pp. 138–45.

28. Beer, op. cit. , pp. 105–25.

29. Ellis, op. cit. , p. 115.

30. Beer, op. cit. , p. 158.

31. Ibid. , p. 145.

32. For an economic analysis of the impact of the depression in Wales, see M. P. Fogarty, Prospects of the Industrial Areas of

Great Britain, Nuffield College, Social Reconstruction Survey
Publications (London: Methuen, 1945).

33. Ellis, op. cit. , Chapter 16.

34. Ibid. , p. 107.

35. For an extremely interesting examination of the tenacity
of Liberal party partisanship in the important rural Welsh constituency
of Cardiganshire, see P. J. Madgwick, The Politics of Rural Wales
(London: Hutchinson, 1973).

36. Cox, op. cit. , p. 149. See also Michael Hechtor, Internal
Colonialism, The Celtic Fringe in British National Development:
1536-1966 (Berkeley: University of California Press, 1975), Chapters
6, 7, and 9 for an analysis of over-time analysis concerning partisan
voting patterns in Wales.

37. P. G. J. Pulzer, Political Representation and Elections
(New York: Praeger, 1967), p. 98.

38. Ellis, op. cit. , p. 106.

39. David Butler and Donald Stokes, Political Change in
Britain (New York: St. Martin's Press, 1971), p. 237.

40. For an analysis of the inflation issue and its impact on
party vote in the 1970 General Election, see D. E. Butler with M.
Pinto-Duschinsky, The British Election of 1970 (London: Macmillan,
1971).

41. The Economist, October 19, 1974, p. 31. For analysis of
the second General Elections in 1974, see Howard R. Penniman, ed.
Britain At the Polls (Washington, D. C. : American Enterprise Institute
for Public Policy Research, 1975).

42. The Economist, October 19, 1974, p. 31.

43. Richard Rose, Governing Without Consensus (Boston:
Beacon Press, 1972), p. 54.

44. Ibid. , p. 67. For specific and detailed discussions of the
British economic performance during most of periods III and IV,
see Derek Aldcroft and Peter Feasnon, eds. , Economic Growth in
Twentieth Century Britain (New York: Humanities Press, 1970);
Richard E. Caves et al. , Britain's Economic Prospects (Washington,
D. C. : Brookings Institution, 1968); and Sir Alex Cairncross, ed. ,
Britain's Economic Prospects Reconsidered (Albany: State Univer-
sity of New York Press, 1972).

45. For an extremely interesting discussion of the various
factors that appear to have contributed to the stagnation of the
British economy, see Stephen Blank, "The Politics of Economic Policy
in Britain: The Problem of 'Pluralistic Stagnation'," unpublished
manuscript, University of Pittsburgh.

46. Blank concludes rather forcefully that Britain's position
in the international economic environment during the post-World

War II period was the most important constraint on the performance of the British economy, op. cit., pp. 44-51.

47. The Economist, November 1, 1975, pp. 68-69.

48. The Welsh Economy in the Post-War Period, Welsh Working party consultative document, 1973, p. 3.

49. For a detailed comparison of the Welsh and British economies between 1956-68 and a current assessment of the Welsh economy, see Western Mail, September 17, 1968. For the pre-World War II period, see Fogarty, op. cit.

50. Western Mail, July 20, 1970. For an evaluation of the forces and events that made the British national political parties seriously consider the devolution in Scotland, see Milton J. Esman, "Scottish Nationalism, North Sea Oil and the British Response," in Ethnic Conflict in Western Europe and Canada, Milton J. Esman, ed. (Ithaca, N.Y.: Cornell University Press, forthcoming).

51. Western Mail, November 1, 1973. For an exhaustive presentation of the Kilbrandon Commission's work on the devolution issue, see Royal Commission on the Constitution, vol 1, Report, Cmnd. 5460, and vol. 2, Memorandum of Dissent, Cmnd. 5460-1, (London: HMSO, October 1973).

52. Western Mail, November 10, 1972.

53. Robert Lafont, La Révolution Régionaliste (Paris: Gallimard, 1967), p. 214.

54. For examples of the various and changing policy positions that the Welsh Labour party has adopted on the devolution issue, and the difficulties of coordinating policies with the national Labour party, see Devolution: The Great Debate 1964-74, op. cit.

55. The Economist, October 19, 1974.

56. Western Mail, September 7, 1968.

57. Richard Rose, writing in The Times, May 28, 1975.

58. The Times, November 27, 1975.

59. Butler and Stokes, op. cit., p. 77.

60. Ibid., and Rose, Electoral Behavior, op. cit., pp. 515-16.

61. Western Mail, September 17, 1968.

62. Ibid.

63. Western Mail, September 9, 1968.

64. Butler and Stokes, op. cit., p. 126.

65. Ibid., p. 131.

66. Ibid., pp. 131-32.

67. New York Times, December 18, 1975.

68. For a sophisticated historical and theoretical analysis of European integration and the European Economic Community, see James Caporaso, European Integration (Pacific Palisades, Calif.: Goodyear, 1974) and Leon Lindberg, The Political Dynamics of

European Economic Integration (Stanford, Calif. : Stanford University Press, 1963).

    69. Cmnd. 6348. HMSO, as cited in The Economist, November 29, 1975, p. 14.

    70. Richard Rose, writing in The Times, May 28, 1975.

    71. Ibid.

    72. The Economist, December 8, 1975, pp. 32 and 35.

    73. Western Mail, May 18, 1975 and June 16, 1975.

    74. For a detailed discussion of the organization of Plaid Cymru, see Phillip M. Rawkins, "Minority Nationalism and Advanced Industrial States: A Case Study of Contemporary Wales," Ph. D. dissertation, University of Toronto, 1975, Chapters 11-13.

    75. There is some confusion concerning the political goal of Plaid Cymru. Plaid Cymru Secretary General Dafydd Williams agrees that many Plaid Cymru voters believe they are voting for a separate Welsh state. According to Williams, "Plaid Cymru's constitutional target is dominion status. We have always emphasized that we seek freedom of action rather than absolute independence. Therefore the pure constitutional issue is of less importance than the ability to run our own affairs. This is why we have never been a republican party but have always defined our objectives in terms of dominion status." Personal correspondence with the author.

    76. Trevor Fishlock, writing in The Times, January 3, 1975. For an analysis of the ideological variation of Plaid Cymru activists, see Rawkins, op. cit.

    77. Western Mail, September 9, 1968; November 9, 1967. For a more detailed analysis of opinion polls throughout most of this period, see Alan Butt-Philip, The Political and Sociological Significance of Welsh Nationalism Since 1945 (Cardiff: University of Wales Press, forthcoming).

    78. Welsh Nation 47, no. 29 (April 11, 1975): 1.

    79. Welsh Nation 47, no. 40 (July 27, 1975): 1.

    80. The Economist, October 19, 1974.

    81. Butler and Stokes, op. cit. , p. 126.

    82. See Esman, op. cit.

    83. Lord Chalfont, writing in The Times, October 10, 1974.

    84. Ibid.

    85. Rose, Governing Without Consensus, op. cit. , pp. 54-55.

    86. See Hechtor, op. cit.

    87. The Times, January 5, 8, and 9, 1976.

    88. Trevor Fishlock, Wales and the Welsh (London: Cassell, 1972), pp. 121-22.

    89. Newsweek, July 21, 1975, p. 24.

    90. Fishlock, Wales and the Welsh, op. cit. , p. 113.

91. For an empirical evaluation of the relationship between Welsh nationalism and the Welsh language issues, see the author's "Nationalism and Communalism in Wales," Ethnicity, 2, no. 4 (December 1975). A more detailed examination of the theoretical and empirical relationship between economic, social, and psychological variables and Welsh nationalism can be found in the author's The Politics of Ethnicity: A Challenge to Advanced Industrial Societies (New York: Marcel Dekker, forthcoming).

92. In discussing the gradualist component of Plaid Cymru policy, Secretary General Dafydd Williams states " . . . as a matter of political tactics we have always tended to assume that we would approach dominion status fairly gradually perhaps achieving domestic self-government first." Personal correspondence with the author.

93. For an exhaustive analysis of the various policy options that both membership and nonmembership in the EEC pose for Plaid Cymru, see Wales and the Common Market (Cardiff: Plaid Cymru Research Group, 1975).

94. Butler and Stokes, op. cit., Chapter 6.

95. Ibid.

IDEOLOGY AS A RESOURCE:
A COMMUNIST CASE STUDY
Robin Remington

The Croatian case offers an example of the difficulty of increasing audibility without provoking a repressive reaction
that threatens durability. The difficulty is compounded
when a number of separate decision-making groups operate
essentially independently and with somewhat different goals.
Insofar as a group attempts to broaden its appeal by seeking
the endorsement of other groups, it runs the risk of being
held responsible for the actions of the other groups—actions
that it cannot control. The powers that be—in this case, the
central government—have been ambivalent all along, and—
unacceptable behavior by the members of any group can
provoke a strong reaction against all groups. The Croatian
case is particularly complex, including not only multiple
decision makers within Yugoslavia but also Croatians living
outside the state and a sizable member of Yugoslav Croatians
who migrate temporarily to other states in search of
employment.

The existence of groups outside of Yugoslavia that want
an independent and noncommunist Croatia exacerbates any
suspicions Yugoslav leaders may harbor about Croation
nationalists who claim to be local communists simply seeking
self-management within the Yugoslav state.

—Judy S. Bertelsen

Even more basic than identifying nonstate nations is the question
of who or what constitues a nation. It is in part to avoid the headaches
stemming from this problem that students of international politics have
retreated to considering nation-states and their decision makers as
the primary components of the international system. Such an arbitrary
cutoff tremendously simplifies the amount of interactions that must
be analyzed. Unfortunately, there is the danger that it oversimplifies

understanding international reality, leads directly to normative judgment that legitimate international actors are those representing the
status quo, and confuses political identity with real estate.

This chapter assumes that a nation is a group of people recognizing a common bond of historical development, language, and national identity. They may or may not be recognized as such by the
international system. In our terms it is the self-perception of these
people of their "nationhood" and the impact of that awareness of
their behavior that counts.

HISTORICAL BACKGROUND

Croatian historians trace the origin of their people back to
2,000 years before Christ in today's Iran. By 375 A. D. they came
as the allies (or perhaps subjects of) the Huns to the Vistula where
they assimilated with the Salvic tribes in this area to become a new
European people that with the death of Attila in 453 split off from the
Huns to form a federal state of Croatians and Antes from Silesia to
the Black Sea. By 602 A. D. this union disintegrated and the Croats
declared themselves an independent state that they describe as "the
first slavic state in the Balkans, fifty years before the Bulgarians,
almost two hundred years before Charlemagne, and two hundred years
before the Serbians of Rascia began with their state organization."[1]

Their modern history is dated from the coronation of King
Tomislav in 910 by a Papal legate. Croatia was united and stretched
from Istria to the Drina in Bosnia, from the Drava and the Danube to
the Adriatic Sea, including key Dalmatian cities. After military
defeats by the Magyars to the north, the Croats signed the Treaty of
Zagreb relinquishing independence for a tokenly autonomous Croatian
King in 1102. Thus began the rule of foreign dynasties in Croatia
that lasted for 839 years until 1941. Those 800 years did not wipe
out a sense of nationhood. Rather they saw a dogged struggle for
expanding Croatian autonomy via political tactics—negotiation, passive resistance, obstructionism. Armed rebellion played its role,[2]
although less so than with the neighboring Serbs.

Just what were the goals of decision makers of the Croat nation
during these centuries of subjugation is unclear. They lived in a
memory of past glories and independence. They struggled for what
would have amounted to home rule, with some signs that partisans
of Illyrianism, the symbol of political and cultural unity of the South
Slavs, at least toyed with ideas of pan-Slavic nation-building. Ivo
Lederer has referred to intellectual leanings in this direction as
early as the sixteenth century.[3] Under the direction of Bishop Josip
Juraj Strossmayer, romantic Illyrianism flowed into a more modern
Yugoslavism in the organizational form of a popular People's party,

whose goal was no less than unity of Croatians with Serbs and Slovenes.
Simultaneously a chauvinistic, pan-Croatianism developed to counter
the Yugoslavists. Ante Starcevic and Eugene Kvaternik formed their
party of the Right (Prava) dedicated to the star-crossed cause of an
independent Croatia.

These two streams of Croat political philosophy continued into
interwar Yugoslavia and continue today. Nonetheless, with Serbian
victories in the Balkan war of 1912 and 1913, the idea of a South Slav
state, Yuroslavia, became increasingly popular. The Croatian Parliament went so far as to vote an end to its tie with Hungary to cast
its lot with the Council of Croats and Slovenes in negotiations for a
united, federal Yugoslavia. The assumption on the Croat and Slovene
side was that this was to be a federation of equals in which each nation
would retain autonomy.

Serbs, still dazzled by their victories, wanted to recreate
Greater Serbia. They unethusiastically agreed to the Declaration of
Corfu creating the Kingdom of Serbs, Croats, and Slovenes in which
in principle the three peoples came as equal partners. Also, the Croat
and Slovene position was radically weakened by the Italian invasion of
1918, thereby strengthening the hand of the Serbs on matters of implementing equality. *

The incompatibility of these goals, not surprisingly, broke down
into first conflict then chaos. By 1923-24 Croatia was on the edge of
insurrection. The Croat Peasant party was outlawed, its leader
Stjephan Radic jailed. Although he was released in 1925, Radic soon
died violently, shot by a hot-headed Montenegrin member of the Parliament during a debate in the Skupstina. In anger, King Alexander
suspended the Constitution and declared his dictatorship. It is hard
not to agree with the conclusion that by 1929 Yugoslavia was virtually
a Serbian police state. Harsh martial law in Croatia did not eliminate
or even control national unrest. Rather, these measures spawned the
notorious Ustashi, terrorist extremists who were at least in part behind the assassination of Alexander himself in France in 1934.

Since Alexander's son Peter II was under age, Prince Paul
acted as regent. In a last—ditch effort to avoid a war that the country
was by no manner of means able to fight, Paul moved closer to the

---

* One should not think such matters irrelevant to the "national
question" of contemporary Yugoslavia. When this author was in
Ljubljana in June 1971 discussing the differing interpretations of the
constitutional amendments of that year with Slovene academics, one
extremely knowledgeable source referred to the problems inherent in
the founding of the interwar Kingdom of Serbs, Croats, and Slovenes
as the "original Sin of the Yugoslav state" and specifically linked
current problems to that conflict of interests.

Nazis. His desperate maneuvering to keep both the throne and the country together even led to a sporazum (agreement) in 1939 granting somewhat greater political autonomy to Croatia. The Tripartite Axis Pact in March of 1940 brought this house of cards down about his ears with an army coup that many Croats rather bitterly considered to have been directed against Paul's promise of increased Croat autonomy.

True or not, motive was less important than result. Germany invaded. Hitler parceled out Yugoslavia to those of its neighbors he wished to woo and established the Independent Kingdom of Croatia under the leadership of the Ustashi quisling Ante Pavelic. In this form the interwar repression in Croatia came full circle. Serbian repression had created the Ustashi terrorist resistance. Under Pavelic's short-lived Kingdom of Croatia, the Ustashi reaped a genocidal revenge on Serbs within its reach. Moreover, tactical, if not organizational, descendents of the Ustashi continue to escalate tension by attacks on Yugoslav representatives abroad, hijacking of airplanes, random bombings, and attempts to instigate uprisings within the country.

These are the extreme. One must note that even a more moderate point on the spectrum describes the Croat reaction to the German invasion: "To a man the Croatian nation rose against the terrorist regime of the Serbians who ruled in Croatia as if it were a Serbian Colony. . .", and considered that at the end of World War II: "Croatia is once again a Serbian Colony . . . . From Croatia was taken the Croatian territories of Syrmium, South Dalmatia with the Fjord of Kotor, Bosnia, and Hercegovina with the Sandzhak of Nova Pazar. . . ."[4]

In sum, if one considers Bertelsen's criteria for a nonstate nation: (1) Is the group in question generally recognized as a nation state? No; (2) Does the group claim to be a nation? Yes; then the Croatian nation qualifies as a nonstate nation (NSN) and may be compared within the overall framework. When dealing with a nation whose last significant era of independence (if one excludes the chaotic period of Pavelic's puppet state during World War II) was in the tenth and eleventh centuries; however, the theoretical possibilities for analyzing the history of Croatian struggle for national liberation are limited only by fragmented data and lack of space. If would be intellectually interesting, for example, to focus on three periods. First was the late 1800s when Ante Starcevic was the leading oracle and political strategist demanding the unification of all Croats, which in his view meant unification of all South Slav lands. Starcevic rejected any other ethnic validity in the region, refusing to admit to even the existence of a Serbian nationality.[5] Second was the interwar period where one might distinguish between the extremism of Ustashi terrorists with Ante Pavelic as the dominant NSN decision maker and the more moderate efforts of Vladko Macek, who took over leadership of the Croatian Peasant party after Radic's assassination.[6] Third there is the fate of the Croatian nation in Tito's Yugoslavia.

Without in any way dismissing the importance of historical developments for understanding the present, it is the third period that will be the focus of this analysis. So much has happened during the postwar years that it would be impossible to chronicle completely these events, still more difficult to make sense of them in anything other than a regretably token historical context. Moreover, choosing to analyize the present situation has the advantage of adding to the painfully slow-growing body of information necessary for cross-systems comparisons. What is the importance of the ideological dimension in understanding nonstate nations as international actors? Does the fact that the adversary is a communist state facilitate their task, make it more difficult, or make no difference? In short, are the resources, environment, or outcome changed when the struggle changes from nation versus nation or nation versus a recognized state that in the eyes of the international system has legitimate claim to its present real estate to a confrontation of a nation versus class?

REVOLUTION AS AN ANSWER:
NATIONALITY POLICY IN POSTWAR YUGOSLAVIA

Interwar Yugoslavia had existed as a patchwork of nations and conflicting national goals rooted in religious and ethnic differences that perpetuated blood-feuding and fierce localism. Politics mirrored national hostilities. Quite simply there was no effectively institutionalized cross-ethnic or national political party. World War II left Yugoslavia almost physically destroyed. The loss in lives and to the social and economic fabric of society had been among the highest in Europe. Despite these problems, for the first time a national political infrastrucure seemed to have a chance.

Western and Yugoslav scholars have rightly pointed to the integrating myth of partisan solidarity as the core of a "revitalized belief system" so necessary if there were to be a Yugoslavia in more than name, * if there were to be a Yugoslav identity, a common Yugoslav cause. [7] For the task facing Yugoslav communists extended beyond

----

*Unfortunately for clear usage, Yugoslavia is composed of "nations" (among which are both the Croatian and Serbian nations) and national minorities such as Hungarians, Slovaks, and so on. The expression "the national question" is commonly used to refer to inter-ethnic relations within the Yugoslav state, whereas reference to "a national party" inevitably means a political institution emcompassing members of all nations and nationalities of Yugoslavia, at least in principle not based on ethnic criteria.

revolution to nation-building. [8] It was an article of faith that in order
for the party to build socialism it had to create a truly unified South
Slav state. Thus Tito's partisans were in principle "international."
They fought against the Germans. But in Tito's own words, they
fought for "the liberation of Croats, Slovenes, Serbs, Macedonians,
Shiptars (Yugoslav Albanians), Mohammedains . . . for liberty,
equality, and brotherhood for all the nations of Yugoslavia." [9] The
provisional government established in the Bosnian town of Jajce on
November 29, 1943, was to be a political framework within which
ideological-revolutionary objectives in reality took a back seat to
national liberation.

Yet the shared experience of partisan resistance was faced with
1,000 years of ethnic separatism. Moreover, "international principles"
notwithstanding, during World War II the nations of Yugoslavia often
fought against each other. Hitler may not have given the Croats any
meaningful independence when he installed Pavelic as the head of his
puppet Kingdom of Croatia on April 10, 1941. But he did thereby un-
leash the fanatic Ustashi's genocidal revenge against Croatian Serbs.
Nor were the Serbs the only victims. These Ustashi madmen ravaged
the countryside, murdering Serbs, Jews, Gypsies, and known Croat
nationalists who had no stomach for their atrocities. Not suprisingly
there were also ugly retaliations, while the partisan army received
many recruits from those survivers with "blood in their eyes"—
soldiers who fought as passionately against Croats as they did against
the occupying Germans.

According to Croat claims, Serbian reprisals cost the lives of
a million Croats during and after the war. [10] Figures are subject to
dispute; however, it can not be disputed that mutual wartime atrocities
exacerbated existing interwar hostilities and severely complicated the
building of trust among Yugoslav nations regardless of official efforts
to bury the past in optimism about the future. Many Serbs and Croats
alike were sickened by these excesses. But on balance in this author's
opinion one has to reject the implicit assumption that wartime atrocities were in the long run favorable to communist nationality policy.
Memories are harder to censor than the press.

Moreover, within Croatia itself not only the partisan forces but
also the Croatian party contained a large percentage of Croatian Serbs,
which is reportedly still the case with the League of Croatian Communists in the 1970s. * In this sense the wartime experience entailed

---

* "Croatian Serbs" are individuals ethnically Serbian, living in
the Republic of Croatia. At the time of the Croatian crisis in 1971 un-
official estimates both of Yugoslav scholars and American diplomatic
personnel were that Croatian Serbs accounted for about 35 percent of
the League of Croatian Communists as compared to 15-17 percent of
the republic's population.

two conflicting trends. It did contribute to a revitalized belief system
and the beginnings of a multiethnic national political infrastructure,
even as it institutionalized the basis for ethnic tensions particularly
within the Republic of Croatia. The shadow of guilt by silent acqui-
esence if not active approval of Ustashi terror tactics meant that
many Croats were treated, or thought that they were treated, as
second-class citizens within the new state.

This attitude was in part a direct consequence of the political
actions of the partisan army at the end of the war, actions which continued to deepen the scars of ethnic hatred. By 1945 the army had
grown to some 800,000 soldiers fighting for a revolution often dimly
understood. In the eyes of the party the army was a valuable political
instrument and every effort was made to rechannel partisan dedication
into revolutionary struggle against real and imagined enemies of yes-
terday and tomorrow. As the German threat subsided, the army was
turned on Tito's wartime competitors—Chetniks, Ustashi, Slovene
White Guards, German collaborators, and along with them those who
might be expected to oppose the election of a communist government. [11]
Inevitably, innocent people were damaged in an excess of revolutionary
enthusiasm. Mistakes were committed, orders sometimes carried
out with more brutality than intended. Undoubtedly some blamed the
party. Others saw not the political forces but the army and considered
that army not in ideological but national terms, concluding bitterly
that Croatia had again suffered Serbian martial law. [12]

In short, revolution and partisan solidarity brought with it a
legacy of both plus and minus for socialist Yugoslavia. Then in 1948
the Soviet Yugoslav split provided an artificial national unity that
Yugoslavs—Serbs and Croats alike—almost came to consider real.
The problem with unity as a function of external threat is that when
the pressure is off, unresolved differences may embarrassingly
reemerge as they did in the 1960s when national/ethnic differences[13]
translated into intense struggle revolving around economic issues
central to the reform of 1965. [14]

At each stage a generic weakness of the Yugoslav political process reemerged; an irrational yearning to believe that there is one
answer, a panacea that can end deeply rooted national tensions, social
inequalities, and economic difficulties at one blow. During the partisan struggle the national question was submerged in the revolution.
It was thought that the proletarian class nature of the revolution would
solve remaining problems. Then the shift from Stalinism to self-
managing socialism was to be the answer. Then the Economic Reform
of 1965 would take care of the structural weaknessess of self-management. At each stage success was seen as sidetracked by evil forces,
resisting either correct theory or preventing its implementation.
There was a series of political villians: Miehailovic, Stalin, Rankovic.

There was always one hero: Tito. This was the political culture within which Croatian NSN decision makers of the 1970s operated.

DECISION MAKERS AND GOALS

For analytical purposes we will look at one recent cross-section of Croatian NSN activity in detail, the events of 1971-72. During these dramatic, confusing months Tito's policy toward the national question was put to its severest test. Political behavior that once would have been unacceptable was included within the spectrum of legitimate politics. Political dialogs openly expressed conflicts of interest that formerly were conducted in esoteric polemics, couched in either ideological or economic euphemisms.

Political actors can readily be identified, although there is a conceptual problem inherent to the situation. When NSN decision makers are considered to represent a subsystem, one must not forget that the scholar has resorted to an inevitably artificial analytical device. Such a device does not remove some NSN leaders from their roles within existing political systems, in the case at hand, those represented by the League of Yugoslav Communists (LCY) and the League of Croatian Communists (LCC). Therefore, reference to insystem leaders confuses rather than clarifies since often at least two systems are involved. In an at best only partially successful attempt to avoid this dilemma, what would be insystem decision makers in the more common usage of the term—that is, members of the Yugoslav or Croatian Communist party or those who basically felt that a solution could be found within the Yugoslav framework— will be referred to as NSN-y; those NSN emigre decision makers who want an independent, noncommunist Croatia and those within Yugoslavia who identify with that goal, as NSN-i. Even this leaves us with the difficulty that individuals who publicly identified themselves as NSN-y may be, and sometimes were, considered by others NSN-i. As always toward the center of any continuum, the mix is often so evenly balanced as to make it impossible to classify.

Nonetheless, in my judgment throughout 1971 the Croatian NSN had four sets of decision makers:

● NSN-y_1, leaders who were also LCY and LCC members such as Tripalo, Dabcevic-Kucar, Pirker, Sibl.

● NSN-y_2, radical student leaders represented by Cicak, Budisa, and Paradzik who were constantly attacked as NSN-i yet at least tactically continued to pledge support to the LCC leadership positions as represented by NSN-y_1.

● NSN-y_3, cultural leaders of the Matica Hrvatska association intent on defending usage of the Croatian literary language

and recognition of Croat cultural heritage within Yugoslavia. This
group was consistently seen as NSN-i particularly in Serbia and
undeniably its rapidly growing rank and file as well as some leadership positions did include those of NSN-i persuasion.

• Emigre NSN-i leaders symoblized by Branko Jelic (president
of right-wing Croatian National Committee and former associate of
Ustashi Leader Ante Pavelic) in West Germany or by leaders of
Australian Croat communities.

Not surprisingly a wide gap existed between the goals of NSN-y
and NSN-i decision makers. What is equally important to keep in
mind is that within the three groups of NSN-y leaders, goals were
also far from identical. Any understanding of these differences must
be rooted in their political context. Thus, it is important to look at
a topic still hotly debated among scholars both within and outside of
Yugoslavia. What in fact happened in 1971?

Year of False Hopes

At its most basic level the problem in 1971 was biological.
Tito, the giant of Yugoslav communism, was approaching his eighties.
Even he realized the dangers inherent in a system that considered
his person indispensable. The mammoth constitutional amendments
of 1971 in practice amounted to the Yugoslav president's attempt to
stagemanage his own succession.

These amendments were politically negotiated. Rather than
being drafted by a commission of legal experts, as the Constitution
of 1963 and earlier amendments had been, they were drafted by a
mixed commission of political leaders and legal advisers. The
drafting took two months. Tito presided at the final meeting, yet
in the end what he got surely was not what he had intended. Designed
to solve the problem of "After Tito, What?" the amendments had
become much more than that. Swept forward by demands for a
genuine participatory federalism, they reflected federation—republican and state-party power struggles. In the process it seemed at
first that the federation had all but disappeared. Although it retained
responsibility for defense, foreign policy, and a "united market" (no
one seemed quite sure what "united market" meant) one might almost
say it had "withered away."

Interrepublican committees were set up to negotiate political
and economic conflicts of interest. The rule was decision by consensus so in effect everyone had a vote. A collective presidency
consisting of members from each republic and each of the provinces
was to replace Tito, who was allowed by Amendment 36 to retain his
position as president for life.

All of this was legitimate, proper activity for expanding Croatian influence within Yugoslavia and equally properly led by the head of the Croat League of Communists, Miko Tripalo, and the party president, Savka Dabcevic-Kucar. By early April, however, these advances had indirectly sparked other, from Belgrade's view, infinitely more threatening activities. On April 7, 1971, the Yugoslav ambassador to Sweden, Vladimir Rolovic, was assassinated by Croatian nationalists, both born after 1945. Tension escalated to a boiling point. [15] Relations between Yugoslavia and Sweden deteriorated in a spate of formal protests that Sweden should have had better security and accusations that indeed the Swedes protected, even encouraged, Ustashi activities. The Yugoslav press questioned whether Sweden provided so much as "minimal protection" for the tens of thousands of Yugoslavs who work in Sweden and are exposed to "the terror of a handful of murders." [16] Claims by NSN-i leader Branko Jelic in West Germany that the Soviets supported Croat demands for an independent Croatia added other undertones to the already inflammable incident. [17]

Under the circumstances it is not surprising the Tripalo's telegram of condolences to the dead ambassador's widow did little to calm the situation. The LCC tried to parry anti-Croat repercussions with a report that "centralist" forces in Belgrade (particularly those connected with the UDBA--secret police) were allegedly plotting to discredit the Croat leadership by spreading rumors that the LCC itself maintained contacts with separatist elements abroad. [18] Charges and countercharges so bitter that Tito himself commented it would only worsen the situation to publish them apparently flew at the LCY seventeenth plenum on Brioni in late April where at least token agreement at the top was reached to "contain" national differences.

Moscow kept discretly or ominously silent, depending on one's view, while nervousness about Soviet intentions persisted. Whether or not Moscow was aiding Croatian terrorist groups, many informed Yugoslavs considered the stories of Soviet support plausible. Rumors of Soviet pressure for a naval base on the Adriatic at Split or Pula combined with reports of Warsaw Pact maneuvers scheduled for the Bulgarian-Yugoslav border "sometime" in the summer fed into these fears. [19]

In June, then Foreign Minister Tepavac took a symbolic trip to China. His visit was more psychological shadow-boxing than seeking a credible ally. Yugoslavia has had little in common with China, nor is it likely that the Yugoslavs expected more than moral support. As Chou En-lai later bluntly told his Balkan would-be allies, "Distant waters cannot quench fire." [20]

Soviet leader Brezhnev's visit to Belgrade in September had a superficially calming result, seemingly bringing Yugoslav-Soviet relations back to their normal agreement to disagree. Still, some

worried about Brezhev's reference to common socialist principles.
And it is fair to say that most thought his remark that the Soviets had
solved "their national question" more than tactless.

Still at least the situation had normalized to the point where Tito
began mending his fences with the West with a trip to Washington,
Ottawa, and London. While the president was reaffirming Yugoslav
nonalignment abroad, factionalism in the Croat party came to a head.
As Vladimir Bakaric, a virtual godfather of Croatian communism,
later admitted when Tito came back, the Bakaric faction went to him
personally for support against the "nationalists" in LCC leadership.
Tito promised he would take care of things. [21]

How the Yugoslav leader "took care of things" is now a matter
of record. He waited until stalemate in the interrepublican committee
over what Croatians perceived as economic exploitation broke down
into open protest. The specific issue was the Yugoslav foreign
currency system--a system whereby in Croat eyes an extremely large
percent of the foreign exchange that came into the country via the
Croatian coast was drained off into Belgrade. The enterprise was
allowed to keep only 7 percent of hard currently earned on export
of goods; 40 percent on tourism. That had long been a sore point in
Zagreb and one on which Tito had publicly supported the Croatian
leadership during his visit in September 1971. [22] Still nothing happened.
On November 23, 24 faculties at the university and various high schools
struck to "exert pressure on these forums whose duty it is to reform
the plundering foreign exchange regime and which are today unwilling
to do so."

Within a number of days the strike involved an estimated 30,000
students. According to the Tanjug version of student proclamation,
this was a peaceful, nonviolent action. The proclamation warned of
possible provocations, urging students not to go into the street. It
also explicitly supported the League of Croatian Communists and its
president, Sanka Dabcevic-Kucar.

At this point such support was decidely unwelcome. The Croat
NSN-y_1 leaders could have well been excused for thinking that with
friends like these they could do without enemies. Miko Tripalo, 45-
year-old representative of Croatia to the new Collective Presidency,
personally warned the students that their actions could have tragic
consequences, that they were already dangerous. He urged them to
return to lectures before they put the whole policy of the Croat party
in jeopardy.

Although deaf to pleas for cutting short their action, the students
on the whole stuck to their pledge of nonviolence, even to the extent,
according to Radio Zagreb, of throwing the leader of an ultraleft
faction calling for more radical views out of a meeting of the philosophy
faculty. Individuals did discuss the more extreme issues, but the
joint proclamation limited itself to demanding reform of the foreign

exchange system that Tito himself had promised two months before
when he said specifically, "this question must be solved, irrespective
of who resists it."

Tito attacked the strike as "counterrevolutionary" activity, [23]
warning of civil war and potential foreign intervention. Nationalist
and incidentally reform-minded Croat Leaders Tripalo and Dabcevic-
Kucar resigned. [24] Heads rolled at all levels of the Croat party, total-
ling some 800 resignations, expulsions, and replacements. At the
fifth LCC conference on January 21 and 22, 1972, Tito personally
ridiculed reports that Yugoslavia was in a state of crisis as "altogether stupid," insisting that the incidents were only "a matter of
past weakness, particularly at the top of the party." [25]

Seen in terms of NSN decision-making goals the events of 1971
demonstrated differences between the NSN-y leaders on what would be
acceptable Croatian autonomy and still wider divisions with respect
to tactics. Tripalo, for example, put forward a concept of Croatian
statehood that entailed a "sovereign" Croat republic still within
Yugoslavia but possessing far-reaching powers over political, economic, and, in the form of territorial defense units, even military
matters. Although the Croat party leaders continued to insist, perhaps
even to believe, that this could be a class sovereignty rooted in the
principles of self-managing socialism, they also supported a thinly
veiled nationalist ideology. Thus, whether the issue was one of right-
ing what Croats considered economic exploitation of their republic or
legitimating a "demand for linguistic equality" in the form of Croatian
literary language, or defending the rights of the cultural organization,
Matica Hrvatska, to revive specifically Croatian heroes, Tripalo
came down on the popular side of the issue in terms of his republican
constituency. In so doing he tried to cover his party base by insisting
that all along the defenders of the Croatian nation had been the communists, who during the war had fought for the unity of all Croatian
lands. He rejected all arguments that Croatian nationalism was in
any sense anti-Socialist;[26] rather in his interpretation the mass
movement in Croatia was an affirmation of socialism. He explicitly
dissociated himself from NSN-i decision makers:

> Our conception of statehood differs from all right-wing
> conceptions. It is a state of a special type, Croatia with-
> in the framework of Yugoslavia. It is the sovereign national
> state of the Croatian people and of the Serbs who live in it.
> Hence a state was involved and a socialist community that
> is based on the sovereignty of the people and on the power
> of the working class in which full national equality has
> been established . . . . [27]

At the same time NSN-y_1 perceived itself deeply threatened by the
strategies employed by both NSN-y_1, and NSN-Y_3. Tripalo himself
prophetically warned, "Tactics of revolutionary struggle can not be
determined in a thousand places. "[28]

Conversely, despite differences in their goals symbolized at the outside by NSN-y_2 demands for a Croation army and Croatia's membership in the United Nations, the student NSN-y_2 leaders publicly supported NSN-y_1 decision makers in their struggle for expanding Croatian rights and arena of sovereign control while remaining within Yugoslavia. NSN-y_2 publicly recognized NSN-y_1 as legitimate spokesmen for the nation. Such support may or may not have been purely tactical. Had the more far-reaching NSN-y_2 demands have met—a de facto army, recognition in international organizations, "that not a single Croatian child should study any language other than Croatian"— there is no assurance that NSN-y_1 representatives identified with Tripalo would have continued to be seen by the students as operating in NSN-y_2 genuine interests.

Given Tito's method of domestic crisis management in December 1971, we will never know what would have been the relationship of these two NSN-y groups. By definition NSN-y_1, symbolized by the Croatian triumvirate (Tripalo, Dabcevic-Kucar, Pirker) became guilty of tolerating a class enemy, of fostering counterrevolution. Student NSN-y_2, leaders became "counterrevolutionaries or at best counterrevolutionary dupes." NSN-y_3 spokesmen, that is, leaders of the cultural organization Matica Hrvatska became guilty of attempting to establish a conspiratorial opposition party.

Meanwhile, toward the other end of the continuum, NSN-i leaders continued to think in terms of an independent, autonomous Croatia free from communist control irrespective of whether that control resided in Belgrade or Zagreb.

Whether or not there was weakness at the top of the LCY, Tito was undoubtedly in a position to know. Yet with the "weakness" ostensibly overcome, Croatian NSN activity did not disappear, although the individuals identified with NSN-y_1, were eliminated from Yugoslav political life; student NSN-y_2 leaders went to jail, as did a variety of the cultural leaders associated with NSN-y_3. The result seems to have been a radicalization of remaining NSN-y_2, and NSN-y_3, decision makers who, if they managed to stay out of prison, either went underground or left the country. This in turn strengthened those among NSN-i leaders who favored more extreme tactics than student strikes.

Miniinvasion: Guerrilla Infiltration into Bosnia

At the end of June 1972 a group of anti-Yugoslav, allegedly Ustashi guerrillas crossed into Yugoslavia from Austria, reportedly with "an arsenal" of submachine guns, rifles with telescopic sights, pistols with silencers, and portable radios. They stole a truck, raised the Croatian flag, and drove 375 miles into Bosnia. Although

the raiders did not find the anticipated support of the population, they
retreated into the mountains to fight a running gun battle with police
and territorial defense units that left 13 members of the security
forces dead [29] along with 15 of the guerrillas. Of this band, which
called itself the "Croatian Revolutionary Brotherhood," four were
captured, three subsequently executed, and the fourth sentenced to
20 years apparently in return for his cooperation. [30]

As might be expected, Croatian NSN-i reports of these events
vary widly from official Yugoslav versions. For example, Croats
abroad claimed that telephone connections had been disrupted between
Sarajevo and Belgrade as well as in the militia to wipe out the guerrillas. They quote from the Western press on "the grave" situation
in Yugoslavia, citing rumors that over 1,000 Croat communists have
been expelled from the party as "rotten liberals," pro-Western, and
nationalists. By August this figure jumped to 10,000 expelled with
"hundreds" of political trials underway. [31] The point is not the accuracy or the lack of it of the figures on either side. Rather the
importance is in the technique used by the NSN-i leaders involved.
This is a form of psychological warfare. To the extent that it buoys
the morale of potential supporters, or angers them at the repressive
nature of the Yugoslav regime, or identifies "pro-Western with
nationalist" in the minds of otherwise neutral readers, or infuriates
Yugoslav official spokesmen into rash denials thereby giving the incident still wider publicity, such tactics pay in the eyes of some
NSN-i decision makers.

Nineteen guerrillas are more of an annoyance than a serious
threat to the stability of the state. In Yugoslavia, however, their
symbolic importance vastly outweighed the numbers involved. Not
only did this attack sharply worsen strains on the ever-fragile fabric
of interethnic relations, it demonstrated the permeability of Yugoslav
borders and created a state of seige mentality that played a not insignificant part in the downfall of the liberal chairman of the Serbian
party, Marko Nikezic, in October 1972. [32]

The age of the invaders, most of whom were apparently in their
early twenties and according to reports "had emigrated only in the
past year" (1971), seems to dispute the Yugoslav official version
that Ustashi followers are limited to Croatian fascists of the older
generation or, on the other hand, that they were Ustashi. The timing
of their infiltration—two days before four of the Croatian student
leaders were to have gone on trial in Zagreb in connection with
charges stemming from the Zagreb student strike of 1971—was most
likely not a chance coincidence. [33]

In sum, by 1972 the nature of Croatian NSN decision makers
and of their missions had changed dramatically. All three NSN-y
groups that dominated the political spectrum in 1971 had disappeared.
And while it is not impossible that there will emerge another NSN-y$_1$

faction within the League of Croatian Communists in the future, the instinct for political self-preservation is against it, at least in the short run. Jelic, who has subsequently died, appears to have been a more symbolic than real leader of the NSN-i faction. The NSN-i members who fought it out with the Yugoslav police and territorial defense units in Bosnia for two weeks called themselves "the Croatian Revolutionary Brotherhood." It is unlikely that this grouping ceased to exist with the death of 18 guerrillas and the imprisonment of the sole surviver of the raid. The three men who were executed were Australian citizens. Thus, although this author has no specific information, one may assume that with some assurance that NSN-i decision makers (unknown) do coordinate Croatian emigre activities in Australia. These may or may not be the same persons that planned the assassination of Rolovic in 1971 and the skyjacking that liberated those assassins from a Swedish prison in 1972.

Whether or not the actors are operating according to the same script, they appear to have a similar senario with emphasis on terror as a tactic. This is not to say that all Croatian NSN-i activity outside of Yugoslavia is the work of the most extreme factions. One might identify Juraj Krnjevic—who headed a meeting of delegates of the Croatian Peasant party in London on April 22 and 23, 1973 which put forward a memorandum to be presented to the forthcoming conference on European security—as a still viable moderate NSN-i decision maker. Yet the question is not whether Croatian nationalists exist who are not terrorists. Of course they do. The question is who has primary access or control of the resources.

RESOURCES, ENVIRONMENT, AND COMPONENTS

One of the more difficult problems in applying the NSN conceputalization to Croatia is distinguishing between resources and environment. This is not a problem that is limited to ex post facto analysis. It was a central concern of the various NSN decision-makers involved, who were operating in circumstances where the line between real and perceived resources was badly blurred. Nor, despite the fact that we are dealing with short time periods, did resources remain consistent. Or to put it another way, today's resource had a way of becoming tomorrow's dubious asset.

Throughout 1970-71 NSN-y_1 decision makers' primary resource was the rising Croatian nationalism with the republic. Institutionally, this meant an alliance with NSN-y_3, whose base was the Croatian cultural association Matica Hrvatska, and an open discussion of a mass people's movement. NSN-y_1's increasing majority within the League of Croatian Communists itself was another resource. Even their relationship to the student NSN-y_2 leaders at certain periods could be viewed as a resource. Indeed until late in the game, Tito's personal support was also perceived (if incorrectly so) as a vital resource.

The increasingly republican-oriented Yugoslav domestic balance of power as symbolized by the envisioned constitutional amendments of 1971 gave NSN-y_1 leaders a favorable environment within which to maneuver. The interrepublican committees were probably the most important organizational forum within the environment. The negative aspects of that environment included the intensifying fears of Croatian Serbs, backlash Serbian nationalism in the neighboring republic, increasing nervousness of the League of Yugoslav Communists that the LCC was becoming infected with nationalism, and the inability of NSN-y decision makers to control the impact of more extreme NSN-i tactics on their own options.

Components of NSN-y_1 strategy were threefold: (1) utilizing the favorable environment to expand Croatian autonomy into de facto sovereignty via veto power in the interrepublican committees; (2) consolidating popular support to improve its bargaining positions vis-a-vis the center and other republics (this meant strengthening the alliance with Matica Hrvatska and contributing to the growth of the "mass people's movement)"; (3) using the threat of more radical alternatives from the center.

The student NSN-y_2 leaders had as resources their control over the official student organization as well as the overwhelming support of at least their more moderate objectives on the part of most Croatian university students. Their environment in the republic was largely sympathetic, since they in turn were considered a resource by NSN-y_1. Within the larger Yugoslav context, however, the environment was predominately hostile from the moment the radical student leadership gained control of the Zagreb University student organization. The NSN-y_2 leadership components focused on radicalizing their student constituency, striking, and attempting to push the League of Croatian Communists further than NSN-y_1 decision makers in fact wanted to go.

NSN-y_3, cultural leaders associated with Matica Hrvatska, had as a resource both rising nationalism within Croatia and its apparent legitimization both of the republican party leadership and within the broader Yugoslav context as implied by the constitutional amendments. They used the organizational framework of the association for mobilization purposes, its newspaper frequently as both media and message. Within the republican environment they faced fear and hostility from the Serbian minority. This manifested itself particularly in sharp confrontations with the veteran's organizations, dominated by Serbian partisans, * and also rising tensions with the Serbian cultural association, Prosveta. In neighboring Serbia the rapidly swelling Matica membership fanned flames of matching Serbian nationalism,[35] even as did $NSN-y_1$'s references to a mass people's movement and $NSN-y_2$'s takeover of the official Croatian student organizations. More than either of the other NSN-y leaders, $NSN-y_3$ decision makers were viewed with suspicion for foreign contacts and held tacitly responsible for behavior of emigre nationalists. $NSN-y_3$ missions consisted primarily in attempts to strengthen their own organizational base and programs geared to making the average Croat more aware of his or her cultural heritage or language, thereby increasing national identification and influence over $NSN-y_1$ decision makers.

NSN-i leaders are the hardest to deal with when it comes to distinguishing between real, potential, and /or perceived resources. One can assume that to some extent both sympathy and financial aid from Croat emigre communities operated as a resource, supplemented by some form of contribution from some portion of the Croat workers in Europe, even though many of these labor migrants intended to return to Yugoslavia. Despite rumors, there is no hard evidence that Soviet contributions either financial or political could be considered a resource of the more extreme NSN-i faction abroad, although one might say that the ability to make the Yugoslav government increasingly nervous and unsure of the facts in the case was a psychological resource, as was the ability to appeal to lingering anticommunist sentiments in capitalist systems.

The environment of the NSN-i groupings abroad tends to be benign, because countries where NSN-i factions plan their missions have the normal difficulties of keeping track of emigrant activity. Furthermore, these countries are hesitant to take harsh measures against suspected NSN-i terror-oriented activists for fear of unjustly harassing Yugoslav migrant workers and thereby destabilizing their own domestic situations. Massive Yugoslav outmigration has provided

-----

* Perhaps the most explosive incident came at a veterans' celebration in Podravska Slatina, a small town in northeastern Croatia where a veterans' demonstration was suddenly faced with demonstrating Croatian nationalists carrying the Croatian flag and coat-of-arms. There was no violence; yet this symbolic confrontation provoked sharp concern among Croatian Serbs and veterans' organizations alike. General Rade Bulat went so far as to demand in the Croatian Assembly that the republic be officially federalized to safeguard the interests of its Serbian minority.[34]

a continual flow of potential NSN-i recruits, while there are varying degrees of access to media depending on the host country involved. Components of the NSN-i factions seem to have ranged from non-violent radicalization of migrants, interest group tactics within the countries bordering Yugoslavia, and psychological pressure on the Yugoslav regime, to terrorist missions such as assassination and hijacking airplanes.

EVALUATION OF NSN ACTIVITY

Differences in goals notwithstanding, it was tactical consider-ations that resulted in the three NSN-y groups' sabotage of each other's objectives, eventually contributing to the elimination of all three as serious political contenders either within the NSN subsystem or the broader Yugoslav context. In attempting to utilize the stated principles of self-managing socialism via the 1971 constitutional amendments as a wedge with which to obtain their goals, $NSN-y_1$ had to balance between satisfying their Croatian republic base (the mass people's movement) and not relinquishing their communist credentials with the LCY. One might say this was the one version of Bertelsen's audibility/durability dilemma. At best it was a delicate, extremely difficult task.

The more radical demands of student $NSN-y_2$ leaders potentially could have cut in two different directions. With luck, they would have been seen as the handwriting on the wall if $NSN-y_1$ Croat demands, in principle still legitimate, were not met. However, there was always the danger that the center, in this case the LCY, would lump radicals and moderates together, using the unacceptable demands as an excuse for eliminating them with one blow. In this sense, student support for Tripalo and Dabcevic-Kucar was a kiss of death.

Once the students refused to abandon their strike, thereby demonstrating that acceptable (marginally) $NSN-y_1$ decision makers were not in control of the situation, the actual nature of their demands at the moment became as irrelevant as the political life-expectancy of the $NSN-y_1$ Croatian communist leadership was short. Despite Tripalo's defiant stand that no matter how many leaders were re-placed, "the policies supported by the Croation people cannot be turned aside,"[36] he could no longer walk the necessary tightrope. His one chance would have been to break the student strike by force so as to prove his ability to eliminate counterrevolutionary tactics. To have done so would have destroyed the loose-knit alliance of in-tellectuals, technocrats, economic elites, and cultural nationalists that formed the core of his republican support.* It is impossible to lead a mass people's movement in a direction it does not want to go and to retain a vestige of credibility.

Moreover, extreme statements of NSN-y_2 leaders aside, the strike itself was limited to demanding a goal systematically put forward by the NSN-y_1 decision makers and publicly supported by Tito. To have broken it by force would have cut deeply into the NSN-y_1 group's self-image as well.

Was it thus the fault of student NSN-y_2 leaders that the "Croatian Spring" disintegrated once again into a winter of discontent? Was November premature? Would it have been wiser to follow the more cynical tactic attributed to the student leaders, that is, waiting until January when many Croatian workers from abroad were home for the holidays, thus demonstrating both maximum public support and the working-class composition of that support? Or should the strike not have been held at all?

Certainly if survival of either the NSN-y_1 leaders of the NSN-y_2 student leadership is considered, the strike backfired, providing the rationale for repression. (It did, ironically, appear to bring about a move toward the economic concessions the students demanded.) There is little evidence that waiting would have improved the situation. There is a good deal of reason to think it might have been more costly in terms of violence and bloodshed. To have canceled the strike after committing the bulk of student NSN-y_2 energies to the project would have finished the student leadership's credibility with its own constituency to say nothing of the damage to the individual egos involved.

Indeed, if one considers survival of the NSN-y_2 faction, once the student leadership was firmly committed to the strike, it was probably doomed. If keeping NSN-y_1 in power was an important enough goal, the only slight chance of doing so would have been to begin the strike and then call it off at Tripalo's request. And even that might not have worked.

Tripalo's dilemma paralleled that of the student leaders. He too was caught in the vise of center versus constituency. Further, that vise was tightened intolerably by the existence and behavior of the more extreme NSN-i leaders. Throughout 1971, tactics such as

----

* It was one thing to expel select radical faculty members from the party for their nationalist views as with Djodan and Veselica in July 1971 as a token of good faith, and even that measure had been far from popular, particularly among the students. To have used violent police action or to have called in the Yugoslav army against the students would have split both the Croat party and the republic.

the assassination of Rolovic in Sweden, claims of Soviet support for an independent Croatia, and so on, had exacerbated the NSN-y$_1$'s already precarious situation. Both goals and tactics of these two groups were completely incompatible, yet symbolically entwined. Successes of the terrorists jeopardized the progress of the moderate, thereby making more persuasive the argument of those favoring extreme tactics, that is, that nothing else would work.

Here an outsider analyzing strategy is always caught in cultural baggage and long-standing personal preferences. For the individuals hurt and their families, increased violence is always bad. For the NSN-i decision makers of any nationality to whom independence comes first there is always the revolutionary rationale that to get radical change one first has to radicalize a population to demand it.

The impact of these events on Yugoslav foreign policy over time has been much deeper than the image problem that Tito complained of when he accused the Western press of blowing the "Croatian events" out of all proportion. The means taken to restore order may have resulted in a better domestic balance from his point of view. In hindsight one can say that they were the first step in the aging Yugoslav leader's drive to reform or, if necessary, recreate the League of Communists of Yugoslavia into a united party rather than the sum of its republican parts. His insistence on a central party with the power to interfere and to which republic parties must be strictly responsible is undoubtedly an attempt to insure that post-Tito Yugoslavia will survive all decentralizing demands. The result is that it is unlikely that representatives of the Croatian party in the near future will dare to publicly identify themselves with the Croatian nation.

In terms of Croatia as a NSN, eliminating NSN-y decision makers both strengthened the hand of more radical groups and potentially increased the Ustashi recruitment base. Following the settlement of this "noncrisis," there was a sharp rise in terrorist activity: one airplane bombed, 28 dead; a train bombing with six injuries; a bomb in the Borba plant in Zagreb that killed a father of five.

Moreover, many people who may not have done so before began to believe that Yugoslavia could not last without Tito. In this manner the Yugoslav president himself contributed simultaneously to the belief that he once again "saved" his country and that he was an indispensable kingpin holding it together. Thus 1971, a year of great expectations and dead hopes, became a prelude to the more violent forms of nonstate nation missions in 1972. Throughout 1972 NSN-i activity appeared most dramatically focused in terrorist missions and propaganda designed to weaken Yugoslavia abroad.

Guerrilla invasion into Bosnia sharply worsened Yugoslavia's official relations with both Austria, whose borders were also crossed by the invaders, and Australia, since most of these young men were from Australia,[37] leading to Australian displeasure at the execution of her naturalized citizens. According to Prpic's version, the new Australian Labour government's investigation into the situation led to the confiscation of secret files that allegedly proved the former government had protected Croatian terrorists. The attorney general announced possible deportation of undesirable Australian citizens of Croatian descent, setting off a national scandal: "For weeks all newspapers covered the developments, reported on the Croatian question, the struggle of Croatian people. A furor broke out in the Australian parliament where Senator Murphy was strongly criticized for his controversial and unconstitutional acts against the Croatian immigrants who number over 150,000."[38]

Such furor did nothing to improve the tone of Yugoslav Premier Bijedic's visit to Australia in late April, a visit that brought thousands of angry Croat demonstrators in front of the Australian Parliament. Bijedic's demands that the Labour government put a stop to Croatian activities and extradite offenders appears to have resulted in a few arrests. Some Croats fled the country and then the situation returned to its former norm—a sign that the Australian government was too split over this issue to take any decisive action. Also during 1972, relations with Sweden once again hit zero when the Swedish government released the assassins of Rolovic to three Croatian hijackers who flew to Spain.[39]

In short, if one evaluates NSN-i activity in 1972 in terms of maximum objective—progress along the road to an autonomous, independent Croatia—the Croatian nation is not perceptibly closer to that goal. But if one takes the middle-range goals of undermining Yugoslav unity, increased psychological pressure on the government, and damage to Yugoslavia's foreign relations, the NSN-i decision makers who planned the terrorist missions score high. Ironically, they score perhaps higher than do the 1971 NSN-y leaders' moderate tactics aimed at more modest gains.

THE CROATIAN NSN WITHIN THE INTERNATIONAL CONTEXT

From the perspective of impact on the international context, the Croatian NSN primarily affects two arenas: (1) Yugoslav foreign policy and (2) the domestic balance in industrialized nations where Croatian workers make up a significant part of the labor force. It undoubtedly has a marginal impact on other nonstate nations as well.

One must keep in mind that one of the factors distinguishing the Croatian NSN from other cases discussed in this volume is the existence of what Tito has somewhat bitterly termed the "Yugoslav three armies abroad," the Gastarbeiter or guest worker. Prior to 1964 only 7,000 Yugoslav citizens were formally registered as working abroad,[40] a tiny fraction of even the official 1971 figure of 671,000. This escalation in absolute numbers resulted from two internal Yugoslav developments, thereby underlining the often-ignored linkages between domestic and foreign policy that increasingly impinge on international relations: (1) the economic reform of 1965 which, in its attempt to rationalize and make more efficient the country's economy by closing "political" factories, led to a sudden jump in unemployment; (2) the fall of Alexander Rankovic at that time considered Tito's most likely successor, in 1966. Rankovic's fall changed many aspects of Yugoslav politics. But from the perspective of the average citizen as well as of this study, one of the most important of these was the citizen's ability to cross state borders in search of work.

Thus by 1971 more than 3 percent of the total population, and according to Yugoslav sources roughly 15 percent of the state's nonagricultural labor force, was outside the country.[41] Yugoslavs were emigrating at an estimated 4.2 percent, the second highest migration rate in Europe.

Short-run advantages were undoubtedly tempting. Yugoslav workers brought or sent home some 20 percent of their earnings, which reportedly totaled $800 million in 1972[42]—not a small sum for any country with Yugoslavia's economic difficulties. In addition, allowing the migrants to work abroad did accomplish its explicit objective of decreasing domestic unemployment. It side-stepped potential social unrest while improving the standard of living of individual workers and their families.

Nonetheless, politically the massive outmigration complicated the Yugoslav government's relations with host countries in a variety of complex ways. First, on matters directly concerned with the behavior or well-being of the migrants themselves, negotiations are anything but a problem-free process in an international environment where conflicts of interest are more often evident than where to begin on the road to reconciliation of differences. Second, and more relevant from our current focus, a disproportionately large number of these foreign workers had either emigrated from Croatia or were Croatian by nationality. This was particularly so between 1965 and 1968, when Zimmerman refers to five studies estimating that of all Yugoslav migrants, 40.5 percent to 59.4 percent came from Croatia.[43] Even after 1968, 33.3 percent of those emigrating came from that republic.

This imbalance did nothing to improve interethnic tensions within Yugoslavia. It certainly fed into already existing Croatian feelings of economic exploitation that sparked the Zagreb student strike in 1971, both strengthening Croat arguments about unfair distribution and intensifying bitterness at delayed solutions. For the republican leadership a reversal in migration trends was an implicit condition for improvement in republic-federation relations. Take the blunt statement of the former head of the Croatian Executive Council, Dragutin Haramija: "I must frankly say: no federal government which in the period to come would consider the possibility of even more of our citizens departing for abroad and relying on their checks to solve Yugoslavia's balance of payments problem could expect support from Croatia."[44]

The large numbers of Croatian migrants, however, had other explosive implications. To the NSN-i decision makers the migration provided a mass potential constituency to serve as a base for their demands for Croatian independence. Whether or not the Croatian migrants were separatists or even ardent nationalists, they were certainly exposed to separatist, nationalist viewpoints much more openly and systematically than while at home in Croatia. The disorientation and dislocation of working abroad most likely did increase their sense of ethnic identity, although there are some reasons to think that for those intent on going back it may have made them more aware that dispite Yugoslav sensitivity on these questions, Yugoslavs working in Austria, for example, are perceived as Yugoslavs to such an extent that until recently there was an attempt to keep track of them by ethnic nationality in Austrian records.

It is less important whether or not the NSN-i decision makers working for Croatian separatism won the battle for the hearts and minds of the Croatian migrant laborers than that the visibility of that attempt combined with a few highly publicized successes (such as with the young assassins of Rolovic) to create a kind of psychosis on this point among other Yugoslav nationalities and even at high levels within the party. This in turn led to a self-fulfilling prophecy. If Croatians who considered it possible, not incompatible, to be Croatian and loyal Yugoslavs were treated with suspicions, as they were, it is not surprising that they began to feel increased alienation and annoyance. The government wanted to keep foreign currency flowing; it was less enthusiastic about the freedom of movement of the individuals earning that money once back in Yugoslavia, where after the events of November-December 1971 singing of a nationalistic song could cost a celebrating worker home for the holidays his job while he cooled his heels in jail.

From our perspective the importance of the Gastarbeiter phenomenon is that of an intensifier and sensitizer on multiple dimensions. The existence of this number of foreign workers makes what is a foreign policy problem for Yugoslavia a domestic problem for the countries in which the emigrant workers form increasingly significant parts of the labor force. The governments of those countries become more sensitive to emigre lobbyists, including Croatian NSN-i factions. In part as a result, official Yugoslav fears are exacerbated; NSN-i hopes raised. In both cases these psychological variables influence the choice of options and interactions of the actors.

Moreover, should there be the much-talked-of and dreaded deepening of the current European recession, these foreign workers will become an ever more likely resource as NSN-i appeals dovetail with economic pressures to, at a minimum, make the Croatians among the Gastarbeiter more apprehensive about returning to Yugoslavia where there is little reason to think the socioeconomic fabric of the country could absorb the strain of a "great leap forward" in unemployment.

This situation along with the more specific undermining of Yugoslavia's relations with host countries such as Sweden and Australia can have direct, visible impact on the foreign policy priorities of the Yugoslav state. There are indirect foreign policy consequences as well. For as Yugoslavia appears more vulnerable, it also appears more tempting to those who would like to pick up the pieces should this maverick socialist state not survive Tito's passing. This in turn puts present Yugoslav policy makers in the unpleasant role of perceived transitional figures on the international state, a perception that makes dependable policy relations all the more difficult to develop. Nor are the repercussions only political. Yugoslav political tensions in large part mirror economic phenomena. It is easy to forget that Yugoslavia is a developing, or at best semi-developed, country. Only the most northern part of the country, Slovenia and present day Croatia, have reached what economists consider a take-off point in terms of economic development. Yugoslavia's economy is one of scarcity in which standards of living oscillate wildly from one part of the country to another. For the more modernized north, teetering on the edge of a West European standard, it is agonizing to see their small margin of comfort drained off to "equalize" levels of development in the south that could not be made equal by even much greater inputs of capital. For the southern, less developed republics, the unfairness of a situation in which, although their absolute standard rises, the gap between them and the industrialized north continues to increase, in a political environment which has led them to expect better, is equally infuriating. In such circumstances, need for and benefits of foreign investments and credits are obvious. Yet the very uncertainty of the country's

political future discourages investment other than by the most politically dangerous investors--the two superpowers hoping to secure a
foothold in the Yugoslavia of tomorrow.[45]

SOME TENTATIVE PREDICTIVE SPECULATIONS

From the foregoing it seems fair to conclude that Croatia does
fit within Bertelsen's category of nonstate nations and in this capacity
directly influences Yugoslav foreign policy options. On the surface
the fact that Yugoslavia is officially dedicated to a socialist ideology
and led by a Communist party does not significantly change the relationship of the Yugoslav state to the factionalized Croatian NSN
decision makers from that, say, of the Britist to Croatia's northern
Irish counterparts. [46] True, in the jargon the NSN-y leaders became
"counterrevolutionaries"; however, in noncommunist societies they
are equally attacked using different labels. In short, an official
dedication to an international ideology neither prevents nor solves
the problem. It may, however, facilitate containment.

With respect to Croatia in the 1970s, elements of Yugoslav
ideology initially worked in favor rather than against at least the
NSN-y_1 leaders. First, the philosophy of self-management strengthened demands for republican autonomy, blurring the lines between
a self-managing Croatia within Yugoslavia and de facto sovereignty.
Second, the official LCY policy toward the national question in which
there is no question about the legitimacy of Croatian nationhood, even
if there are intense differences on what rights flow from that status,
also strengthened the hand of Croatian communists who felt that
"nation" should have increasing equality with "class. " One could go
as far as to say that at least early in the game the party legitimacy of
these NSN leaders eased tensions rather than exacerbated them. It
made a range of recognized successes possible and facilitated
compromise solutions. It was not inevitable that Tripalo and
Dabcevic-Kucar would lose control of the League of Croatian
Communists, nor that they would fail in their attempt to bring about
a controlled transition to what Croatians could perceive as genuinely
equal federation in which a significant degree of Croatian sovereign
control over the fate of the nation would have drained off sentiment
for an independent Croatia.

One of the few feasible alternatives to demands for independence
territorially is to arrive at domestic accommodations where nonstate-
nations feel that their interests (economic, cultural, political) are
better protected by the collective than they could be in independent
isolation. The tragedy of Bangladesh is not that independence led
to mammoth starvation; the starvation is tragic in itself. It resulted

in part from the dislocation and extraordinary resource demands created by the struggle for independence. That struggle, however, might have been of a very different nature had the Bengalis not found that their position within Pakistan was rapidly deteriorating from difficult to unendurable. Civil war was not the only solution until Pakistan's indiscriminate violence made any version of tommorrow better than today as far as the individuals involved were concerned. Estimates of the numbers massacred by Pakistanis in Bangladesh before the 1971 war began to reach 1 million and above. The accuracy of the number is less important than the desperation those deaths produced. Nations talk in terms of struggles for independence; authorities use the rhetoric of repressing treason; independence struggles and treason do occur. They usually involve relatively small parts of the population unless that struggle for independence is actually seen as a fight for political-economic survival of the nation.

Croatia is not Northern Ireland or Bangladesh, despite perceived similarities among Croatian NSN spokesmen—not yet and maybe never. Nonetheless, concern with the future of the Croatian nation and its impact on Yugoslav foreign policy is far more than an academic exercise. This chapter has traced in summary form events since 1971 that in some sense parallel those of interwar Yugoslavia although they are less violent. Radic was seen as a legitimate spokesman of the Croatian nation within the framework of the Kingdom of Serbs, Croats, and Slovenes. His death, Alexander's suspension of the Constitution, and martial law in Croatia led to the Ustashi who in turn helped destroy Yugoslavia and certainly made it harder to put the country back together in the postwar period.

Tripalo and the NSN-y leaders had legitimacy and were changing the impression that within socialist Yugoslavia, as before, Croatia was a Serbian colony. Their disappearance from the political spectrum did bring a flurry of increased terrorist activity; worse, it recreated within Croatia a sense of hopelessness about ever achieving a South Slav state in which equality is reality not myth. There is evidence that it significantly strengthened the position of those most disposed to violence among remaining NSN-i leaders abroad. So far these negative effects have been largely contained. The problem is less today than tomorrow. Very much depends on both the state of the economy and political scene when Tito dies. He is now (in 1975) 83 years old. This means that the likelihood of an extreme Croatian NSN-i faction forcefully entering the international context in the near future is almost a sure thing.

It would be absurd not to anticipate that some NSN-i decision makers favor immediate, violent provocation as the logical reaction to Tito's death. In their view, why wait until power is reconsolidated? From that perspective it makes sense to strike when the enemy is weakest, and whether or not Yugoslavia will be weak enough to allow Croatia to fall away (something this author considers unlikely); it is almost a sure thing that among those who live on hope and feed on desperation, there will be some who are willing to try.

Then will come the test: Will postwar Yugoslavia reenact the scenario of the interwar period? For if Croatia as a republic is held responsible for potential provocations by radical NSN-i leaders from outside and subjected to even temporary occupation, one does not have to be a confirmed pessimist to fear civil war. And if anyone thinks the repercussions of such a conflict in the heart of the Balkans would be limited to Yugoslavia, I could only suggest that person is not a dreamer but a political fool.

It is not the nature of the provocation that will count, rather the official reaction. If that response follows the pattern of lumping the moderate together with the extreme, used to end the political careers of NSN-y1 decision makers in 1971, or the escalation of harassment for "nationalist" offenses in Croatia that followed the miniinvasion in Bosnia in 1972, it has all the possibility of ending in a downhill slide to disaster.

Yet history does not repeat itself without the help of men and women who make decisions. As one commentator succinctly put it: "To paraphrase Talleyrand, there are many ways of coping successfully with a nationalist movement, but sitting on it is not one of them."[47] A useful axiom to keep in mind for communist and noncommunist policy makers alike.

NOTES

1. Ivo Omrcanin, Diplomatic and Political History of Croatia (Philadelphia: Dorrance, 1972), p. 35.

2. Note peasant uprising of Matija Gubec in 1573, in Stephen Clissold, ed., A Short History of Yugoslavia (Cambridge: Cambridge University Press, 1966), p. 25. Also Z. Crnja, Cultural History of Croatia (Zagreb: Office of Information, 1962), pp. 248-55.

3. Ivo J. Lederer, "Nationalism and the Yugoslavs," in Nationalism in Eastern Europe, ed. Peter F. Sugar and Ivo J. Lederer (Seattle: University of Washington Press, 1966), p. 141.

4. Omrcanin, op. cit., pp. 176, 180.

5. Lederer, op. cit., p. 420.

6. For a good basic account of the interwar period, see Jacob B. Hoptner, Yugoslavia in Crisis 1934-1941 (New York: Columbia University Press, 1962).

7. See M. George Zaninovich, The Development of Socialist Yugoslavia (Baltimore: John Hopkins University Press, 1968), p. 44 ff, and Gary K. Bertsch, "Currents in Yugoslavia: The

Revival of Nationalisms," Problems of Communism, November/
December 1973, pp. 1-15.

8. For a provocative approach to that process, see Gary
K. Bertsch, "Nation-building in Yugoslavia: A Study of Political
Integration and Attitudinal Concensus," Sage Professional Paper,
Comparative Politics Series 01-0222, 1971.

9. Phyllis Auty, Tito (New York: Ballantine, 1972), p. 81.

10. Omrcanin, op. cit., p. 181. For an account of massacres
of Croatian regular army soldiers and civilians turned over to
partisan forces after their surrender to the British, see Major—
General Charles A. Willoughby, The Croatian Slaughterhouse,
reviewed in East Europe, June 1975.

11. Matter-of-factly referred to by Auty in her largely pro-
Tito biography, op. cit., p. 115.

12. Omracanin, op. cit., p. 180.

13. As the leading figure in the Croatian Communist party
commented as early as 1966, "If the Economic Reform does not
work, nationalism will become question number one." Vladimir
Bakaric, Borba, March 6, 1966.

14. Branko Horvat, "Nationalism and Nation," Gledista,
May-June 1971.

15. For extensive coverage of the assassination, see Borba
and Politika, April 10, 1971. Also letter of Yugoslav workers
requesting permission to personally square accounts with the
criminals, Borba, April 16, 1971.

16. Politika, April 14, 16, 1971.

17. The Times (London), April 19, 1971.

18. Slobodan Stankovic, "Tito Attacks both Croatian and
Serbian Nationalism," RFE Report, May 10, 1972. See also
attempts of LCC leaders to diffuse attacks by shifting the issue
to that self-management. Pero Pirker, "Behind Attacks on the
Croatian Leadership an Attack on Self-Managing Socialism is
Hidden," Politika, April 17, 1971.

19. See Vjesnik editorial, August 10, 1971. The maneuvers
were canceled after Yugoslav protests as perhaps a prelude or
condition to the Brezhnev visit. This view and much anxiety were
personally expressed to me when I returned from Belgrade after
spending a month in Warsaw, May 1971.

20. Vjesnik, August 28, 1971.

21. Bakaric interview in Frankfurter Rundschau,
December 17, 1971.

22. Borba, September 16, 1971.

23. Speech to the LCY Twenty-first Plenum at Karadjordjevo,
December 1, 1971, Borba, December 3, 1971.

24. To date the best existing analysis of these events, although I have reservations about some of its interpretations, is

Dennison Rusinow's four-part study, "Croatia in Crisis,"
American University Field Staff Reports, June-September 1972.
Other valuable but less detailed accounts include F. Stephen
Larrabee, "Yugoslavia at the Crossroads," Orbis, Summer 1972,
and Alvin J. Rubinstein, "The Yugoslav Succession Crisis in
Perspective," World Affairs, Fall 1972. An excellent recently
published account giving a somewhat more balanced view of the
Croat leadership's narrowing room for maneuver, is Viktor
Meier's, "Political Dynamics of the Balkan's in 1974," in
William C. Griffith ed. , The World and the Great Power Triangle
(Cambridge: MIT Press, 1975).

25. Tito's concluding speech to the second LCY Conference,
Borba, January 27, 1972.

26. Politika, June 11, 1971.

27. Speech on August 22, 1971, on the thirtieth anniversary
of the wartime uprising in Croatia, quoted from George Schopflin,
"The Ideology of Croatian Nationalism," Survey, Winter 1974, p. 139.

28. Speech of November 25, 1971; Review (of the Study Center
for Yugoslav Affairs), 2, no. 1 (London, 1974), p. 84

29. Belgrade Tanjug in English, April 12, 1973. A figure
reported only at the time of the execution of the three captured
guerrillas some ten months later.

30. On April 10, 1973, the day Croatian Nationalists
celebrate as their independence day. George Prpic, Ireland, Croatia,
and Bangladesh (Arcadia, Calif.: American Croat, 1973), p. 36.

31. Ibid. , pp. 23-24

32. For an excellent comparison of these events to the fall
of the Croat leaders in 1971, see Slobodan Stankovic, "Yugoslavia—
One Year After: December 1971-December 1972," RFE Report,
December 8, 1972.

33. Time, July 24, 1972.

34. NIN, September 19, 1971.

35. Reportedly the cultural association had increased its
membership from 1,200 to 30,000 within 12 months and "increasingly
resembled a radical, nationalist political party. " A. Ross Johnson,
"Yugoslavia in the Twilight of Tito," Washington Papers, no. 16
(Beverly Hills: Sage Publications, 1974), p. 18.

36. Vjesnik, November 28, 1971.

37. Tanjug special correspondent from Melbourne,
Australia, July 14, 1972, reports discovery of such training
grounds and links it to the invasion of Bosnia. Also the angry
article of Gen. Franjo Herljevic, "The Enemies Don't Stand Still,"
Borba, September 2, 1972.

38. Prpic, op. cit. , p. 36.

39. For news coverage of the hijacking, see Raymond
Anderson in New York Times, September 16, 1972; specifically

regarding Yugoslav protest to the Swedish government, Eric Bourne, Christian Science Monitor, September 19, 1972. The hijackers surrendered without a battle once they reached Madrid, trusting to the anticommunist sentiment in Spain to prevent their extradition.

40. George W. Hoffman, "Migration and Social Change," Problems of Communism, November-December 1973.

41. Miloje Nikolic, "Some Basic Features of Yugoslav External Migrants," Yugoslav Survey (Belgrade, February 1972).

42. Ivo Baucic, "Some Economic Characteristics of the Yugoslav Foreign Migration of Workers," a paper presented at the International Conference on Conditions for the Development of Countries in the Mediterranean Area," held in Italy, January 19-21, 1973, cited by Hoffman op. cit., p. 27.

43. William Zimmerman, "National-International Linkages in Yugoslavia: The Political Consequences of Openness," a paper presented to The American Political Science Association 1973 Annual Meeting, New Orleans, September 4-8, 1973, pp. 14-15.

44. Politika, April 18, 1971.

45. Note, for instance, the long-term Soviet-Yugoslav-credit agreement signed on November 2, 1972, just two days after Slovene premier Stane Kavcic resigned under pressure for tying the economy of Slovenia too closely to the West. Or see recent reports that the United States is financing a Yugoslav nuclear power plant to the tune of $205 million in credits from the U. S. Export-Import Bank, Christian Science Monitor, December 30, 1974.

46. Certainly Croatian NSN spokesmen are not unaware of these parallels, see Prpic's provocative monograph, Ireland, Croatia and Bangladesh, op. cit.

47. Schopflin, op. cit.

8

THE NAVAJO
NONSTATE NATION
Mary Shepardson

The Navajo offer an example of a nation living basically
as a conquered people but seeking to maximize its
authority over its land base and population. The U. S.
government has defined in court cases the status of the
Navajo as a "domestic dependent nation." The U. S.
government thus recognized a rather unique, albeit
somewhat vague, national status for the Navajo (and
for other Indian tribes) within the U. S. nation-state.
　　The removal of tribes to reservations has made
impossible the maintenance of all aspects of the traditional way of life. Nonetheless, tribal organizations
have attempted to cut losses and to represent tribal
interests to the U. S. government. The Navajo have
succeeded in maintaining the international nature of
their relations with the U. S. government. The states in
which the Navajo reside do not have authority to tax
Navajo land and property, and the tribal government,
not the U. S. Constitution, has supreme jurisdiction in
domestic matters on the reservation. The extent of
Navajo "sovereignty" is unclear, however. The tribe is
subject to acts of Congress, and the area of Navajo
jurisdiction has been determined by U. S. court cases.
Thus, while the Navajo may claim sovereignty, the
areas in which their authority can be exercised effectively seem to depend upon the U. S. government.
　　The Navajo have entered the international context
through the courts of the United States. By insisting on
their treaty rights they have asserted their status as a
nation in relation to the United States. The Navajo have

tended to avoid such direct-action techniques as seizure
of land and buildings employed by some other Indian
groups and consequently have not received sustained
media attention.

—Judy S. Bertelsen

Americans are so accustomed to thinking of Navajo Indians in
terms of "tribe" that it comes almost as a shock to realize that they
are also, in truth, a nonstate nation (NSN). Not only do the Navajo re-
themselves as a nation, but they are so defined in U. S. law. As a
nonstate nation they may well be compared with the other groups
struggling for nation-statehood that are described in this volume.

HISTORICAL BACKGROUND

The Navajo Indian nation or tribe bases its relationship to the
U. S. government on the Treaty of 1868 that was signed by Indian
leaders and U. S. envoys as a pact between two sovereign nations.
The Navajo possess today a well-demarcated territory over which
their government exercises all those rights of sovereignty that have
not been extinguished by acts of Congress. In a number of specific
substantive areas, the Navajo are governed solely by their own laws.
As a treaty tribe they are not subject to the Constitution of the United
States, a fact that differentiates them from the federated states in
both extent and quality of sovereignty. The Navajo nation is not a
nation-state because it does not have the right to raise an army,
negotiate with foreign powers, or engage in warfare unilaterally, and
because its members share certain rights and obligations with all
other citizens of the United States.
    American Indian treaty tribes have been characterized by the
U. S. Supreme Court as "domestic dependent nations," which as
weaker states have placed themselves under the protection of a
stronger state (Worcester v. Georgia, 1832). In this chapter we will
discuss the origin of this peculiar status and its implications for the
Navajo nonstate nation in both national and international contexts.
The present goals and strategy of the Navajo nation will be compared
with the goals and strategy of some other tribal groups in the United
States as they also strive for self-determination and sovereignty.
    The Navajo comprise the largest Indian tribe in the United
States with an estimated population of 140,000. The majority live on
a 12-million-acre reservation in the states of Arizona, New Mexico,
and Utah. This fast-growing and far-ranging people are believed to
have wandered into the Southwest in small bands of hunters and

gatherers from the vast Athabascan-speaking region of the American
Northwest. Estimates of their time of arrival, based on archeology,
the oral tradition of the myths, and glottochronology (measuring the
length of time involved in language changes) vary from 1000 A. D.
to 1400 A. D. In any case they were latecomers as compared to the
Pueblo Indians whom they found already in residence. The Navajo
borrowed a number of traits from the Puebloans, such as the techniques of weaving and agriculture, religious beliefs and rituals. For
as long as we can trace the record, the Navajo have been borrowers,
but they have also been adapters and innovators. Navajo women
weave; among the Pueblos, the men weave. Navajo religious rites
have been transformed from calendrical, agricultural rituals into
individual curing ceremonies. Navajo residence patterns and house
styles have not followed the compact villages of stone and adobe
"apartment" houses of the Pueblos. Although the Navajo are closely
related to Apaches by language and by origin, they have developed
over a period of some 500 years in the Southwest a separate national
identity, differing from their cousins in dress, crafts, economy, and
religious beliefs. In short, they have created their own distinct
culture.

The arrival of a Spanish expedition under Coronado in the
year 1539, and the later Hispanic settlement of what is now New
Mexico, had a profound effect on the Apaches de Nabajú, as the
Spaniards called them. Unlike the Apaches, the Navajo did not eat
the horses and sheep they captured in raids on the settlements, but
adopted the alien herding techniques to become a pastoral people.
Scattered clusters of hogan dwellings dot desert and mesa. Each
cluster houses a residence group which has been formed around
parents, (preferably but not exclusively) their married daughters,
their sons-in-law, and their grandchildren; that is, a matrilineal,
matrilocal extended family. In Navajo relationship reckoning, a
child belongs to the clan of his mother and is "born for" the clan of
his father. This wide network of kin relations is continually being
extended through rules which require "marrying out," that is,
family and clan exogamy. These links form a web which preserves
the cultural entity of the expanding tribe.

The family-based residence group is the basic subsistence unit
for Navajo labor in small-scale agriculture and stock raising. Wage
work, money, trading patterns that tie into the world market,
schooling, modern law, and government have been added to the
cultural inventory since the arrival of the Americans. These addi-
tions have, of course, affected Navajo traditional life but they have
not completely altered the old culture.

The most significant dates in Navajo historical progression
toward the present status of nonstate nation are the arrival of the

---

Spaniards in the Southwest, 1539; the conquest of the New Mexicans by U. S. troops, which was formalized in the Treaty of Guadalupe Hidalgo, 1848; the conquest by U. S. troops of the Navajo and their removal to Fort Sumner, 1862-63; the signing of a treaty between the Navajo and the United States which was followed by their immediate return to part of their old homeland delimited as a reservation, 1868; the establishment of a Navajo Tribal Council, 1922; the federal program of stock reduction which broke the back of the pastoral economy as a subsistence base, in the 1930s; and the discovery of large quantities of oil and gas within the reservation boundaries, in the 1950s.

Some of this history—conquest, loss of land, reduction of sovereignty, precipitation into the world economy—is the native American story. Some of it is the general history of treaty tribes, but some is unique to Navajo life. Three special factors have had a profound effect on Navajo political development. These are relative isolation, rapid increase of population, and retention of a large territorial base, the original reservation of 3.5 million acres having been extended by executive order, acts of Congress, and tribal purchase to its present size of 12 million acres.

NAVAJO NATIONHOOD

There is no question but that the Navajo, with their thriving tribal council, and an increasing ability to handle their own affairs, view themselves as a nation. They use both "tribe" and "nation" for self-identification. The stationery of the highest official is headed "The Navajo Nation" and is signed "Chairman, Navajo Tribal Council." The seal is the "Great Seal of the Navajo Tribe." But the answer to another question, whether or not they are regarded as a nation by the United States, lies buried in the slough of agreements, treaties, statutes, and administrative promulgations dealing with Indians in the United States.

We may well ask if native Americans were ever considered to be sovereign nations. Frank B. Higgins, writing in the Arizona Law Review, concludes from a well-documented study:

> War Powers, boundary and treaty regulations, passports, extradition, and regulations with third countries and powers, all recognized in treaties between the United States and various tribes or nations of Indians, would seem to give weight to our contention that at one time in history the United States did in fact accord the Indian nations international status, i.e., they did

think of them as true "nations" (Higgins 1961, p. 85).

Higgins concedes, however, that although the "status of Indians at the beginning of the United States history might have been international indeed it quickly changed to national with neither the Indians' knowledge nor consent" (p. 84).

This erosion of the status of Indians as sovereign nations soon raised basic legal problems for white settlers. In the early 1800s Chief Justice John Marshall made three major decisions in U. S. Supreme Court rulings which form what Harold Fey and D'Arcy McNickle call "the basic edifice of American policy toward the Indian people" (1959, p. 54). These decisions concerned Indian land title, whether or not an Indian tribe is a foreign nation, and the status of an Indian tribe in U. S. law.

The first of these decisions, in 1823, concerned Indian land rights. Marshall reaffirmed the doctrine of Indian use rights in land (rights of occupancy or possessory rights). The United State, however, as successor to the European powers (whose claims on "discovery" of the continent, had been obtained by preemption, conquest, or purchase) held the ultimate legal title. This doctrine, so convenient for the government, was explained as follows:

> While the different nations of Europe respected the right of the natives, as occupants, they asserted the ultimate dominion to be in themselves; and claimed and exercised as a consequence of this ultimate dominion, a power to grant the soil, while in possession of the natives. These grants have been understood by all to convey a title to the grantees, subject only to the Indian right of occupancy (Johnson's and Graham's Lessee v. McIntosh, 1823).

Marshall was here concerned only with a practical solution, not with the morality thereof, as Fey and McNickle point out. Once more, as in most dealings between Europeans and native Americans, pragmatism is the keynote, that is, what is practical and what works to the benefit of non-Indians. Marshall himself as an officer of the highest court of justice was uneasy.

> However extravagant the pretension of converting the discovery of an inhabited country into conquest may appear, if the principle has been asserted in the first instance, and afterwards sustained; if a country has been acquired and held under it . . . it becomes the law of the land and cannot be questioned . . . . However this restriction

> may be opposed to natural right, and to the usages of
> civilized nations, yet if it be indispensable to that sys-
> tem under which the country has been settled, and be
> adapted to the actual condition of the two people, it
> may, perhaps, be supported by reason, and certainly
> cannot be rejected by the courts of justice (Johnson
> v. McIntosh, 1823).

Vine Deloria, Jr. , a Sioux Indian, writes:

> Title depended on who discovered whom, and since the
> two continents of the western hemisphere were never
> lost to begin with, the whole doctrine appeared sus-
> piciously like a shell game. The only way any American
> tribe could claim title to its lands would be for it
> to greet the first explorers with a certified deed
> signed by either the Pope or King Henry VIII. And
> this, of course, was patently impossible (1972, p.
> 79).

The second major decision on Indians was made by John
Marshall in 1831. He ruled that Indian tribes could not be considered
"foreign nations"; rather they were "domestic dependent nations":

> Though the Indians are acknowledged to have an unques-
> tionable, and therefore unquestioned right to the lands
> they occupy until that right shall be extinguished by a
> voluntary cession to the government, yet it may well
> be doubted whether those tribes which reside within
> the acknowledged boundaries of the United States can,
> with strict accuracy, be denominated foreign nations
> . . . . They may more correctly be denominated
> domestic dependent nations . . . . They are in a
> state of pupilage; their relations to the United States
> resemble that of a ward to his guardian . . .
> (Cherokee Nation v. Georgia, 1831).

It should be noted that Marshall did not say that the Cherokees were
wards of the government but that their relations to the United States
resembles that of a ward to his guardian. Vine Deloria, Jr. comments, "and in so doing he created a swamp of pseudo-legal theories
into which countless lawyers and judges have disappeared in the
years since" (1972, pp. 79-81).

A year later Marshall elaborated the doctrine to say of Indian
sovereignty:

> The Indian nations had always been considered as dis-
> tinct, independent, political communities, retaining
> their original natural rights . . . the settled doc-
> trine of the law of nations is, that a weaker power
> does not surrender its independence—its right to self-
> government—by associating with a stronger and taking
> its protection. A weak state, in order to provide for
> its safety, may place itself under the protection of
> one more powerful, without stripping itself of its right
> of government, and ceasing to be a state (Worcester v.
> Georgia, 1832).

Neither the doctrine of discovery nor the doctrine of domestic
dependent nation bothered the Navajo Indians at the time. They were
busy herding their sheep, planting their crops, raiding the Hispanic
settlements, and running their own affairs as a sovereign people,
and of course they had no thought of voluntarily placing themselves
under the protection of a more powerful state.

NAVAJO DECISION MAKERS BEFORE THE CONQUEST

At the time the doctrines on U. S. federal relations to Indians
were being developed in treaties and judicial decision, the Navajo
were a self-ruled tribe. They were not a nation-state in the sense of
an organized, centralized political power. They were a sovereign
political community, a bounded cultural group sharing a common
language, economy, land base, values, beliefs, with a sense of
belonging. They recognized no higher authority than the consensus
of their peers, meeting in groups, counseled by their headmen as
decision makers. As men who exercised informal leadership over
their voluntary followers, the headmen enjoyed no formalized
authority. These informal decision makers concluded treaties with
Spaniards and Mexicans who mistook their authority-by-consent for
the power of ruling chiefs. In these treaties the Navajo "chiefs"
promised an end to the raiding of villages and the running off of horses
and sheep belonging to the more sedentary Hispanic settlers. Such
treaties were only temporarily honored if at all by the Indians,
partly because the Navajo signatories lacked the power, partly
because they lacked the will, to enforce them. Even so, these headmen represented the highest level of political decision making at
this period.

In 1848 the Treaty of Guadalupe Hidalgo formalized the agreement between the United States and Mexico. Mexico surrendered its
claimed, but unexercised, jurisdiction over all Indians in their

territory in New Mexico. The fact that the United States continued the Hispanic policy of treaty-making with Navajo "chiefs" suggests that the conquerors were still aware that their de jure sovereignty over the tribe was by no means de facto. The Navajo continued their previous policy of treaty-making and treaty-breaking, of raiding and withdrawing, despite all the efforts of federal troops to overawe them. De facto the tribe was still a sovereign political community.

THE CONQUEST

Once the U. S. Civil War was in progress, raids and skirmishes that interfered with the transport of gold from California to the capital became intolerable to the federal government. Detachments of troops under the leadership of the famous scout, Kit Carson, instituted a scorched-earth policy of killing sheep, cutting down peach orchards, and burning cornfields. The Navajo were literally starved into submission. Some 8,500 surrendered to the U. S. troops at Fort Defiance and were taken by forced march to Fort Sumner at the Bosque Redondo beyond the Pecos River. Although a few thousand were able to hide out in remote canyons, the large mass of the tribe submitted to removal, a conquered people.

Four years later, when the experiment of making "civilized" farmers out of "savages" was becoming too costly and had actually failed, the government proposed to negotiate a treaty. This would indicate that in 1868 the United States considered the Navajo a formerly sovereign, now conquered, nation. According to the terms of the treaty, they would be allowed to return to a fraction, little more than a third, of their former homeland now declared to be a reservation. Here they were to receive rations and sheep from the government and were required to live in peace. Ten Navajo, chosen at a tribal meeting at the Bosque Redondo, were empowered to sign the treaty. The other signatories represented the United States. The authority of the Navajo "chiefs and headmen" to sign the document is explicitly stated in the treaty:

> . . . commissioners Lieutenant General W. T. Sherman
> and Colonel Samuel F. Tappan, on the one part, and the
> Navajo nation or tribe of Indians, represented by their
> Chiefs and Headmen, duly authorized and empowered
> to act for the whole people of said nation or tribe . . .
> (Treaty of 1868).

In this manner, in the year 1868, the Navajo tribe, a "weak state," chose to "place itself under the protection of one more powerful" in John Marshall's euphemistic phrase for Indian capitulation. This act was voluntary only in the sense that it was a choice between, on the one hand, exile and starvation and, on the other, a surrender of a portion of their sovereignty. The treaty offered them some guarantees over their land against encroachment by individuals or by the territorial governments. The people and the land, however, were placed squarely under the jurisdiction of the federal government. (We should note, parenthetically, that even this shadow of quasi-sovereignty began to appear excessive to land-hungry U. S. settlers, prospectors, and investors. In 1871 Congress legislated to end all treaty-making with native Americans.)

Article II of the Treaty of 1868 reads:

> . . . and the United States agrees that no persons except those herein so authorized to do, and except such officers, soldiers, agents and employees of the government, or of the Indians, as may be authorized to enter upon Indian reservations in discharge of duties imposed by law, or the orders of the President, shall ever be permitted to pass over, settle upon, or reside in, the territory described in this article (Treaty of 1868).

So, by treaty, the Navajo had recovered and preserved the core of a land base which was to prove of so much importance to the later development of their nationhood.

MODERN DECISION MAKERS

The first step toward the formalization of all-tribal decision making came in 1922 when a Navajo Business Council was appointed by federal officials. This council was instituted for the purpose of signing oil leases in the name of the tribe, and a year later by promulgation of the secretary of the Interior it developed into the Navajo Tribal Council, clearly within the framework of a domestic dependent nation.

Two years later American Indians were made citizens of the United States by Congress, but through the aforementioned misreading of the Marshall decision, Indians in Arizona were denied the vote because they were "wards of the government." The constitution of New Mexico denied the vote to "Indians not taxed." Only in 1948, after successful suits were brought by Navajo plaintiffs against these states, were Indians allowed to participate in general elections. Since the humble and sketchy beginnings of self-government, the fledgling Navajo Tribal Council has increased its authority and its areas of competence to become fully institutionalized in Navajo life.

PROBLEMS OF JURISDICTION

The surrounding states have never completely abandoned their efforts to extend jurisdiction over Indian territory, but as late as 1959 the doctrine of domestic dependent nation was reaffirmed by the U. S. Supreme Court. The case of <u>Williams</u> v. <u>Lee</u> elicited the decision. A trader on the Navajo reservation had seized the sheep herd of a Navajo in partial payment of a debt. The Navajo tribe sued in the Superior Court of Arizona and lost the case. An appeal to the U. S. Supreme Court reversed the Arizona verdict on the precedent of Marshall's doctrine of domestic dependent nation. Because of this ruling the Navajo reservation and its Indian inhabitants are not under the jurisdiction of the states, whereas the non-Indian residents must pay state taxes and are tried in state courts for offenses they commit on the reservation.

There is a further anomaly in the present status of the Navajo people in that they are citizens of the United States, subject to acts of Congress, but not subject to the Constitution of the United States. This last was made clear in a case brought by the Native American Church against the Navajo Tribal Council in the U. S. District Court of New Mexico. The church was challenging the right of the tribal government to outlaw the use of peyote in religious services. The court dismissed the action of the plaintiff on the grounds that the recognized government of the Navajo tribe had sole jurisdiction over domestic affairs, including matters of religion, on the Navajo reservation. This decision came as a shock not only to peyotists but to young Navajo veterans who had been, during their term in the armed forces, heavily indoctrinated with the principles of the "four freedoms." To find that, although they had served under the Constitution of the United States, they would not be protected by its Bill of Rights brought bitter disillusionment. Only after intensive political activity and a reservationwide campaign by Navajo peyotists were the defenders of religious freedom able to reverse the 1940 tribal resolution banning the use of peyote on the reservation. In 1967 the Navajo Tribal Council passed a resolution on Human Rights based on some of the provisions of the Bill of Rights of the United States Constitution.

GOALS OF THE NONSTATE NATION

The great goal of the people at the beginning of the reservation
period was to rebuild their pastoral way of life on land bounded by
their sacred mountains. With this end in view, they observed the
terms of the treaty to desist from warfare and gathered regularly
at Fort Defiance for the distribution of rations and sheep promised
by the government. Only a small number of Navajo at this time had
any desire to change their ways or prepare their children through
education for coping with an alien and irresistible power. Nevertheless, there were only a few sporadic incidents of armed resistance
against federal control. Black Horse and his followers captured the
Navajo agent and his interpreter and threatened to burn down the
trading post in which they were incarcerated as a protest against
the forced removal of Navajo children for schooling. Byalille, a
medicine man, called a "witch" by the superintendent of the Northern
Navajo Jurisdiction, was seized at gun point and imprisoned without
trial. Bizhozhi's son, who resisted the pressure to abolish polygyny,
had his wives seized and kidnapped by federal order. During stock
reduction there were death threats and violent acts performed against
range riders and government officials. Except for such scattered
incidents, the peace called for in the Treaty of 1868 has prevailed.
There is no present movement to "cut loose."

In an earlier essay I wrote, "The struggle for complete
independence is over." I based this on my observations of Navajo
government in the 1950s and 1960s when the Navajo were openly
opposing the federal policy of terminating Indian reservations.
Navajo of all ages, traditionalists and modernists, feared the
encroachment of the states, the onslaught of taxation, and a massive
withdrawal of federal aid for health, education, roads, and so on.
Peter MacDonald, chairman of the Navajo Tribal Council, has
challenged my statement:

> The only other point I would really take issue with is your
> statement . . . that the struggle for complete indepen-
> dence is over. The Navajo Nation is exerting its sover-
> eignty in many fields it had entered in the past. We
> are sovereign except Congress has taken away this
> sovereignty. Unfortunately, many people do not under-
> stand this. In fact, some Congressmen feel it's the
> other way; that we are sovereign only as Congress has
> given us sovereignty.
> The sovereign status of the Navajo Nation is, as
> you intimate in your article, "very muddy" with

conflicting court decisions, opinions by experts and so-called experts, as well as by actions of the various states. Frequently, states recognize our sovereignty when it comes to a requirement to expend money within the Navajo Nation. We hear in effect, "You are a sovereign and our state has no authorization to be within the Navajo Nation providing various services." On the other hand when it comes to earning money from the Navajo Nation, for instance taxes, etc., these same states are very quick to forget our sovereign status and attempt to exert their control over us. It has only been through litigation that the tax question has been partially resolved.

In summary, our "non-state nation status" as you call it, works to the detriment of the Navajo Nation as well as it works to our benefit. There are a number of possible solutions to the problem one of them being statehood for the Navajo Nation (Peter MacDonald, personal communication, 1974).

The Navajo government operates at the present time within the framework of a domestic dependent nation. The goals are to gain as much authority and as wide a sovereignty as possible; to retain control of domestic affairs, personal relationships, land rights, and religious ceremonies. The Navajo have reacquired the right (in a modern context) to direct the education of their children, hire their own personnel (particularly their own legal counsel), prepare their own tribal budget, and handle their own monies; they are pressing for complete control of the use and disposal of their own natural resources. Some of these rights are aboriginal and have never been taken away; some are regained painfully step by step from their federal "tutors."

MacDonald, in speaking of statehood, as I interpret his letter, is referring to a federated state, operating under the Constitution of the United States. Ruth Roessel of the Navajo Community College develops this concept in Navajo Studies (1971, pp. 77–78): "An increasing interest has been shown in the prospect of the Navajo Nation becoming the 51st state." The Constitution of the United States provides for the addition of new states into the union provided that "no new state shall be formed or erected within the jurisdiction of any other state, nor any state be formed by the junction of two or more states without the consent of the legislatures of the states concerned as well as of the Congress." The crucial question, Roessel feels, is whether or not Arizona, New Mexico, Utah, and Congress will give their consent. The states may assent, she believes, as resentment grows against added state expenditures for Indian education, health, and welfare and the inability of the states to tax Navajo land and property. Other questions to be considered are the Navajo concept of land ownership (use rights versus individual rights in fee simple), guarantees that the Navajo will retain governance of the state, and the right to exclude or remove non-Navajo from Navajo state territory.

One further question which I foresee is a comparison between the projected economic status of the Navajo nation as the fifty-first state with its present economic status as a domestic dependent nation. As far as I know, the Navajo have not addressed themselves to this question in serious detail. Would their economic status be improved as a state controlling its own resources, enjoying revenue-sharing and other federal funding now open to the federated states or would they stand to lose more by extinguishing their special status as treaty Indians, under which they enjoy free education, health services, and so on? That such a study is not already underway suggests to me that statehood may be at this particular point in time more effective as a national slogan than as an immediate goal.

PLANS TO ACHIEVE THE GOALS OF
ECONOMIC AND POLITICAL INDEPENDENCE

There are two principal directions in which the Navajo are moving. One is toward the preservation of the Navajo way of life through teaching respect for Navajo history, ceremonies, and beliefs and through the extension and improvement of the sheep herding and small-scale agricultural economy. The second main direction is toward modernization through wage work, industrialization, large-scale irrigation, and other measures to raise the standard of living. At one time the modernists were in the minority, but after World War II power began to tip to their side, a shift which has become intensified with each subsequent war in which young Navajo have fought. Most of the older people have come to accept the necessity for compromise with modern ways, for sending their children to school, for encouraging them to perform wage work, even to leave the reservation on relocation or vocational training jobs. Politically, this is clearly shown in the moves of many councilmen not formally educated who refused to run again for office because they had come to believe that the ability to read, write, and speak English was essential to the successful discharge of their duties.

There is very nearly complete agreement on the wisdom of maintaining and developing the reservation with the goal of economic independence, to "get off the welfare rolls," and the need for self-government, to "get out from under" an irksome veto power still enjoyed by the secretary of the Interior. Distasteful also are capricious acts of Congress affecting Indians.

Both traditionals and progressives viewed with alarm the threat of "termination of the special status of the Indians," a policy which was formulated in House Concurrent Resolution 108 of the 1953 Congress. The Navajo feared the withdrawal of federal services and protection for their land base since the alternative was an illusory freedom which could quickly be eroded through the encroachment of the surrounding states. To this end the Navajo have refused to divide up their tribal lands for individual ownership or to distribute tribal income per capita. The present course is to operate within the framework of federal protection as they seek to obtain more important decision-making positions in the Bureau of Indian Affairs and in state legislatures. In both of these efforts they have achieved some success.

At the same time that they are "modernizing," interestingly enough, the younger tribal leaders are showing an increasing concern about coping with the problems of the pastoralists. In the interests of bettering conditions for stockmen and farmers, they have acquired off-reservation land for grazing, have spent money for water development, sheep dusting, lamb sales to cull the flocks, and have tried to develop markets for cattle, horses, crafts, and wool. They have trained the Navajo for irrigated farming in the San Juan Basin area. On the nonmaterial side, these leaders have shown interest in the preservation of the Navajo way of life by stressing the importance of teaching children to read and write Navajo as well as English. Navajo traditional history, religious beliefs, and mythology, instead of being denigrated as ignorant superstition, are now presented in some of the Indian schools as the valued heritage of every Navajo child. (The winds of ethnic identity—"Black is Beautiful," "The Aztec Heritage"—are blowing over the reservation too.) The Navajo are seeking greater control of federal and state schools through the election of Navajo to school boards. As this move becomes success-ful in the isolated areas, more traditional Navajo come into local decision-making positions, because in their districts they are often the solid citizens and the trusted leaders. While traditionals are in the leadership in the Rough Rock, Ramah, and Rock Point school districts, there has been a striking increase in the power of Navajo youth. In a recent sociocultural impact statement I wrote:

> Respect for age, the association of wisdom with the num-
> ber of years lived on earth is a basic Navajo traditional
> value. The change-over is to high respect for youth.

Not only are the Navajos in their twenties appointed to
responsible Tribal positions, but they win elections to
powerful political office. One important aspect of the
youthful Navajo culture is the "new ethnicity." It takes
the form of the adoption of outward symbols of Indianness
such as long hair, circling the head with sweatbands,
adornment with squash blossom necklaces, bracelets
and rings. Increased use of the Navajo language and
more frequent participation in Navajo Sings is part of a
desire to recapture a past identity that is gradually
eroding under the pressures of changing times . . . .
Young people, who a few years ago strove to be at least
outwardly like Anglos, now prefer to be "bilingual and
bicultural." They want their children to be Indians—
Navajo Indians—but also to be able to cope with
encroaching Anglo society.

The new ethnicity fits well with developing
Navajo nationalism. The preoccupation with Navajo
sovereignty, the goal of economic independence for the
Tribe, "controlling our own resources," has a nationalistic, bicultural flavor. To attain these ends Navajos
require not only self-confidence and a strong self-image,
but modern skills are indispensable (Leonard 1975,
p. 4. 8. 2).

Not all of these young people have been content to work peacefully
for the bicultural society, as we shall presently see in the discussion
of strategy and the quest for visibility.

STRATEGY

The factionalism the Navajo have experienced in the last 30
years has had as a core controversy the right to use peyote in
religious ceremonies on the reservation. The Tribal Resolution
of 1940 outlawing the use of peyote was challenged by the Navajo
branch of the Native American Church. Other hotly debated issues
that became linked by accretion to the peyote schism were such
matters as the amount of power to be accorded to non-Indian tribal
lawyers; the extent of cooperation or resistence to the Bureau of
Indian Affairs; the adoption of a constitution which some feared
would widen rather than curtail the authority of the federal government over Indian affairs. The struggle became at times bitter and
paralyzing to self-government, but the factionalism was allayed,

perhaps resolved, politically within the framework of tribal government and courts.

By and large, the Navajo, in their move toward self-determination and sovereignty, have rejected the violent tactics of the urban Indians and the warrior Sioux of Wounded Knee. Peter MacDonald, the tribal chairman, has criticized the Indian Bureau for broken promises, but the Navajo Tribal Council did not endorse the takeover and vandalism committed by Indians during their occupation of the Bureau of Indian Affairs office in Washington. They did not rush to the support of the insurgents of Wounded Knee. They have not put a premium on civil disobedience.

The Navajo have not followed the Trail of Broken Treaties. This may be because they are better off now than they were at the time of the treaty agreement. Some of the onerous requirements, such as having to obtain a pass before leaving the reservation, have been dropped. The reservation has been increased in size. Educational facilities are vastly improved and expanded. (Their own community college and its northern branch are going concerns.)

Several years ago a few young Navajo, who had been indoctrinated with concepts of Red Power as students in off-reservation colleges, picketed the Navajo Tribal Council sessions, painted "Racist Ripoff" on historical markers at Fort Defiance (the first military fort on reservation land), and printed angry articles against their "sell-out" leadership. But these young people were in a small minority. It was not until three Navajo were murdered and butchered by white teen-agers in Farmington, New Mexico, in 1974, that Navajo anger against an indifferent white community expressed itself in highly visible form. An organization called the Coalition for Navajo Liberation was formed under young militant leadership. Demonstrations and parades were held in the white community but there were no shootings or killings. The chief effect of these militant, unarmed demonstrations was not on the white people of Farmington but on the Navajo of the San Juan Basin. Young militants, veterans of the Coalition for National Liberation, came to power in tribal and chapter elections on an antiadministration program. These youthful leaders and their followers presently are spearheading the fight against rapid and uncontrolled industrialization of the Navajo reservation.

INTERNATIONAL AUDIBILITY

In the 1900s Zane Grey could write a novel about the Navajo with the title, The Vanishing American. He did not realize that he might be describing what would soon be the fastest-growing and most

visible Indian tribe in the United States. He did not foresee their
development into a strong, though dependent, nation. They themselves
have made few efforts to achieve international audibility. Preoccupied
with nation-building, they have raised their issues of sovereignty and
have cited the international treaty of 1868 more to enhance their status
vis-a-vis the federal government than to appeal to the nation-states of
the world. The Navajo publish their own newspaper, Navajo Times,
in which statements of their leaders on policy and national developments are printed. To date, most of the nationwide and international
publicity about the Navajo has been the work of syndicated columnists
and the makers of television documentaries. These pundits tend to
emphasize the more sensational aspects of reservation life—the mud
huts, the dire poverty, the nefarious traders, and rampant exploitation by coal and power companies. Or if they do not wish to be
controversial, they drown the Indians in picturesqueness and highly
colored scenery.

The Navajo have been slow to join the broad civil rights movements of blacks, Chicanos, Asians, and women. Vine Deloria, Jr.,
suggests that this is partly because the Indians are primarily working
for group rights and group sovereignty rather than individual civil
rights, of which they are suspicious. "The policy of terminating
federal services to Indians, which had dominated the previous decade,
was based upon giving Indians civil rights under the theory that, by
abolishing treaty rights, Indians would receive full citizenship"
(Delona, 1974, p. 23).

From time to time Navajo leaders have called for Indian unity
on Indian problems, but in general the Navajo have remained on the
periphery of the pan-Indian movements. Some of the older leaders
told me that they did not like being manipulated by other Indians any
more than they liked being manipulated by the white man. Only within
the last two or three years has the national American Indian Movement (AIM) been able to set up Navajo branches. Most of the top
Navajo leadership has refrained from condemning the movement.
Larry Anderson, Navajo treasurer of the national AIM organization,
was allowed to write articles for the Navajo Times until the abortive
"occupation" of the Fairchild plant in New Mexico.

In Shiprock, New Mexico, the tribal government had constructed
a building for the Fairchild Electronics Company where, at the peak,
more than a thousand Navajo, mostly women, were employed. With
the depression, and the end of the Vietnam war, both the market for
war industries and federal funds for manpower training were drying
up. In consequence, Fairchild Electronics had been cutting its work-
force until it numbered between 400 and 500 employees. In March
1975, AIM made its drastic move. With the aid of Chicanos and other
Indians it staged an armed occupation of the Fairchild plant and

presented demands for full employment and better working conditions.
While the move brought some popular support from the Shiprock
community, there was no evidence of the widespread elation "that
developed a new pride . . . which transcended tribal loyalties and
instilled in Indian children everywhere the image of the brave
Indian warrior which had been missing in Indian society for two
generations" as Vine Deloria, Jr., reports was the psychological
effect of Wounded Knee on North American Indians (1974, p. 80). The
violent disruption gave Fairchild an excuse for closing the plant some
two years before its contract with the Navajo nation had expired.
Women who lost their jobs turned in fury on AIM members and on
the Shiprock councilman who was accused of encouraging the takeover.
The failure of this first violent protest action seems to have brought
AIM's influence on the Navajo to a low ebb. Only a tenth of the
number predicted, and a large part of them non-Navajo, gathered
for the national convention in the summer of 1975 on the periphery
of the Navajo reservation.

Other tribes have taken the leadership in striving for national
and international visibility. Taos Indians quietly petitioned for 60
years for the return of the sacred Blue Lake which had been incorporated into the Carson National Forest. It was not until President
Nixon was photographed, flanked by blanketed and braided Indian
leaders, signing the bill to return 48,000 acres to the Pueblo, that
they attained international visibility. Vine Deloria, Jr., one of the
most articulate of the Indian leaders, published his book, Custer Died
for Your Sins, in France as well as in America.

The "shot heard round the world" was the seizure of Alcatraz
in 1969 by a group of Indians recruited from many different tribes.
When this notorious federal prison, on an island in San Francisco
Bay, was abandoned as obsolete, the government considered offers
from real estate developers who proposed to make a tourist attraction out of the surplus land. Indian occupation of the "Rock" drama-
tized for the world, as no other act could have done, the injustice of
selling off federal land without considering the rights of the descendants of the original owners. It was a clean issue, without the component of tribal factionalism which muddied the demands of Wounded
Knee. That the government recognized a measure of justice in the
Indian claim was later demonstrated by the setting aside of surplus
army buildings for an Indian-Chicano university at Davis, California.
DQ, or Deganawida-Quetzalcoatl University, is a symbol of the
recognition of that right.

Among the demands of the Trail of Broken Treaties was for a
definition of the basic legal status of all Indian tribes in the United
States, so that they could know what they owned and what their
relationship was to the federal government (Deloria 1974, p. 50).

The Oglala Sioux at Wounded Knee carried these demands further. They constituted themselves a nation which declared its independence from the United States and announced that it would determine its own borders, as defined by the Treaty of 1868 with the United States, and threatened to shoot anyone who violated their borders. They began to press their claims at the United Nations for international recognition (Deloria 1974, p. 78). If the notion of complete independence for native Americans is only a dream, it is one that never dies out.

RESOURCES AND ENVIRONMENT

Resources and environment in the terminology of the system's framework include those elements which can be controlled (resources) and those elements which cannot be controlled (environment) by the decision makers as they strive to implement their goals.

The environment in which the Navajo nation must operate but cannot control is, of course, the overall coercive authority of the dominant nation-state, the United States. Perhaps the difficulty that this environment presents, a difficulty with which it is so hard to cope, is the constantly changing policies promulgated by the Bureau of Indian Affairs. At one time the pressure may be for complete assimilation and the extirpation of Indian culture. Again it will be a paternalistic policy of preserving Indian ways through isolation and absence of modern services. One generation may face the complete termination of federal aid, another the development of extensive programs of government services and the encouragement of self-government of Indian tribes. The Navajo, after Fort Sumner, were directed to build up large sheep herds to replace those destroyed by Kit Carson. Some decades later, with very little advance warning, they were forced to reduce their herds on pain of imprisonment for trespass, in some cases below subsistence level. The Navajo are advised to stand on their own feet and eschew paternalism, but if they move too fast in that direction they are reminded that they are "wards of the government," however erroneous that concept may be. In sum, the federal government at times plays the role of protector and purveyor of important services; at other times it acts as inhibitor, even oppressor. It is hard for any tribe of native Americans to know for any long period of time "where they're at." Navajos have only recently come to see that they are not always helpless, always voiceless before Washington.

The principal resources, that is, what they can control and use toward the implementation of their goals of self-maintenance and self-governance, are land, people, and natural resources.

Twelve million acres of tribally owned land has provided a base, such as no other American Indian tribe has, for the nonstate nation. This land, so bare, so infertile, of so little rain, has yielded oil, gas, coal, helium, and uranium, and the Navajo still retain rights to use water from the San Juan River. Through leasing to outside companies for the development of oil and coal mining, the tribal government has acquired a substantial income. They have a home- land into which unwanted Anglo residents and unwanted local state power cannot intrude. This forms the economic base which, supplemented as it is by federal funds, has enabled the Tribal Council to develop and has provided Navajo leaders with the funds to help meet the expanding needs of self-government.

A second resource of great importance is people and their skills. Rapid population increase and the deterioration of grazing land from overuse mean that pastoralism can no longer serve as an adequate subsistance economy. Either the land base must be expanded or the economy must be diversified. Navajo decision makers have prepared a 10-Year Plan of economic development. They hope to use their tribal population, which has already shown its ability to learn new skills and work well in heavy industry, for the development of industry, big and small, on the reservation. Proposals have been made for the investment of federal funds in the economic improve- ment of the Navajo base.

CONCLUSIONS

We have, then, in the case of Navajo Indians, an example of a nonstate nation acting within the environment of a dominant nation- state, the United States. This nonstate nation retains some measure of international sovereignty based on a treaty signed between nation- states. This has been recognized in Supreme Court decisions and, as we have shown, can be appealed to in specific cases of law. Although the goal of this nation or tribe before the conquest was to preserve complete independence at all costs, the present activities of the people and their decision makers are directed toward increas- ing the sovereignty of the "domestic dependent nation" within the legal framework of the United States.

Historically, there has been a rapprochement, an accommoda- tion between the two principal components, traditional and modern, of their goal orientation. The present strategy is a far cry from the guerrilla struggles of the Palestine rebels or the armed resistance and declaration of independence of the Oglala Sioux. Nevertheless, they share with these resisters the long-enduring goal of cultural identity, self-government, and nationhood.

REFERENCES

Cohen, Felix. 1942. Handbook of Federal Indian Law. Washington, D. C. : U. S. Department of the Interior, Office of the Solicitor.

_____. 1960. The Legal Conscience. New Haven, Conn. : Yale University Press.

Deloria, Vine, Jr. , ed. 1972a. Of Utmost Good Faith. New York: Bantam Books.

_____. 1972b. "The Basis of Indian Law. " In Look to the Mountain Top, ed. Charles Jones. San Jose, Calif. : Gousha Publications.

_____. 1974. Behind the Trail of Broken Treaties. New York: Delacorte.

Fey, Harold E. and D'Arcy McNickle. 1959. Indians and Other Americans. New York: Harper.

Higgins, Frank B. 1961. "International Law Consideration of the American Indian Nations by the United States," Arizona Law Review 6: 237-55.

Kane, Albert E. 1965. "Jurisdiction Over Indians and Indian Reservations," Arizona Law Review 6: 237-55.

Leonard, James R. Associates. 1975. Assessment of Cumulative Sociocultural Impacts of Proposed Plans for Development of Coal and Water Resources in the Northern New Mexico Region. Salt Lake City: Department of the Interior, Bureau of Reclamation. Upper Colorado Regional Office.

Navajo Nation. 1972. The Navajo 10-Year Plan. Window Rock, Ariz.

Roessel, Ruth, ed. 1971. Navajo Studies at Navajo Community College. Navajo Community College Press.

Shepardson, Mary. 1963. Navajo Ways in Government. Memoir No. 96, American Anthropological Association.

_____. 1971. "Navajo Factionalism and the Outside World. " In Apachean Culture, History and Ethnology, ed. Keith Basso and Morris Opler. Tucson: University of Arizona Press.

Young, Robert W. 1961. The Navajo Yearbook. Window Rock, Ariz.:
    Navajo Agency.

_____. 1972. "The Rise of the Navajo Tribe." In Plural Society in
    the Southwest, ed. Edward H. Spicer and Raymond H. Tompson.
    New York: Weatherhead Foundation.

9

THE NONSTATE NATION
IN INTERNATIONAL POLITICS:
SOME OBSERVATIONS
Judy S. Bertelsen

The nonstate nation (NSN) cases presented in this book cover wide range of goals, levels of success, kinds of decision makers, kinds of resources, and intensities of impact on the international context. The cases also vary in time span covered, detail of reporting, and interpretation of the NSN framework. These kinds of variations were accepted at the beginning of our endeavor because of the desire to encourage individual researchers to describe their cases within a common framework but to interpret freely the categories of the framework. Our aim was to produce comparable studies but to avoid predetermining the authors' conclusions in a framework that might be overly specified and therefore more applicable to some cases than to others.

The first chapter in this book indicated an interest in greater specificity and a commitment to increasingly systematic and operationally explicit research. This concluding chapter will attempt to draw some generalizations suggested by the cases and outline research directions to be pursued in the future.

DIFFUSION OF NSNs

All the nonstate nations described in this book have deep historical roots and have endured substantial periods of dispersion and suppression. Many have been directly encouraged in their resurgence by a twentieth-century trend of championing the right to national self-determination.

The cases in this book constitute only a tiny fraction of the currently audible groups that fit the definition of nonstate nation. Are both the number and intensity of audibility of such groups

increasing with greater and greater rapidity? An attempt to enum-
erate NSNs and their respective levels of audibility would allow us to
trace the pattern of diffusion of NSN audibility. We know that some
NSNs have been coordinating strategies publicly. (The "unrepresented
nations" approach to the European Economic Community and the
Japanese "Red Army" terrorists who act in behalf of Palestinian
groups offer contrasting examples.) Furthermore, reports of
clandestine meetings of European nonstate nation groups have
appeared in the press. This evidence of cooperation and coordination
among NSNs would suggest not only that the number and audibility of
NSNs may be increasing but that the rate of increase may itself be
increasing. The pattern may approximate the exponential diffusion
process described by "innovation theory."[1]

CORRELATES OF NSN DIFFUSION

The studies reported in this book suggest not only the diffusion
of NSN audibility but also some possible explanations, or at least
concomitant phenomena. A number of the NSNs have perceived
economic disadvantage at a time when hopes were rising. The Kurds,
the Welsh, and the Croatians all apparently perceive their populations
as receiving less than their rightful shares of public goods, given
their special resources and contributions to public goods. All three
have been experiencing rising expectations about the possibility of
greater autonomy or greater participation for the NSN in the life of
their respective nation-states. These examples suggest a possible
link between relative economic disadvantage for the members of the
NSN and the diffusion of NSN audibility. Relative disadvantage could
be measured as a difference between the income per capita or
proportion of public budget per capita allotted to the NSN population
and the corresponding income or allotment of other subpopulations.
Diffusion may be hastened by the development of movements and
organizational structures that might foster NSN activity or by the
development of examples of NSN audibility that serve as inspiration.
The Welsh are one part of a general Celtish nationalist trend.
Palestinian Arab autonomy may have been significantly spurred by
the Palestine Liberation Organization (PLO), even though that group
was originally established by Arab states as a vehicle that they could
control. The Kurds have been given both international recognition
for their national aspirations and repeated lip-service from Iraqi
governments.

If an enumeration of each NSN could be prepared showing
variations over a certain time span in international audibility,
relative socioeconomic welfare, and political/institutional

opportunities, the interrelationship of these variables could be investigated. It seems plausible to anticipate that some combination of perceived loss of welfare and an increase in political/institutional opportunities would accompany the increasing audibility of many NSNs. *

VARIETIES OF NATIONAL AUTONOMY

Our cases suggest three general types or categories of national autonomy: complete sovereignty and independence, intermediate federal autonomy, and national assertion and recognition short of autonomy. A fourth category, complete annihilation (by either assimilation or genocide) can be added to complete the list.

Complete Sovereignty

Of the NSNs included in this book, only the Zionist movement has achieved independence and sovereignty. The Palestinian Arabs seek complete sovereignty; furthermore, most of the highly audible Palestinian Arabs also seek the elimination of the Israeli state and, presumably, Jewish nationalism.

The other NSNs either have enjoyed or have sought complete independence in the past or include groups that currently seek complete independence for the nation. None of these groups is explicitly and completely united behind such a goal at present, however.

In general, groups that seek complete sovereignty include anticolonial liberation movements (most of the movements leading to independent African states, for example), secessionist movements (such as Biafra and Bangladesh), movements to establish national states in territories being divided after wars (for example, many Arab states as well as Israel, with reference to the Ottoman Empire), and movements to conquer currently existing states and establish the NSN as a state in the territory (for example, some current Palestinian Arab groups with reference to Israel).

---

*This relationship parallels the explanation of revolution suggested by James C. Davies; see 1962 "Toward a Theory of Revolution," American Sociological Review 27: 5-19.

Intermediate Federal Autonomy

The majority of nonstate nations described in this book claim to seek a measure of autonomy within a federal state. The degree and range of control sought by the NSN varies with the specific details of the state within whose boundaries the NSN resides.

The Navajo (or, more specifically, some Navajo spokespersons) say they wish to see the Navajo established as a state among the United States. Precise details are not clear, however. Apparently some Navajo wish to be able to exclude non-Navajo people from such a state. No such racial or ethnic criterion for residence has been acknowledged by U. S. federal law, and it seems likely that such a criterion would be deemed unconstitutional. On the other hand, U. S. court cases have established that Indians are not under the protection of the U. S. Constitution but under their own community jurisdiction. Just how these apparent confusions would be clarified remains to be determined.

The Basques, Kurds, Welsh nationalists (Plaid Cymru), and Croatians offer clearer cases of NSNs that seek (but have not found) federal solutions to their national aspirations. Each of these groups remains willing currently to operate within a federal structure. Each also has contained in the past and/or in the present contains elements seeking complete independence. This circumstance can obstuct the forward path of the true "federalists." Their federal aims sometimes are suspected of being interim objectives, while the true but hidden goal is thought to be complete independence. A federal NSN group thus may be in danger of being perceived as a subversive element, although the NSN sees its goals as consonant with the continued health of the central (federal) government.

The exact nature of autonomy and the distinction between that status and complete independence are in some cases difficult to define. The general defining difference seems to be simply that groups settling for autonomy do not request complete separation and sovereign independence. With that common restriction, NSNs seeking autonomy have claimed a wide range of rights and authority. While the specific "package" sought varies from group to group, the rights asserted have included official preeminence of the local ethnic language, establishment of laws derived from the NSN's religion, claims upon the national economic resources (both claims proportional to NSN population and also special claims to monies accruing from natural resources of the NSN region), representation by the NSN in the federal government, control over local government, control over local military or police forces, and the right to conduct independent foreign relations by bargaining and negotiating internationally on behalf of the NSN. NSNs seeking autonomy usually claim a rather comprehensive set of rights and authority giving the NSN jurisdiction over life within specified territorial boundaries within the federal nation-state.

Measures Short of Federal Autonomy

Many NSNs, however, may not achieve (and, indeed, may not seek) federal status as a "state" or "province" and yet may operate in the international context by doing at least one kind of activity usually done only by sovereign nation-states. Most of the cases in this book currently find themselves in this situation. The Navajo, whatever their ultimate objectives may be, make claims as parties to international treaties with the U. S. government and demand their just rights on those terms. A number of NSNs seek to participate in international organizations: the Palestinian Arabs have participated in UN proceedings; both the Basques and the Welsh have sought recognition from the European Economic Community (EEC). Furthermore, these latter NSNs have encouraged the participation of other "unrepresented nations" in the EEC.

Many NSNs that do not claim or achieve autonomous status within a nation-state may seek institutional guarantees of their prerogatives. Until the 1975 civil conflict erupted in Lebanon, that country provided an example of a state that built into its institutions a rather explicit distribution of political offices and jobs among major ethnic-religious groups in the society. The balance has become brittle, the brittleness exacerbated by the Palestinian Arab-Israeli conflict and its continued impact on Lebanese life. The solution of a kind of "disproportional representation" (disproportional because the distribution of positions is fixed and does not reflect population fluctuations) has not proved sufficiently stable and flexible to sustain orderly government in the face of the Palestinian Arab-Israeli conflict and its intense impact on Lebanese politics. Nonetheless, the general principle of ethnic-religious proportional representation in civic and political life remains at least a possible interim solution to the problems confronted in governing a multinational or multiethnic polity.

The Lebanese approach can be seen as a more explicit and rigid version of the practice common in U. S. politics of making partisan political appointments and nominations roughly along ethnic lines. A problem of this practice, as with the Lebanese practice, has been the disproportionate attention to some groups, while others receive benign (or even malignant) neglect.

Some NSNs may enter the international context not to establish stable or long-term policies of separation or institutionalized quotas of positions and jobs but simply to "up the ante" or change the rules and context of a domestic game they are consistently losing. [2] The international context may provide both new allies and greater audibility. Furthermore, the international context may change the rules from a domestic pluralist game of "how many votes can you deliver?" to a question of violation of international law or international principle. The attempt of some black groups to raise before the United Nations the question of possible genocide in the United States can be seen in this light. Presumably these groups did not expect eventually to obtain sovereign national independence by entering the international context but instead hoped to gain a wider audience which would in turn put additional pressures on U. S. decision makers.

Nationalist arguments, including the claim that a group seeks complete independence, may also have the effect of changing the strategic context for the group, whether or not the independence goal is serious or feasible. Within the United States at least one segment of the Mexican nationalist movement (the nation is known as "Atzlan") has made claims to complete independence. While it seems unlikely that Atzlan will ever gain independence or autonomy, the claims do "up the ante" and change the context in which the group's goals are pursued. Groups have claimed land for U. S. citizens of Mexican ancestry, based on the Treaty of Guadalupe Hildalgo between the Mexican and U. S. governments. These claims do not constitute NSN activity, insofar as the claimants do not assert that they are parties to the treaty but simply that they should be beneficiaries of the terms of the treaty. [3]

Complete Annihilation: Assimilation or Genocide

Obviously, none of the NSNs described in this book have been annihilated. All, however, have disappeared from international view for periods of time. Some have undergone significant programs of assimilation by the dominant nation-state culture. Some also have experienced attempts to annihilate or decimate their populations by genocide. Assimilation has reduced the visible impact of NSNs such as the Welsh and the Basques for periods of time and in specified geographical areas. The national movements have not died, however.

While the Jews as a people were subjected to genocidal policies by the Nazis, it is important to bear in mind that it is likely that most Jewish victims of the Nazis did not think of themselves as a Jewish nation but instead identified themselves with their respective nation-states. However, the genocidal policy of the Nazis produced an increase rather than a decrease in movement to Palestine and later to Israel.

Other current nonstate nations—for example, American Indian tribes and the Croatians—in the past have been the targets of massive violence. Indians were attacked by invading settlers, while the Croatians have been both victims and perpetrators of violent competition among traditional ethnic groups. Although conquest and relocation have modified radically Indian ways of life, tribes have maintained their languages and traditions and are in many cases developing a resurgence audible to a wider public.

These brief observations about genocidal attack on NSN groups do not imply that a people cannot be completely suppressed or even exterminated. Because we have studied currently functioning NSNs, we have not directed attention to the phenomenon of disappearance of a national group. The possibility of complete disappearance is mentioned because it could happen and seems to be the logical polar opposite of complete independence and sovereignty. Questions about the conditions under which a NSN disappears permanently would be relevant to our framework, although such questions are not addressed in this book.

VARIETIES OF IMPACT UPON THE INTERNATIONAL CONTEXT

Our concern in this study focuses not only on the NSN itself but also on its impact upon the international context. Each of the varieties of national autonomy discussed above produces its characteristic impact upon the international context: Both the replacement of one state by another and also the fragmentation of one state into two or move obviously alter the number and character of the nation-states operating in the international context. The development of autonomous units within federal systems also affects the international context insofar as autonomous units seek to operate directly in international organizations such as those of the European Economic Community.

NSNs also affect the international context by the means they use. In order to avoid being dismissed as the domestic problem of an established nation-state and in order to prevent nation-states from imposing solutions upon them, NSNs may direct violence against nation-states other than the ones in which they reside. Some Palestinian Arabs have employed such tactics, thereby both extracting costs from third parties and also making difficult the maintenance of stable cease-fires between Arab states and Israel.

While NSNs in some cases can manipulate nation-states, NSNs run the risk of becoming pawns in games played among nation-states. When the Palestine Liberation Organization establishes a "joint command" with Syria, the PLO may give up more in control than it gets in capability. When the Kurds step up their fight with the Iraqi government on the basis of aid received from Iran (and, covertly, the United States) the Kurds allow Iran (and, inadvertently, the United States) the capability to halt the conflict by turning off the aid flow. In such cases the NSN may indirectly serve to exacerbate international conflicts in that the NSN functions as a tool by which a nation-state may (indirectly) perpetrate violence against another state at reduced cost to itself.

In contrast, NSNs may indirectly promote cooperation between or among nation-states, insofar as the states involved are mutually inconvenienced by the NSN activity. The Basques of Spain and France may very well promote increased coordination between those two nation-states, insofar as increasing Basque militance may seem threatening to the stability of both nation-states.

An area for continued research is the description of the many federal and short-of-federal or interim solutions being devised by NSNs and the nation-states in which they reside. While national sovereignty and independence continue to be an explicit goal of many NSNs, the independence achieved is in some cases more legalistic than behavioral. For a NSN with a small population and land area and limited natural, industrial, or technological resources, a federal solution or a nearly confederal regional arrangement may be more efficacious than simple sovereign independence.

Insofar as NSNs and the states in which they reside can come to workable federal agreements, these arrangements can serve as models for other peoples. Ideally, they could help to avoid repetitions of tragic civil wars that not only cost the lives and well-being of the immediate population but also deepen and exacerbate group conflicts and make later federal arrangements brittle and difficult to maintain.

PATTERNS ASSOCIATED WITH
SOVEREIGNTY OR FEDERAL AUTONOMY

In addition to enumerating and describing interim solutions to NSN aspirations, we seek patterns associated with the move either to complete sovereignty or to some sort of federal status.

The cases reported in this book suggest relationships between the amount and source of NSN resources and the willingness of the NSN and the nation-state decision makers to seek accommodation or wage an all-out battle for dominance. An all-out battle for dominance on the part of the nation-state means that the nation-state seeks to suppress completely the NSN. An all-out battle for dominance by the NSN means that the group seeks independence either by overthrowing or replacing completely the present government or by seceding and thus overthrowing or replacing the present government in part of its territory.

One of the cases in this book, the prestate Zionists, leading to the state of Israel, came into being under the peculiar circumstances of the League of Nations Mandates system. The prestate Zionists did not, therefore, attempt to overthrow or replace an existing state but instead bargained first with the Mandate authority and later with the UN authority in order to establish sovereignty in a part of the Mandate territory. The Israelis declared themselves to to be a state (the Palestinian Arabs, of course, did not accept the Israeli declaration) and in the war that followed extended their claimed territory to include part of the land allotted to the Arabs by the UN partition. The Israelis thus can be said to have established their state partially by bargaining and partially by the overthrow of the existing authority. The Israelis did not, strictly speaking, overthrow an existing government, since no Palestinian Arab government had been established parallel to the Israeli government in the Arab part of the partitioned Mandate territory. Insofar as Palestinian Arab groups seek now to establish a state in the entire Palestine Mandate area they, of course, seek to overthrow and replace the current Israeli state.

The general relationships between the NSN and nation-state(s) in which the NSN resides and the four resultant outcomes can be represented in Table 9.1. Within each cell the expected distributions of levels and sources of NSN resources are enumerated. This table summarizes relationships that seem likely, based upon the cases reported in this book, and suggests variables about which data might be systematically gathered for a much greater number of cases.

In this tabular summary the seeking of federal solutions and measures short of federal autonomy are combined into one category. These kinds of goals involve the NSN in bargaining with the nation-state in which the NSN resides. If the NSN has resources that are highly valued by the nation-state leaders, an exchange may be negotiated. In particular, if the NSN organizes effectively within the nation-state party structure, the NSN may muster sufficient electoral strength to persuade a major party or parties to support the NSN claims as part of the party or coalition platform.

In order to make the federal goal plausible, the NSN must establish clearly the limits of its aspirations. If the nation-state leaders see the federal goal as merely an interim argument masking

TABLE 9.1

Relationship Between NSN and
Nation-State of Residence

Nonstate Nation

	Bargain with Government (seek federal solution or other solution)	Overthrow/Replace Government (seek complete independence)
Suppress NSN	4 Outcome: NSN disappears (either is "underground" or is destroyed). Resources: NSN has few resources; may have resources from outside sources.	1 Outcome: Either NSN prevails or nation-state prevails. This is a showdown. Resources: In this case NSN usually has considerable resources from outside competitors or enemies of nation-state.
Accommodate NSN	3 Outcome: Federal or interim solution. Resources: Extensive resources, including opportunities from within nation-state.	2 Outcome: NSN becomes independent state. Resources: Extensive resources, although few from outside nation-state. May have resources from within nation-state, including tradition of decolonization.

Nation-State
of Residence

the true goal of complete independence, the NSN is likely to be seen
as a subversive force. The credibility of NSNs that seek federal
solutions will be undercut if their main sources of support are other
nation-states and/or if they engage in violent disruption within the
nation-state of residence.

By contrast, NSNs that seek complete independence and sovereignty often will receive major aid from nation-states other than the
nation-state of residence. (Indeed, a motive of the donor state or
states often is to use the NSN as a thorn in the side of the nation-state
of residence.) In some cases in which an established colonial power
has made the policy decision to decolonize, the granting of independence will be negotiated in an orderly manner. In the situation where
the nation-state resists the NSN's independence moves, however, the
conflict will amount to a showdown, with each side seeking to prevail
against the other.

Cells 3 and 4 of the table all involve some degree of bargaining
or accommodation; only cell 1 involves a "hard line" on the part of
both actors. Cells 2 and 4 combine hard-line tactics from one actor
with accommodation and bargaining from another. The conflict and
bargaining patterns described and analyzed by Richard Walton and
Robert McKersie[4] may be helpful in fleshing out the relationships
between the nation-state and nonstate nation actors. Walton and
McKersie identify three general types of bargaining process:
integrative (bargaining over a variable sum—problem solving rather
than strict competition), disintegrative (bargaining over a fixed sum—
strictly competitive), and mixed. The authors claim that their formulation can be adapted to the study of international conflict. If applied
roughly to Table 9.1, cells 1 and 4 can be seen as representing fixed-
sum, disintegrative bargaining situations; cell 3 approximates a
variable-sum integrative bargaining situation; and cell 2 represents
a mixed situation in which the parties attempt to develop mutually
beneficial interactions while accepting the independence of the NSN.
The specification of relationships and the development of indicators
to make possible empirical investigation of validity of the relationships is a major undertaking beyond the scope of this book.

EPILOGUE

While this concluding chapter has sketched lines of research
that are anticipated for the future, the production of additional systems case studies also would be useful for detailing particular
federal or interim solutions adopted by NSNs and their host states.
These interim solutions short of complete independence may well
be the kinds of solutions most practical in many cases for satisfying

needs for national self-determination while avoiding fragmentation into small states that are not viable.

The behavior of nonstate nations in international politics may appear baffling, quixotic, and annoying when viewed from the perspective of nation-states, especially the big powers. By focusing on the international arena from the perspective of the NSN we gain insight into the combinations of goals and circumstances that motivate NSN decision makers to move out of the domestic context and into the international arena.

The purpose of the NSN system analyses has been simply to increase understanding and knowledge. Any policy implications depend upon the values and goals of policy makers, whether those policy makers be nation-state, international organization, or NSN decision makers. Nation-states may ignore, deny, attack, aid, recognize, or defend a nonstate nation. Furthermore, they may vary their treatment of an NSN as suits their interests over time. Prudent NSN decision makers will be aware of these possibilities and, wherever possible, choose strategies with a range of contingencies in mind. In a world in which verbal representations cannot always be trusted, the NSN decision maker may find it useful to seek something resembling a minimax strategy and structure a situation where the worst possible outcomes for the NSN are also costly for the nation-states involved. Of course, nation-state decision makers may adopt similar minimax approaches to NSNs, thereby severely restricting NSN maneuverability in areas judged costly by nation-states.

The impact of nonstate nations on international politics has become increasingly visible in recent years. The framework and studies in this book are offered as a beginning step toward systematic study of the strategies adopted by NSNs as they seek to realize their goals in an environment of powerful states—an environment that includes elements that often can be exploited by skillful NSN decision makers and transformed into manipulable resources.

NOTES

1. See, for example, Robert L. Hamblin, R. Brooke Jacobsen, and Jerry L. L. Miller, A Mathmematical Theory of Social Change (New York: John Wiley, 1973).

2. For a general discussion of the problem of consistently losing minorities, see Christian Bay and Robert Paul Wolff in Obligation and Dissent, ed. Donald W. Hanson and Robert Booth Fowler (Boston: Little, Brown, 1971), pp. 222-58.

3. For a discussion of the nationalist Atzlan movement, see Rona M. Fields, "A Comparative Case Study of the Chicano and Irish

Republican Non-state Nations," a paper presented at the annual
meeting of the International Studies Association, New York, 1973.

    4. Richard Walton and Robert McKersie, <u>A Behavioral Theory
of Labor Negotiations</u> (New York: McGraw-Hill, 1965).

ABOUT THE EDITOR AND THE CONTRIBUTORS

JUDY BERTELSEN is a Research Associate at the Institute for Scientific Analysis, San Francisco, and is currently Visiting Assistant Professor of Political Science at the California State University, Chico. Previously she has taught at the University of Oregon, Oregon State University, and Mills College. She holds a doctoral degree from the University of Oregon.

Dr. Bertelsen is an active participant in the International Studies Association, having served as program chairperson, vice-president, and president of the Western Regional Association. She was elected to the Council of the Comparative Interdisciplinary Studies Association of the ISA, and chaired an Internet dealing with nonstate nations in international politics. In addition to her work on nonstate nations, Dr. Bertelsen has also written about women in higher education, and sex roles and political attitudes.

CHARLES M. BENJAMIN is a Ph. D. candidate in the School of International Relations, University of Southern California. His primary academic interests are in the fields of United States foreign policy, comparative foreign policy, policy analysis, and theory and methods in the study of international relations.

RAYMOND R. CORRADO is an Assistant Professor of Political Science at the University of Pittsburgh. He received his undergraduate degree from Michigan State University and his Masters and Ph. D. degrees from Northwestern University. He was a Canada Council Fellow while conducting his research on Welsh nationalism at the University of Lancaster's Peace and Conflict Research Programme. Professor Corrado has published in Ethnicity and has a forthcoming book on Ethnicity in the Advanced Industrial Society. His current research includes a comparison of ethnic nationalist and student terrorist movements in Western Europe.

DAVID NACHMIAS is a Senior Lecturer at Tel Aviv University. He holds a Ph. D. degree in political science from the University of Oregon, and was a visiting scholar at the John F. Kennedy School at Harvard University during the summer of 1976. He is the author of numerous articles in professional journals and is coauthor with Chava Nachmias of Research Methods in the Social Sciences (1976).

ROBIN ALISON REMINGTON is Associate Professor of Political Science at the University of Missouri (Columbia) and a research affiliate of the Massachusetts Institute of Technology Center for International Studies. Professor Remington's field work in Eastern Europe dates from 1967. She is a member of the Executive Council of the American Association for Southeast European Studies. Her book length publications include Winter in Prague: Documents on Czechoslovak Communism in Crises (1969) and The Warsaw Pact: Case Studies in Communist Conflict Resolution (1971).

ROBERT ROCKAWAY received his Ph. D. in history at the University of Michigan in 1970. He is presently a Senior Lecturer in the Department of Jewish History and the Department of History at Tel-Aviv University, where he teaches American Jewish history, modern Jewish history, and American immigration history. He has written numerous articles dealing with the American Jewish experience, and is currently completing a history of the Jews of Detroit.

MARY T. SHEPARDSON is a social anthropologist, Professor Emeritus from San Francisco State University. She received her M. A. from Stanford University in 1956 and her Ph. D. from the University of California, Berkeley, in 1960. Her published works include Navajo Ways in Government (1963); The Navajo Mountain Community (coauthored by Blodwen Hammond) (1970); and numerous articles in anthropological journals and collections on Navajo politics, law, and factionalism.

MILTON DA SILVA is Assistant Professor of Political Science at Juniata College. He has published in Comparative Politics and is coauthor of a chapter on Basque nationalism in The Limits of Assimilation: Ethnicity and Nationalism in Modern Europe, edited by Oriol Pi-Sunyer. He holds a Ph. D. degree in political science from the University of Massachusetts, Amherst.

SMALL STATES AND SEGMENTED SOCIETIES:
National Political Integration and the Global Environment

edited by Stephanie G. Neuman

NATIONALITY GROUP SURVIVAL IN MULTI-ETHNIC
STATES: Shifting Support Patterns in the Soviet Baltic
Region

edited by Edward Allworth

*SOUTH ASIAN CRISIS—INDIA, PAKISTAN, AND
BANGLADESH: A Political and Historical Analysis of
the 1971 War

Robert Jackson

+CHINA AND SOUTHEAST ASIA: Peking's Relations
with Revolutionary Movements

Jay Taylor

THE POLITICS OF DIVISION, PARTITION, AND
UNIFICATION

edited by Ray E. Johnston

---

*For sale in the U. S. and Philippines only
+PSS Student Edition